TABLE OF CONTENTS

INTRODUCTION / Annette Stahmer

> "And be sure you knock on the wall if you want anything in the night. My bed is just on the other side, and the partition is quite thin. Just give a knock now, as soon as you are ready, so that we shall know where we are."
> And, sure enough, that evening I gave three knocks – a signal which, the week after, when I was ill, I repeated every morning for several days, because my grandmother wanted me to have some milk early. Then, when I thought that I could hear her stirring, so that she should not be kept waiting but might, [...] I ventured on three little taps, timidly, faintly, but for all that distinctly, [...] And scarcely had I given my taps than I heard three others, in a different intonation from mine, stamped with a calm authority, repeated twice over so that there should be no mistake, and saying to me plainly: "Don't get excited; I heard you; I shall be with you in a minute!" and shortly afterwards my grandmother appeared. I explained to her that I had been afraid that she would not hear me, or might think that it was someone in the room beyond who was lapping; at which she smiled:
> "Mistake my poor chick's knocking for anyone else! Why, Granny could tell it among a thousand! Do you suppose there's anyone else in the world who's such a silly-billy, with such feverish little knuckles, so afraid of waking me up and of not making me understand? Even if he just gave the least scratch, Granny could tell her mouse's sound at once, especially such a poor miserable little mouse as mine is."[1]

This brief episode is one of my favourites in Marcel Proust's *À la recherche du temps perdu*. In it the first person narrator describes how he goes on holiday by a lake with his grandmother and, plagued by physical and mental pain in the new and unfamiliar house, communicates with her by knocking on the wall.

The episode presents a wall that separates: the grandchild from his beloved grandmother, the two rooms with each head of the bed directly on either side. Yet it also connects them, as the instrument of their communication, a kind of membrane made to reverberate by their knocking. The knocking sounds are also well able to transport finer emotions; the anxious grandson's hesitant knocking, or "scratching", is answered by the grandmother's stronger and confident "knocking voice". So the morning ritual becomes a dialogue, a conversation between two people.

> [...] dear morning moment, opened like a symphony by the rhythmical dialogue of my three taps, to which the thin wall of my bedroom, steeped in love and joy, grown melodious, immaterial, singing like the angelic choir, responded with three other taps, eagerly awaited, repeated once and again, in which it contrived to waft to me the soul of my grandmother, whole and perfect, and the promise of her coming, with a swiftness of annunciation and melodic accuracy.[2]

This scene also made me think of another wall in the history of literature. Publius Ovidius Naso (Ovid), in his *Metamorphoses*, tells the unhappy tale of Pyramus and Thisbe, lovers from hostile families whose secret meeting place is a wall separating both houses from one another. The unhappy couple whisper to one another through a gap in that wall.

fissus erat tenui rima, quam duxerat olim,
cum fieret, paries domui communis utrique.
id vitium nulli per saecula longa notatum –
quid non sentit amor? – primi vidistis amantes
et vocis fecistis iter, tutaeque per illud
murmure blanditiae minimo transire solebant.
saepe, ubi constiterant hinc Thisbe, Pyramus illinc,
inque vices fuerat captatus anhelitus oris,
"invide" dicebant "paries, quid amantibus obstas?
quantum erat, ut sineres toto nos corpore iungi
aut, hoc si nimium est, vel ad oscula danda pateres?
nec sumus ingrati: tibi nos debere fatemur,
quod datus est verbis ad amicas transitus auris."
talia diversa nequiquam sede locuti
sub noctem dixere "vale" partique dedere
oscula quisque suae non pervenientia contra.[3]

Between the houses was a common wall,
Flawed with a narrow chink long years ago,
When it was built. This chink, so long unnoticed –
But what does love not see? – those lovers found
And made of it their voices' passageway,
And safely flowed the whispered words of love;
And often, when on her side Thisbe stood
And Pyramus on his, eager to catch
Each other's breath, they said "Oh jealous wall,
Why thwart fond hearts? Why grudge to let us meet,
Or open, at least, to give our kisses room?
Yet we are grateful, for we owe to you
A pathway for sweet words of lovers true."
So on their separate sides, they talked in vain
Till nightfall, then "goodbye", and on the wall
Each printed kisses that could never meet.[4]

Here too the wall is an obstacle, symbolising an apparently insurmountable hindrance. At the same time, the wall (unlike an abyss) indicates the proximity of the lovers, who are only separated from each other by this thin construction. A kind of seam which says, You are so close, yet unreachable. In the case of Pyramus and Thisbe, the wall is also both friend and foe, a dividing wall, but also a site of encounter, of closeness.

A gap in the wall even allows the lovers' breath and whispered words to reach from one side to the other. So this wall also becomes a phonetic membrane, a skin, "singing like the angelic choir".[5] Furthermore, it is interesting that the lovers refer to the wall as a person, an envious third party who stands between the two.

In his play *A Mid-Summer Night's Dream* William Shakespeare includes the story of Pyramus and Thisbe as a play within the play, exaggerating the concept of a personified wall. Played by an actor, the wall appears as a third person who thinks, feels and speaks.

WALL:
In this same interlude it doth befall
That I, one Snout by name, present a wall;
And such a wall, as I would have you think,
That had in it a crannied hole or chink,
Through which the lovers, Pyramus and Thisby,
Did whisper often very secretly.
This loam, this rough-cast, and this stone doth show
That I am that same wall; the truth is so;
And this the cranny is, right and sinister,
Through which the fearful lovers are to whisper.[6]

So the wall is not only a transmitting membrane, in Shakespeare it even becomes a phonetic body, a speaking person. With this I'd like to come to the topic of this second issue of *Parole, Phonetic Skin / Phonetische Haut*, which continues with the theme of the corporeality of language by focusing on skin as a medium of communication.[7]

The skin is our largest and most multifaceted organ. As it covers the human body, it thus represents it outwardly. The skin and its adnexa (hair, nails, etc.) considerably influence a person's appearance. At the same time, the skin protects us – against cold, heat, sun rays, dangerous environmental influences and also mechanical stress, etc. It is a permeable membrane capable of absorbing, storing and excreting substances. It is also our largest sensual organ: through the skin, which is equipped with innumerable sensitive receptors, we can touch, and feel pain, temperature, pressure or vibrations. These stimuli are passed onto the brain by fine nerve strands and can warn, for instance, of possible threats. The sensitive skin is the body's contact area to the outside world. For this reason it plays a decisive role in communication and interaction. It also adds greatly to our experiences of each other, lending to forms of intimacy and sexuality: to touch is to feel oneself and the other at the same moment. Our skin is in direct contact with our emotional world. Not only external contacts have an impact inside us, inner sensations too can be expressed via the skin, such as blushing, blanching, goose bumps, etc. On the other hand, we may also consciously use our skin to create a self-image, for instance, with cosmetics, jewelry or tattooing, etc. The skin in other words conducts meaningful exchange in numerous ways.

This publication aims to investigate the skin as a communicative medium by also using the term metaphorically. Skin stands for surface, for the protective coat not only of the human body but of other bodies as well, like the walls of a house, the package of a product, the surface of the earth, etc. It thus stands for the border between the inside of the body or the object and the outside world. A border that separates and links. A seam at which an exchange between inside and outside takes place.

"Phonetic Skin" is a poetic term that foregrounds these dynamics, opening up the role of the skin as a sensitive tool of communication. Thus the skin can become a phonetic surface when it reverberates and transmits sound waves, for example, with the eardrum, or when a drum plays and transmits messages on a stretched animal hide. Skin as metaphor therefore leads to new poetic combinations, so that the wall that is knocked on for example becomes a "phonetic skin". Usually this requires an external impact, an impulse or stimulus which makes the skin, the membrane reverberate, in either a literal or metaphorical sense. This can be a finger touching the skin, a drumstick hitting the hide, the knuckle knocking on the wall, the needle scratching the record, a drop falling onto the surface of water or the pen writing on the paper.

As editor, I was interested to explore these themes by bringing together artistic and theoretical work by leading scholars and practitioners from around the world. In *Parole #2* the various facets of skin as a contact surface for communication and language are elucidated through critical essays, documentation and reflections on artistic works, as well as projects and audio works.

The volume opens with the text *Mit Haut und Hören [Listen to Your Skin]* by the culture and media theorist PETRA MARIA MEYER, which highlights the close link between skin, hearing and voice and thus introduces the theme. She also presents two important artists, Henri Chopin and Carlfriedrich Claus, who used their own bodies as resonant chambers and instruments so as to render the corporeality of language audible.

This is followed by an artwork from the American sound artist PAUL DICKINSON. In the project *Sleep Talk* Dickinson has been examining, since the 1980s, his own sleep talk, that quiet murmuring, whispering, sighing that transgresses, as it were, the border, the skin, between consciousness and the unconscious. He had these talks recorded in a sleep laboratory and the transcription of those recordings form a kind of night-time diary, excerpts from which are to be read and heard in the publication.

A second artwork, *Topography of a Voice*, by British artist IMOGEN STIDWORTHY, investigates the Liverpool accent known as "Scouse". In the publication she presents a series of waterfall plots, digital graphs that render the pitch, wavelength and duration of the expression "Get here" spoken by different people from Liverpool so as to appear as a topographical survey.

The surface of the earth also plays a role in the next article. In his text *The Phonetic Burrow* the Slovene philosopher MLADEN DOLAR examines the role of sound in Franz Kafka's late short story *Der Bau [The Burrow]*. In the story, a mysterious sound without any obvious source breaks through, so to speak, the protective walls of a burrow; it stands for something alien that attempts to get in and against which the main character, a badger, tries desperately to protect himself.

Following this essay, three works by the artist JÜRGEN PARTENHEIMER are presented. A drawing and two poems combine to form a poetic fabric with two installations produced for the Ikon Gallery, Birmingham – *Copan [Voices]*, in which a room becomes an opaque white acoustic space (with simultaneous whispering of four voices in different languages) and *Small Bodies [Particle Zoo I–III]*, an installation in the listed building Perrot's Folly, where the artist worked with the existing, unrenovated wall and complemented the natural structures, irregularities and spots with small sculptures.

The text *Playing the Strange Statue: Sound, Silence and Touch in Didier Anzieu and The Piano* by the French Studies scholar NAOMI SEGAL introduces two concepts of the French psychoanalyst Didier Anzieu, "consensuality" and "formal signifiers". She applies these concepts in an analysis of Jane Campion's film *The Piano*, in which, from childhood, a young woman communicates through her piano so that her tactile sense substitutes, as it were, for her voice.

The American music ethnologist DAVID LOCKE presents another instrument, another skin that is used as a means of communication. In an article about the "talking drums" of the Dagomba people in northern Ghana, he describes a culture that is closely linked with drums and their means of expression. Drums perform to speak aloud stories of the community.

Documentation of the video work that follows, *Phonetic Skin. A Library of Voices*, is one in which I myself examine various books as to their phonetic features, the language of their paper. The work explores the book as a body and poetically interlaces written language and the "voice" of the page.

A chapter from the previously published work, *Ventriloquized Bodies*, by the American Romance Studies expert JANET BEIZER follows. *The Textual Woman and the Hysterical Novel* describes the phenomenon of dermographism, which was regarded in 19th century France as a symptom of hysterical illness. For demonstration purposes, the doctor wrote on the body of mainly female patients using his fingernail or a pen. The skin reacted immediately by swelling and the writing remained visible for several hours. Beizer critically analyses the doctor's proprietorial gesture of writing, inscribing. In a new afterword *Textual Woman: Twenty-First-Century Reinscriptions* she draws a parallel to a trial that took place several years ago of a gynaecologist who branded the skin of a womb with the logo of his university before surgically removing it.

The Swedish artist LEIF ELGGREN creates a phonetic skin of another kind in his project, *The Sudarium of St. Veronica*. This is based on the etching of the same name by the French artist Claude Mellan (1649) showing a portrait of the crucified Christ composed of just one line beginning at the tip of the nose and running spirally outwards. Elggren had a new etching plate of this print made and then played it as a record, thereby animating the surface as a sonic material. The sound can be heard on the CD enclosed in the publication.

The Brazilian author and curator ANDRÉ LEPECKI introduces the three-part performance series entitled *The White Series* by Colombian artist MARIA JOSÉ ARJONA. The three linked performances *Untitled*, *Remember to Remember* and

Karaoke were last done in 2009 at the Haus der Kulturen der Welt in the context of the symposium *IN TRANSIT*, curated by Lepecki. Images of *Untitled* show the artist blowing soap bubbles onto a white wall. The thin skin of these "speech balloons", which are coloured with red ink, bursts against the wall and leaves bloody-looking traces.

The subsequent pages show the impressive installation *Marsyas* by British artist ANISH KAPOOR in the Turbine Hall at Tate Modern, London: a huge funnel-like shape spanned with a red PVC membrane. The installation refers to the mythological figure Marsyas, who competed with Apollo in flute playing contest, lost, and at Apollo's command was skinned alive. According to the myth, the stream of his blood formed the river Marsyas, which is named after him.

This is followed by the text *The Sonic Skin of Water* by the American theorist ALLEN S. WEISS, who explores Japanese Zen gardens in Kyoto. Weiss transfers the metaphor of the phonetic skin to the water's surface that in some of the gardens is part of an instrument, a so-called water zither. The enclosed CD contains the soundscape composition mentioned in the text, *Suikinkutsu* by American musician, filmmaker and anthropologist STEVEN FELD, who recorded the sound of the water zither in the garden of the Enkō-ji Temple in Kyoto.

For his project *The Sonic Body* the American artist and author BRANDON LABELLE had different people dance to their favourite music, heard through earphones, and recorded the sounds made by their bodies and clothing. The final recordings translate, so to speak, the original music, resulting in a ghostly sound, that can be imagined as a "sonic skin".

The Berlin fashion label TRIKOTON also works with aspects of the body, focusing on the relationship between voice and clothing. Here the frequencies of recorded words are translated into knitting patterns using a programmed knitting machine, and then become part of various items of clothing. The client can thus carry hidden messages by a certain voice on their skin.

The publication closes with an article by the Brazilian author and editor LEONARDO GUELMAN, who has been preoccupied for many years with a Brazilian cult figure, the prophet Gentileza. This prophet developed a typography and mode of writing for his messages and publicised these in a series of large murals on the streets of Rio de Janeiro and on his own clothes.

Between the pages of this publication, as a flexible element, is also a card referring to a project by the Dutch artists' group DE GEUZEN. *Wearable Resistance* provides luminous letters for protesting demonstrators which can be used as gloves in various combinations to form portable banners.

This issue of *Parole* also includes a CD of sound recordings complementing the different articles. The CD compiles extracts from the *Sleep Talk Recordings* by Paul Dickinson, samples of the drum language of the Dagomba people performed by David Locke and his students, the paper language of several books from my video *Phonetic Skin. A Library of Voices*, Leif Elggren's *Sudarium of St. Veronica*, an excerpt from Steven Feld's composition *Suikinkutsu* and some figures from *The Sonic Body* project by Brandon LaBelle.

As a final component to mention, the design concept developed for the *Parole* series works with the idea of a voice body, which is based on appropriating the design layout of existing books. For *Parole #2: Phonetic Skin / Phonetische Haut* the books chosen were from the field of phonetics. The text sections of those books were "taken apart", form and content separated, and the old layout was "filled" with the new text, which now enters into an interesting relationship with the original book. This present publication therefore conceals a series of phonetic books. The cited books and their designers are listed at the end of the publication as sources.

I would like to close this introduction by expressing my sincerest thanks to all those who have made this second issue of *Parole* possible: Brandon LaBelle, André Heers, my parents Eilith le Fort and Carsten Stahmer, Bryndís Sigurjónsdóttir and Henning Reinke, the translators Pauline Cumbers, Adriana Francisco, Octávio Camargo and Patrick Charles, the publisher Gerhard Theewen, Druckerei Conrad and first and foremost the authors!

[1] Marcel Proust, *Remembrance of Things Past II / Within a Budding Grove* (New York: Vintage Books, 1982). Translation: C. K. Scott Moncrieff. French original text in the inside cover: Marcel Proust, *À la recherche du temps perdu / À l'ombre des jeunes filles en fleurs 2* (Paris: Gallimard, 1919), 94–95. [2] ibid. [3] Ovid, *Metamorphosen* (Ditzingen: Reclam, 2010), IV, 65–80. [4] Ovid, *Metamorphoses* (Oxford: Oxford University Press, 1986), IV, 65–80. Translation: A. D. Melville. [5] Marcel Proust, *Remembrance of Things Past / Within a Budding Grove* (New York: Vintage Books, 1982). Translation: C. K. Scott Moncrieff. [6] William Shakespeare, *A Midsummer Night's Dream* (Leipzig: Reclam Philipp Junior, 1989), Act V, Scene I. [7] Annette Stahmer (ed.), *Parole #1: The Body of the Voice / Stimmkörper* (Cologne: Salon Verlag, 2009).

PETRA MARIA MEYER / MIT HAUT UND HÖREN [LISTEN TO YOUR SKIN]

Der Mensch ist ektoderm,[1] sagt Paul Valéry, der darum wusste, dass sich Haut und Gehirn entwicklungsgeschichtlich als erstes aus der gleichen Membran, dem Ektoderm, ausbilden. Als multisensorisch arbeitendes Organ, das Sinnesempfindungen weiterleitet, nimmt die Haut auch akustische Schwingungen auf und leitet sie an verschiedenste Sinne weiter. Wird insofern der Körper über die Haut umfassend von Schallwellen erreicht, muss auch ein Klangerlebnis ganzheitlicher betrachtet werden. Gehört wird nicht nur mit den Ohren.

Das Leben beginnt im empfindbaren Millieu mit Haut und Hören. Ein Embryo ist darin schon bald ganz Ohr, denn dem mit der Haut verbundenen ersten Sinn, dem Tastsinn, folgt wenig später bereits der Gehörsinn, der sich nach den Studien von Alfred Tomatis spätestens viereinhalb Monate nach der Empfängnis in all seiner Komplexität aus Labyrinth und Cochlea sowie in der endgültigen Größe ausgebildet hat.[2] „Wir besitzen nur ein einziges Organ, das seine endgültige Größe erreicht, lange bevor wir geboren werden – unser Innenohr“[3], stellt auch Joachim Ernst Berendt fasziniert fest. So kann der in Atmung, Blutkreislauf, Ernährung und Verdauung von der Mutter vollständig abhängige Embryo, der noch weitere, viereinhalb Monate im Mutterleib verbeiben muss, bereits eigenständig hören und empfinden. Der engen Verbundenheit von Haut und Hören hat Michel Serres mit einer prägnanten Bezeichnung entsprochen. Er nennt die Haut ein „generalisiertes Trommelfell“[4]. Bevor der Mensch in seiner Ganzheit überhaupt ist, kann er durch das „generalisierte Trommelfell“ ein Berührter und Hörender von Geräuschen und Stimmen sein. Anthropologisch betrachtet geht die Stimme somit dem Sein des Menschen vorgeburtlich voraus.

Haut und Stimme

Haut und Stimme sind verschieden und haben doch Vieles gemeinsam. Beide stehen pars pro toto für das Subjekt oder den Menschen. In diesem Sinne sagt man von Jemandem, dass er eine ehrliche Haut sei oder eine gewichtige

Man is ectodermal,[1] according to Paul Valéry, who obviously knew that, in the history of development, skin and brain were the first to form from the same membrane, the ectoderm. The skin, as an organ that works multi-sensorially to transmit sense impression, also registers acoustic reverberations and transmits them on to the most varied of senses. So if the body is comprehensively reached by sound waves via the skin, then the experience of sound must be viewed in a more holistic way. We hear, but not just with our ears.

Life begins in a sensitive milieu, with skin and hearing. Thus an embryo is "all ears", for the first sense linked to the skin, the sense of touch, is soon followed by the sense of hearing, which, according to studies by Alfred Tomatis, is fully formed in all the complexity of its labyrinth and cochlea, as well as in its final size, four and a half months after conception at the latest.[2] "We possess only one single organ that achieves its final size long before we are born – our inner ear",[3] Joachim Ernst Berendt ascertained to his fascination. So the embryo, totally dependent on its mother for breathing, blood circulation, nutrition and digestion, and with another four and a half months to go in the uterus, can already hear and feel independently. Michel Serres came up with an apt designation for describing the close link between skin and hearing; he calls the skin a "generalised eardrum".[4] Before a human being becomes a whole, he can already be moved through the "generalised eardrum" and hear sounds and voices through this. In anthropological terms, the voice thus precedes a human being's birth.

Skin and Voice

Though skin and voice differ, they still have much in common. Both stand, pars pro toto, for the subject or human being. In this sense, we say of someone that he is an honest skin or has a weighty voice.

Skin and voice are inside and outside, anchored in both a symbolic and a symptomatic field, culturally

Stimme habe bzw. seine Stimme abgebe. Haut und Stimme sind innen wie außen, im symbolischen ebenso wie im symptomatischen Feld verankert, sowohl kulturell durchformt als auch Träger somatischer Spuren. Während die Haut Grenze und Kontaktfläche zwischen Innen und Außen oder Ich und Anderem zugleich ist, agiert die Stimme als Äußeres im Inneren und Inneres im Außen an der Grenze und in Kontakt zur Sprache wie zum Anderen.

Haut und Stimme haben Schleimhäute. Die Stimmlippen gleichen einem inneren Mund. Seine Schleimhäute machen die Stimmbänder weich und geschmeidig oder trocken und rauh. Dadurch lässt sich die Stimme wohlklingend und vermeintlich über allem Körperlichen schwebend oder körnig körperlich vernehmen. „Le grain de la voix" nennt Roland Barthes diese Körnigkeit, die Sprache als Körpergeräusch und/oder Musik versinnlicht. Haut und Stimme verbergen und verraten, stoßen ab und ziehen an. Sie werden häufig als Ausdrucksträger eines Ideal-Ichs genutzt, bleiben aber stets auch allzu menschliche Träger von Spuren, die als visuelle oder akustisch wahrnehmbare Narben schmerzvolles Dasein indizieren.

Stimme, Kommunikation, Sprache

Durch die Stimme erfolgt die erste Anrufung, die den Menschen als Angesprochenen konstituiert. Die Ansprache von Angehörigen erzeugt ein Gefühl der Zugehörigkeit. Über Stimmen, Klänge, Geräusche wird Geborgenheit vermittelt. Auch nach der Geburt erfolgt die frühe Kommunikation zunächst über einen Austausch von Berührungen und Lauten, so dass der Psychoanalytiker Didier Anzieu von einem anderen, nicht informationstheoretisch erfassbaren Verständnis von Kommunikation in diesem Zusammenhang ausgeht. „(...) Kommunizieren heißt vor allem, in Resonanz treten, in Harmonie mit dem anderen Schwingen."[5]

Auch wenn uns die Worte noch gar nichts sagen, vermögen die Schwingungen der Stimme den Menschen bereits zu beruhigen oder zu trösten, aber auch zu irritieren und zu ängstigen. Stimmen stillen und zwingen. Sie beruhigen, trösten und vertreiben die Einsamkeit. Das Begehren, die Stimme des geliebten Anderen zu hören, ist entsprechend stark. Die Angst, den falschen Tonfall zu hören, groß. Judith Butler konstatiert eine „grundlegende Abhängigkeit von der Anrede des Anderen"[6]. Erst durch die Art des Anrufes und der Anrede „gelangt das Subjekt zur ‚Existenz'"[7], die ihm somit auch abgesprochen werden kann. Sehnsucht und Abwehr kennzeichnen das Hörfeld gleichermaßen.

Bevor die Stimme Sprache hörbar macht, nimmt sie ihren Weg durch den Körper. Insofern ist sie Sprach- und

shaped and also a carrier of somatic traces. Whereas the skin is both borderline and contact area between inside and outside, or between the I and the Other, the voice as something external acts internally and as something internal externally, at the borderline and in contact with language and the Other.

Skin and voice have mucosa. The vocal folds resemble an internal mouth. Its mucosa keep the vocal chords soft and supple, or dry and hoarse. Thus the voice can be perceived as if hovering melodiously over all that is corporeal, or else as physically gritty. Roland Barthes called the grittiness that symbolises language as a bodily sound and/or as music "le grain de la voix" (the grain of the voice).

Skin and voice conceal and expose, repel and attract. They are often used as the expressive carrier of an ideal I, but also always remain all too human carriers of traces that, as visually or acoustically perceptible scars, indicate painful existence.

Voice, Communication, Language

The first invocation which constitutes the human being as an addressee takes place through the voice. Being addressed by relatives creates a feeling of belonging. Voices, sounds, noises communicate security. After birth, early communication initially takes the form of an exchange of touches and sounds, so that in this context the psychoanalyst Didier Anzieu assumes a different understanding of communication that cannot be grasped by information theory: "... To communicate means, above all, to enter into a resonance, a harmony with the other vibration."[5]

Even if we do not even understand the words, the vibrations of the voice are able to calm or console us, but also to irritate and frighten us. Voices appease and force, they calm, console and drive away loneliness. The need to hear the voice of the beloved Other is correspondingly strong; fear of hearing the wrong tone is great. Judith Butler ascertains a "fundamental dependence on being addressed by the Other."[6] Only through the mode of appeal, of address, does "the subject achieve 'existence'",[7] which can thus also be denied him or her. The field of hearing is characterised equally by longing and resistance.

Before rendering language audible, the voice makes its way through the body, so that it is at one and the same time a medium of language and of the body. Whereas language is not comprehensible to everyone, body sounds are universally understood. According to Michel Serres, the body sounds a kind of universal underground music and sets a rhythm.[8] This latter is often drowned out by

Körpermedium zugleich. Während die Sprache nicht für jeden verständlich ist, lassen sich Körperlaute universell verstehen. Nach Michel Serres stimmt der Körper eine Art universeller Untergrundmusik an und gibt einen Rhythmus vor.[8] Häufig wird er von der Sprachmelodie übertönt. Die Sprache neigt dazu, das Rauhe, Widerständige, Spröde des Körpers zum Verstummen zu bringen und so nutzen die Künste häufig sprachunabhängige Laut- und Geräuschprozesse, um den Körper wieder hörbar zu machen. Als Medium zwischen Sprache und Körper wird Stimme außer- oder innerhäutlich hörbar. Avancierte Tontechnik vermag beide Entfaltungsbereiche zu betonen.

Stimme und Technik

Stimme im technischen Zeitalter – so heißt es – sei eine entkörperlichte Stimme. Das scheint zunächst eine überzeugende Überlegung zu sein, da die Entwicklung der Telekommunikation gerade auf der Trennung der menschlichen Botschaft vom Körper des Menschen basiert. Im Unterschied zum Sehsinn ist der Hörsinn jedoch ein Fernsinn, der keinen Abstand hält, da die Töne, die das Ohr hört, auch bei räumlicher Entfernung in es eindringen und eindringlich bleiben.[9] Dieser Unterschied ist bezogen auf Telephon und Radio besonders wirkungsmächtig, aber auch bei jeder Stimme über Mikrophon und ihrer Wiedergabe über Lautsprecher gegeben. Ein künstlerischer Umgang, der nicht auf Informationsvermittlung und Nachrichtenfernverkehr ausgerichtet ist, macht zudem deutlich, dass dieses Verhältnis zwischen Stimme, Körper und Technik ein dialektisches ist. Gerade eine mit Mitteln der Technik ermöglichte Entfernung der Stimme vom Körper kann den Körper dem Hörer näher bringen, denn die Technik ermöglicht zugleich, in den Körper hineinzuhorchen. Das macht die technische Rückgewinnung der Körperstimmen so anstößig. Diese wirken bisweilen nackter denn je. Die Stimme lässt sich zwar unabhängig vom Körper hören, indiziert aber einen bestimmten Körper und seine Verfassung.

Körperstimmen entäußern eine ungeahnte Vielfalt, die sich sowohl abseits der Stimme der Metaphysik (Derrida) als auch einer gewöhnlichen Stimme der „ordinary language“ (Austin) ausformt.

Mit der medientechnischen Entwicklung elektromagnetischer Aufzeichnung hat sich auch der Bereich akustischer Phänomene, die sich bewahren lassen, enorm ausgeweitet. Was sich nicht wie Sprachlaute oder Noten durch codifizierte Verschriftlichungsformen notieren lässt, kann nun auf Tonband aufgezeichnet werden.

the melody of the language. Language tends to silence all that is rough, resistant and brittle about the body, and that is why the arts often use sound and noise processes that are independent of language so as to make the body audible again. As a medium between language and body, the voice is audible outside and inside the skin. Advanced sound technology is capable of accentuating both realms.

Voice and Technology

It is said that the voice in the technological era is a disembodied voice. Initially, this seems like a persuasive idea, given that the development of telecommunications is based on the separation of the human message from the human body. Unlike vision, however, hearing is a "distant sense" that does not keep its distance, as the sounds which the ear hears penetrate it and remain strong even from a spatial distance.[9] This difference is particularly important in connection with telephone and radio, but it is also there in each voice that sounds through a microphone and is reproduced through loudspeakers. What is more, an artistic handling that is not aimed at communicating information or transmitting long-distance news also shows clearly that this relationship between voice, body and technology is dialectical. A distancing of the voice from the body made possible by technology can bring the body closer to the listener, for technology also enables us to listen into the body. This is what makes the technical retrieval of the body's voices so objectionable. Sometimes these voices seem more naked than ever. Although the voice can be heard independently of the body, it indicates a specific body and its constitution.

The body's voices divulge an unanticipated diversity that is formed both apart from the voice of metaphysics (Derrida) and from any normal voice of "ordinary language" (Austin).

The realm of acoustic phenomena that can be conserved has been greatly extended thanks to the technological development of electromagnetic recording. What cannot be written down in codified forms of writing, like speech sounds or musical notes, can now be recorded on tape.

Henri Chopin, a famous representative of European "poesie sonore",[10] points out that as a result of this the acoustic repertoire of "originally 40 phonemes" has been extended to "more than 40,000 variations".[11] We owe these variations to the body, from which Chopin is able to garner a "constant, uninterrupted confusion of voices".[12]

Henri Chopin, ein bekannter Vertreter der europäischen „poesie sonore“[10], weist darauf hin, dass sich dadurch das akustische Repertoire von „ursprünglich 40 Phonemen“ auf „mehr als 40.000 Variationen“ erweitert hat.[11] Die Varianten verdanken sich dem Körper, dem Chopin ein „unaufhörliches, ununterbrochenes Stimmengewirr“[12] abzugewinnen vermag.

Mit dem Mikrophon unter die Haut gehen
Henri Chopin

Avancierte Tontechnik ermöglicht nicht nur die Psyche, sondern auch innerhäutliche Geschehnisse hörbar zu machen, da die Mikrophontechnik eine Einhörnahme in den Körper erlaubt. Erst durch Mikrophontechnik lassen sich mikroskopisch kleine Stimmelemente hörbar machen, die sonst gar nicht aus dem Körper herausdringen können.

Lange bevor ein Künstler wie Stelarc Kameras in den Körper einführte, nutze Henri Chopin in die Mundhöhle eingeführte Mikrophone, um die Blut-, Luft- und Rülpsgeräusche der inneren Organe zu Gehör zu bringen. Exemplarisch lässt sich sein Audiopoem „Le Corpsbis“ anführen, von dem er sagt, dass es „ein zweiter Körper in der Bedeutung des lateinischen Wortes ‚repetere‘ – wieder den Körper suchen.“[13] sei.

„Ich bin besessen von der Frage, was physische Poesie ist. Ich habe die Mundhöhle benutzt, die Luftröhre, den Atem, das Geräusch des Körpers. Der Körper, der Mund als Klangkörper, als Instrument.“[14]

Was hörbar wird, klingt in seinen rhythmischen Varianten und wechselnden Hallräumen klopfender, schnalzender oder pfeifender Klänge mal wie eine Maschinenhalle, ein anderes Mal wie ein sphärischer Mikrokosmos. Der Stimmakrobat vermag den Körper geradezu anzukurbeln, tabuisierte Ausdrucksmöglichkeiten zu entäußern. Im körpereigenen Echoraum, der durch das gesamte Instrumentarium elektronischer Technik ergänzt wird, strömt die Luft in Atemgezeiten ein und aus, pocht und dröhnt der Puls zu schmatzenden Kaubewegungen in genußvoller Körpermusik aus Lippenklatschen und Stimmritzengeräuschen. Die hier freigesetzten, lautlichen Mikroelemente und winzigen Stimmvibrationen verweisen nicht mehr auf konventionelle Bedeutungen. Der Referent der Stimme ist hier kein Signifikat mehr, sondern der Körper selbst, dessen akustische Vielfalt dem Hörer zustößt. Insofern sind diese Verlautbarungen nicht einfach sinnlos zu nennen. Ein dabei freigesetzter Sinn lässt sich mit Roland Barthes als *signifiance*[15] bezeichnen, als Sinn der sinnlich generiert wird.[16]

Getting under the skin with a microphone
Henri Chopin

Advanced sound technology facilitates not only audible rendering of the psyche, but also of inner-skin events, since microphone technology permits us to listen into the body. Thanks to microphone technology, microscopically small voice elements that otherwise cannot get out of the body can be made audible.

Long before an artist like Stelarc introduced cameras into the body, Henri Chopin used microphones in the mouth cavity so as to make the noises of the inner organs, the sounds of blood, air and belching, audible. An example of this is his audio-poem "Le Corpsbis" of which he said that it was "a second body in the sense of the Latin word 'repetere' – to seek the body again".[13] "I am obsessed by the issue of what physical poetry is. I have used the mouth cavity, the windpipe, breath, the noise of the body. The body, the mouth as sound box, as instrument."[14]

Everything that is audible sounds sometimes like a machine hall, sometimes like a spherical microcosm in its rhythmic variations and the changing "echo chambers" of beating, clicking or whistling noises. The voice acrobat may spur on the body, so to speak, to divulge taboo expressions. In the body's own echo chamber, which is complemented by the whole instrumentation of electronic technology, air goes in and out in tides of breath, the pulse beats and thuds in chomping movements – a pleasurable body music consisting of smacking lips and glottis sounds. The phonetic microelements and tiny voice vibrations unleashed here no longer point to conventional meanings. Here the referent of the voice is no longer a significatum but the body itself, whose acoustic diversity strikes the listener. To this extent, these sounds should not just be called meaningless. One meaning they release can be designated as *signifiance*,[15] to use Roland Barthes' term, a sense that is sensually generated.[16]

signifiance: a sensually generated sense

The states of the body resonate as shouting, throat clearing, twanging, stuttering, singing, but not in words. A mouth, responsible through skin and mucosa for absorbing food and for linguistic expressions, for oral sensuality and the production of meaning, is used not only as an organon of speech, but also as an organ, sometimes as an organ of excretion, as in Samuel Beckett's "Not I", through which words are transposed into sounds and rhythms, into the music of the body, which later digests them or

signifiance: ein sinnlich generierter Sinn

Die Befindlichkeit des Körpers erklingt schreiend, räuspernd, näselnd, stotternd oder singend, aber nicht im Wort. Ein Mund, der in Haut und Schleimhaut für Nahrungsaufnahme wie für sprachliche Entäußerungen, für orale Sinnlichkeit und Bedeutungsproduktion gleichermaßen zuständig ist, wird nicht nur als Organon der Sprache, sondern auch als Organ, gelegentlich als Ausscheidungsorgan wie in Samuel Becketts „Not I" benutzt, durch das Worte in Laute und Rhythmen, in die Musik des Körpers überführt werden, der sie verdaut hat oder als unverdaulich entäußert. Werden die Bewegungen des Körpers hörbar, verläuft nicht nur die Sinnstiftung anders. Vielmehr verlangt diese auch nach einem anderen Verstehen über ein Empfindungswissen, dass sich darüber bewußt zu werden bemüht, was ihm durch Laut und Rhythmen zustößt. Es handelt sich dabei um einen Sinn, der dem Betrachter, Hörer, Teilnehmer widerfährt. Roland Barthes prägte den Begriff im Kontext einer Neuausrichtung der Texttheorie bezogen auf andere Aspekte künstlerischer Produktion. Das Imaginäre, die Struktur des Begehrens (Lacan) sowie der Körper und seine Gesten werden als konstitutive Grundlagen verstanden und enthalten einen entsprechend zentralen Stellenwert. „*Signifiance*" wird insofern von Barthes vornehmlich mit einer Schreib-, Mal-, Sprech- oder Gesangsgeste verbunden, die – exemplarisch bezogen auf den Gesang – „aus der Tiefe der Stimmhöhlen, der Muskeln, der Schleimhäute, der Knorpel"[17] heraus, den Körper und die spezifische Art und Weise, wie er etwas hervorbringt, hörbar macht.

Signifiance entsteht abseits einer Funktionalität von Kommunikation, die mit Klarheit, deutlicher Artikulation oder Expressivität operiert, um konventionelle Bedeutungsbeilegungen zu motivieren. Ein Verständnis von Kommunikation, wie Anzieu es im Zusammenhang mit dem „Haut-Ich" thematisiert, korrespondiert diesen Überlegungen. *Signifiance* zu kommunizieren, heißt, nicht etwa codierte Botschaften zu senden, die decodierbar wären, sondern vielmehr in Resonanz zu treten.

Das Innere Ausland hörbar machen
Carlfriedrich Claus

Einen besonderen Versuch, nicht nur mit dem eigenen Körper, sondern auch mit der Natur in Resonanz zu treten, stellen die psycho-phonischen Stimmexperimente von Carlfriedrich Claus dar. Die Situiertheit des Menschen inmitten von Klängen und Geräuschen ist dabei ebenso

relinquishes them as indigestible. If the body's movements are made audible, then not only meaning-giving functions differently. Rather the latter also demands another way of understanding through a sensitive knowledge that tries to conceive what happens to it as a result of sound and rhythm. This involves a sense that befalls the viewer, listener, participant. Roland Barthes coined the term in the context of a new orientation of text theory in relation to other aspects of artistic production. The imaginary, the structure of desire (Lacan) as well as the body and its gestures are understood as constitutive bases and have a correspondingly pivotal status. To this extent, Barthes mainly links *signifiance* with a gesture of writing, painting, speaking or singing which – with reference to the example of singing – makes the body and the specific way it makes something audible "from out of the depths of the voice cavities, the muscles, the mucosa, the cartilage".[17]

Signifiance emerges apart from a communicative functionality that operates with clarity, clear articulation and expressiveness so as to motivate participation in conventional meaning. An understanding of language as addressed by Anzieu in connection with the "skin-ego" corresponds to these considerations. To communicate *signifiance* means for example not sending coded messages that might be decoded, but rather entering into a resonance.

Making the "inner outland" audible
Carlfriedrich Claus

The psycho-phonetic voice experiments undertaken by Carlfriedrich Claus represent a special attempt to enter into resonance not only with one's own body but also with nature. Man's location in the midst of sounds and noises is a point of departure for experimental sound process, as is the body as a "system of forces" capable of unleashing "elemental forces". Controlled uncontrolled self-experiments aim at "unconscious communication between body and consciousness". Feedbacks between voice and hearing in the process of hearing oneself enable one to respond to the act of breathing in and out, to noise segments of the mucosa and vibrations of the vocal chords. As a result of such reactions, which in the case of Claus resulted from his decades-long exploration of voice, language and articulation processes, a process is set in motion that is, as it were, itself the theme of the a-semantic poetic compositions.

In his composition for radio "Lautaggregat" (Sound Aggregate),[18] which can serve as an example, Carlfriedrich Claus linked 32 sound and speech operations lasting

Ausgangspunkt für experimentelle Lautprozesse wie der Körper als ein „System von Kräften", das „Elementargewalten" freizusetzen vermag. Kontrolliert unkontrollierte Selbstexperimente zielen auf eine „unbewusste Kommunikation von Körper und Bewusstsein". Rückkopplungen zwischen Stimme und Gehör im Vorgang des Sich-selber-Hörens ermöglichen auf die Vorgänge des Ein- und Ausatmens, auf Geräuschsegmente der Schleimhäute und Vibrationen der Stimmbänder zu reagieren. Durch solche Reaktionen, die bei Claus auf der Grundlage einer jahrzehntelangen Erforschung von Stimm-, Sprach- und Artikulationsvorgängen erfolgt, wird ein Prozess in Gang gesetzt, der gleichsam selber Thema der asemantischen poetischen Kompositionen ist.

In seiner Radiokomposition „Lautaggregat"[18], die exemplarisch angeführt werden kann, hat Carlfriedrich Claus 32 Laut- und Sprechoperationen, die eine Dauer zwischen 30 Sekunden und 15 Minuten haben, zu einem ca. 42 minütigen Stück verbunden. Durch eine spezielle Kunstkopfproduktion gelang es, diese einzelnen Sprechoperationen im Studio zu verräumlichen und in dreidimensionalen Raumfiguren im stereophonen Hör-Raum zu versinnlichen. Eine mit technischen Mitteln des Radios hinzugefügte vielfache Überlagerung und Schichtung seiner Sprechoperationen gab der Komposition eine palimpsestartige Charakteristik, die jedoch dynamisch bleibt, sich in Phasen ständig verwandelt und umformt.

Durch einen deutlichen Mangel an Vokalen, fehlt dem „Lautaggregat" alles Gefällige, während die „Rauheit" von Konsonanten dominiert, von der Roland Barthes sagt:. „Die ‚Rauheit' ist der Körper in der singenden Stimme, in der schreibenden Hand, im ausführenden Körperteil."[19]

Im „Lautaggregat" wird ganz konkret hörbar, dass die Stimme auf ihrem Weg durch den Körper auf Widerstände stößt, denn die Konsonanten schaffen „innere Stauungen".Weitere innerhäutige Widerstände im Einsatz der Sprechwerkzeuge kommen hinzu. „Ich baue im Mundraum Widerstände auf, indem ich die Zunge entweder hochstelle oder vorwärtspresse und den Luftstrom hindurchzischen lasse und dadurch geht eine Dynamik nach innen. Es entsteht also eine Kräfteansammlung, eine Kräftekonzentration durch diese Stauungen."[20]

Durch den hörbaren, mit Mundhöhle, Stimmritze oder Zunge agierenden Körper zeigt sich eine sinnlich sinngenerierende Kraft des Körpers, unabhängig von Bedeutungssetzungen. Diese tritt in Wechselwirkung mit den Kräften der Natur- und Umweltgeräusche. In der Dichte der Überlagerungen lassen sich zwischendurch auch Wassergeräusche oder Tierstimmen hören. Wie sonst nur die

between 30 seconds and 15 minutes, to make an approximately 42-minute long piece/ radio play. Thanks to a specially produced artificial head, he succeeded in spatialising these individual speech operations in the studio and in sensualising them in three-dimensional spatial figures in the stereophonic hearing space. A multiple superimposition and layering of his speech operations achieved by the technical means of the radio gave the composition the character of a palimpsest which remained dynamic however, constantly changing and reshaping itself at different phases.

As a result of an obvious lack of vowels, "Lautaggregat" has no pleasing aspect. What predominates is the roughness of the consonants, of which Barthes says: "The 'roughness' is the body in the singing voice, in the writing hand, in the performing body part."[19]

That the voice, on its way through the body, meets resistance because the consonants create "internal congestion" becomes clearly audible in "Lautaggregat". Other inner-skin resistances join these when the speech tools are used. "I build up resistances in the mouth cavity by either raising the tongue or pushing it forwards and letting the stream of air hiss through, so that a dynamism proceeds inwards. This causes a gathering of forces, a concentration of forces due to this congestion."[20]

The audible body, operating with the oral cavity, glottis or tongue, reveals a sensually sense-generating force of the body, independently of posited meanings. This force interacts with the forces of the noises of nature and the environment. Sometimes the sounds of water or the voices of animals can be heard in the dense superimpositions. As otherwise only the skin, here the voice exhibits a permeability that is present both inside the body and also in the exterior surroundings.

Touching and touched

Given that skin, to the extent that it touches something or someone, is always also touched skin, Anzieu can see it as a model for further reflective sensations. In as much as the voice forms an audio-phonetic system with hearing, the voice also exhibits this reflective sensation. In the course of this, sound waves take the labyrinthine path into the inside, past skins and hairs and through the skin – the eardrum.

It is impossible from this point of view to speak of the body as an object. For Valéry too the body is "not exclusively a thing, and it belongs to us somewhat less than we belong to it".[21]

Haut, weist Stimme hier eine Durchlässigkeit auf, die sowohl ins Innere des Körpers als auch zum Äußeren der Umwelt gegeben ist.

Berührend und Berührt

Da die Haut, sofern sie etwas oder jemanden berührt, immer zugleich auch berührte Haut ist, kann Anzieu sie modellhaft für weitere reflexive Empfindungen betrachten. Sofern die Stimme mit dem Gehör ein audio-phonisches-System bildet, weist auch sie diese reflexive Empfindung auf. Dabei nehmen Schallwellen den labyrinthischen Weg ins Innere an Häuten und Härchen vorbei sowie durch die Haut – das Trommelfell – hindurch.

Aus dieser Perspektive wird es unmöglich, vom Körper als einem Gegenstand zu sprechen. Auch für Valéry ist der Körper „nicht ausschließlich eine Sache, und er gehört uns etwas weniger, als wir ihm angehören."[21]

„Dieses Etwas, so meinig und doch so geheimnisvoll, manchmal auch und letztlich immer unser gefährlichster Widersacher, ist das Bedrängendste, das Beständigste und das Veränderlichste, was es gibt: jede Beständigkeit und jede Veränderung gehören nämlich ihm."[22]

Mit Haut und Hören lässt sich der Körper nicht mehr als Objekt, sondern als Transformator bezeichnen, wenn sein Hauptkennzeichen bewusst gemacht wird: seine vielfältige Fähigkeit zur Veränderung. Aus dieser Perspektive lassen sich auch das Hören und die Stimme anders verstehen. Von der Haut aus den Schall, Sprache, Klang und Geräusch erfassen, heißt ihren Druck, ihr Gewicht, ihre Wärme und Kälte, ihre Trockenheit oder Feuchtigeit, ihre Weichheit oder ihr Kratzen zu empfinden.

"This something, so much mine and yet so mysterious, sometimes and ultimately always our most treacherous opponent, is the most pressing, the most constant and the most mutable thing there is; every constancy and every change belong namely to it."[22]

Given its skin and hearing, the body can no longer be designated as an object but as a transformer, once its main feature is brought to mind: its great capacity to change. From this viewpoint, hearing and the voice can also be understood differently. To grasp sound, language, tone and noise through the skin means sensing their pressure, weight, warmth and coldness, their dryness and humidity, their softness or scratchiness.

NOTES

[1] Vgl. Paul Valéry, „La Pléiade", *Œuvres complètes, Bd. 2*, S. 215f.

[2] Vgl. Alfred Tomatis, *Der Klang des Lebens* (Reinbek b. Hamburg: 1990).

[3] Joachim Ernst Berendt, „Ich höre, also bin ich", in: *Über das Hören*, hrsg. von Thomas Vogel (Tübingen: 1998), 69-90, hier 70.

[4] Vgl. Michel Serres, *Die fünf Sinne* (Frankfurt/Main: 1998),157.

[5] Didier Anzieu, *Das Haut-Ich* (Frankfurt/Main: 1991), 75.

[6] Judith Butler, *Haß spricht. Zur Politik des Performativen* (Berlin: 1998), 15.

[7] ebenda.

[8] Vgl. Michel Serres, *Die fünf Sinne*, a.a.O., 162.

[1] Cf. Paul Valéry, "La Pléiade", *Œuvres complètes, vol. 2*, 215f.

[2] Cf. Alfred Tomatis, *Der Klang des Lebens* (Reinbek b. Hamburg: 1990).

[3] Joachim Ernst Berendt, "Ich höre, also bin ich", in *Über das Hören*, ed. by Thomas Vogel (Tübingen: 1998), 69-90, here 70.

[4] Cf. Michel Serres, *Die fünf Sinne* (Frankfurt/Main: 1998), 157.

[5] Didier Anzieu, *Das Haut-Ich* (Frankfurt/Main: 1991), 75.

[6] Judith Butler, *Haß spricht. Zur Politik des Performativen* (Berlin: 1998), 15.

[7] ibid.

[8] Cf. Michel Serres, *Die fünf Sinne*, loc. cit., 162.

[9] Vgl. ausführlich zu den Eigenarten des Gehörsinns, Petra Maria Meyer, „Minimalia zur philosophischen Bedeutung des Hörens und des Hörbaren", in: Dies. (Hg.), *acoustic turn* (München: 2008), 47-73.

[10] Den Beginn der „poesie sonore" verbindet man zumeist mit dem lettristischen Poeten François Dufrêne. In Weiterführung insbesondere auch dadaistischer Lautgedichte gründete Isidor Isou die literarische Bewegung der Lettristen, nach „lettre", franz. Buchstabe, um visuell und auditiv durch eine Atomisierung von Worten zu Buchstaben und Lauten neue poetische Wege einzuschlagen. Stimmen oder Phoneme werden dabei zu akustischen Materialien sinnfreier Kompositionen. Bernhard Heidsiek und Henri Chopin führten diese Poesie-Tradition in Frankreich, Brion Gysin z.B. in den USA fort.

[11] Henri Chopin im Gespräch mit Klaus Schöning, in der Sendung: „Im Gespräch: Henri Chopin", Prod. WDR 1991.

[12] ebenda.

[13] Henri Chopin, zit. nach der Hörstückbeschreibung zur „Audiothek" des WDR, Köln auf der Dokumenta 8, Kassel 1987, S. 330.

[14] ebenda.

[15] „Qu'est-ce que la signifiance? C'est le sens en ce qu'il est produit sensuellement." Roland Barthes, „Le plaisir du texte", *Œuvres complètes, Tome 2 1966-1973, 1495-1529*, hier 1526.

[16] Vgl. ausführlich dazu: Petra Maria Meyer, „Signifiance: der Sinn, der mir zustößt. Zur Sinnlichkeit der Sinnstiftung in der künstlerischen Praxis von Arnulf Rainer und Carlfriedrich Claus unter Berücksichtigung der diskursiven Voraussetzungen eines anderen Verstehens von Friedrich Nietzsche bis Roland Barthes", in: Martin Zenck (Hg.), *Erzeugen und Nachvollziehen von Sinn. Rationale, performative und mimetische Verstehensbegriffe in den Kulturwissenschaften*, erscheint voraussichtlich München 2010, 253-281.

[17] Roland Barthes, „Die Rauheit der Stimme", in: *Was singt mir, der ich höre in meinem Körper das Lied* (Berlin: 1979), 23.

[18] Carlfriedrich Claus, *Lautaggregat*, WDR 1993.

[19] Roland Barthes, *Der entgegenkommende und der stumpfe Sinn*, a.a.O., 277.

[20] Carlfriedrich Claus, zit. nach Begleitheft zur CD „Lautaggregat", hrsg. von Susanne Anna. Städtische Kultursammlung Chemnitz 1995, 25/26.

[21] Paul Valéry, *Cahiers, Hefte 3*, hrsg. von H. Köhler / J. Schmidt-Radfeldt (Frankfurt/Main: 1989), 205.

[22] A.a.O, 206.

[9] For details on the peculiarities of the sense of hearing see Petra Maria Meyer, "Minimalia zur philosophischen Bedeutung des Hörens und des Hörbaren", in Meyer (ed.), *acoustic turn* (Munich: 2008), 47-73.

[10] The beginnings of "poesie sonore" are often linked with the lettrist poet François Dufrêne. As a continuation of Dadaist phonetic poems in particular, Isidor Isou founded the literary movment known as Lettrism so as to visually and acoustically blaze new poetic paths by atomising words into letters and sound. Voices or phonemes thus became acoustic material for compositions without meanings. Bernhard Heidsiek and Henri Chopin continued this poetry tradition in France, Brion Gysin, for example, in the US.

[11] Henri Chopin in conversation with Klaus Schöning, during the radio programme "Im Gespräch: Henri Chopin", produced by WDR 1991.

[12] ibid.

[13] Henri Chopin, quoted from the description of the radio piece "Audiothek" for WDR, Cologne at Dokumenta 8, Kassel 1987, 330.

[14] ibid.

[15] "Qu'est-ce que la signifiance? C'est le sens en ce qu'il est produit sensuellement." Roland Barthes, "Le plaisir du texte", *Œuvres complètes, vol. 2 1966-1973, 1495-1529*, here 1526.

[16] Cf. for more details: Petra Maria Meyer, "Signifiance: der Sinn, der mir zustößt. Zur Sinnlichkeit der Sinnstiftung in der künstlerischen Praxis von Arnulf Rainer und Carlfriedrich Claus unter Berücksichtigung der diskursiven Voraussetzungen eines anderen Verstehens von Friedrich Nietzsche bis Roland Barthes", in Martin Zenck (ed.), *Erzeugen und Nachvollziehen von Sinn. Rationale, performative und mimetische Verstehensbegriffe in den Kulturwissenschaften*, scheduled for publication in Munich 2010, 253-281.

[17] Roland Barthes, "Die Rauheit der Stimme", in *Was singt mir, der ich höre in meinem Körper das Lied* (Berlin: 1979), 23.

[18] Carlfriedrich Claus, *Lautaggregat*, WDR 1993.

[19] Roland Barthes, *Der entgegenkommende und der stumpfe Sinn*, loc. cit., 277.

[20] Carlfriedrich Claus, quoted from booklet to the CD *Lautaggregat*, ed. by Susanne Anna. Städtische Kultursammlung Chemnitz 1995, 25/26.

[21] Paul Valéry, *Cahiers, vol. 3*, ed. by H. Köhler / J. Schmidt-Radfeldt (Frankfurt/Main: 1989), 205.

[22] loc. cit., 206.

S L E E P T A L K / P A U L D I C K I N S O N

1986 - ongoing / Sound recordings

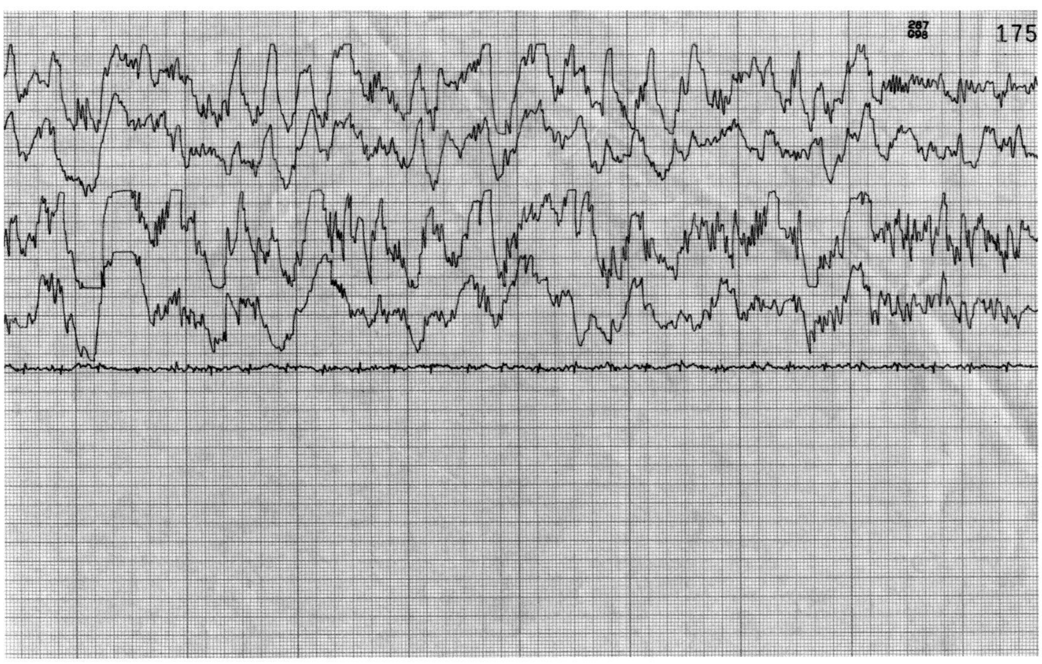

Upon first learning of my sleep talking talents, I was curious about the relationship these utterances might have to my waking life, and to some vague idea of a "true self" existing beneath the layers of social conditioning. It is a widely held assumption that on occasion, the truth seeps through this membrane to lay bare primal motivations and deep insecurities - even profound wisdom. Or, from a mediumistic approach, cures and remedies might be revealed. In my personal experience of the sleep talking process, I have found no such grand revelations yet. Instead, I have encountered humor arising from absurd correlations and juxtapositions. The recordings have further been used as source materials for sculptural objects, performances and video installations.

(The recordings used here are excerpted from "Sleep Talk Recordings, Vol.1: 1986-2000".)

1987, March 31

Cost more Call or people
Paps ur people Mmm People ok
Oggy doogy Wha Ummhmm
Mmmm

Whwhwhwhwhu

1987, June 19

Anzvay zwoke by manzeego
Teresh treek go panzine Oohhh
Throw it out, transvestite
Right? Riiiight.

1993, April 09

Go girl, go girdles yeh

1993, April 27

Anar bug fly head our tant di
tower Ohhh mice head It's my
neighbors and I have to be
able to serve my windows close
Ahh boy Umm hey they getting
away Oh god yeah Whew, I
wonder how they're doin' Wha
they're doin'

1996, October 12

Uuuurrrrrrr Babpersillive
sirrive sirrilly I am sirrilly
I am Offce buh bad poose bad
poost Bbbhbhbhhbhbhb

1998, February 13

Yeaup I got somethin out fer
dissan night Ixon tiss gaaa
waaaaah gotta get somethin
soon up there in my room
Aaduh gaaaaa Get di oteily
slides around on her head
With lonely ohhh (cough) nmmm

1999, August 22

MMMMMM MMMMMM
shp-p-p-p
Lance Campbell
sampling stool
where is my lamb pole?
mmmmm
my boy oh boy
ahh jeez gosh
UHM okay
MMMMMMMM MMMM MM MM MMM
shucks
mmmm mmmm
is it all as a much bigger file
Weow
'tsa total victim vittle
climb down

1999, August 24

Awwww leeta leper leaper
leaper leaper leaper leaper
leper leaper leper leper
leper leaper leper leper

leper leper leaper
(lip squeal)
no Dana jus- just slice it thin
ohhhhhh d-don't no no no nohhh
hff bff bvvv p-p-p-p-l
bzzaowww dzoh du wets

1999, November 01
A gu zillz a wupa zed
yer up yer head
mmmmmmmmm- hyello
gone be a lill
piss what I dill
gettin' oola from yoot

1999, December 01
B-b-b-b-b-b-b-b-b-b-b-b-b-b-
<kiss kiss kiss kiss kiss kiss>
Man with the golden gun

1999, December 28
Mmmm
ahhh well,
budayyduhdahduhdoohyuh
dahhtuhtowhtuhl
he's comin' over there to come
duhcore talkin' tez
singin here
mmmm mmmmm mmm mmmmm
MMMMMMMM
whut eight
I gotta log bout it gin teeth
aww some stuff in back here
see what reviews I can get back
here
like we
my mom didn't know
about it but
but others yes

this

full tilt fool!

2000, January 03
Dove bwhy dwy
why do we have to have a duet?

2000, January 24
Pffffff
well
RRR key boost dowd to Ron to
Sue Anne give
Puff Duty
mmp
of course

IMOGEN STIDWORTHY /

TOPOGRAPHY OF A VOICE (2008/2009)

Copperplate and offset print /

6 x 510 x 320 mm, 1 x 25.5 x 320 mm

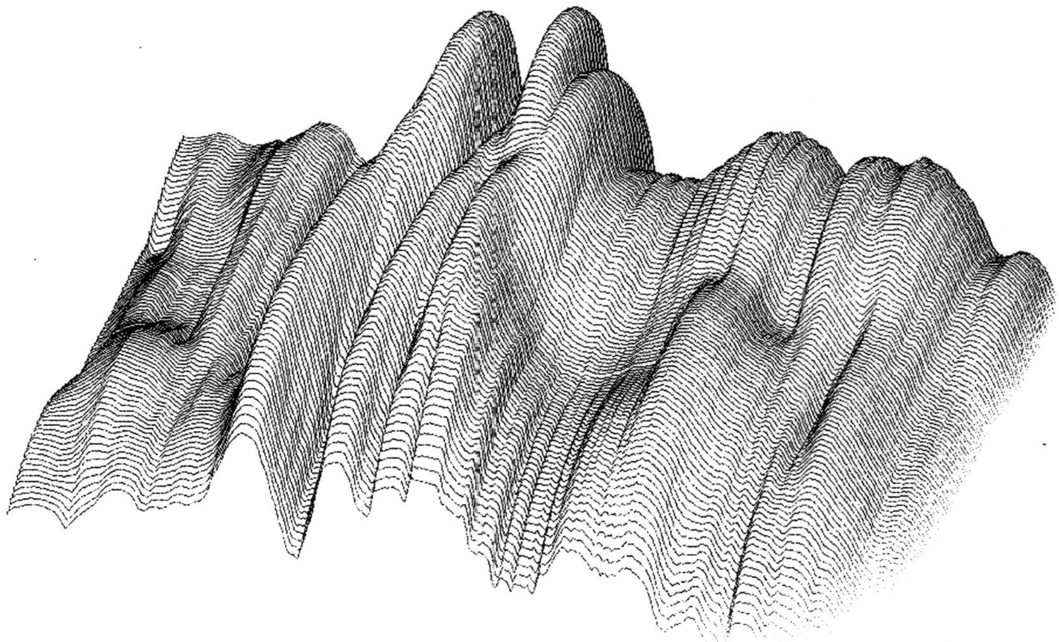

Toxteth

ˈgɛr ↘ɪə

"'b's and 'd's and 't's can be dentalised – if you go 'd-d-d-d-d' your tongue hits the roof of the mouth, the alveolar ridge. Here, rather than hitting against the roof of the mouth – which is quite an effort – it just bangs against the top teeth, so you get that slight hissiness. Almost like the tongue's too big for the mouth space.

'I SAY "GET HERE"... VERY SLOW AND CAREFUL.' EDGE HILL 'I KNEW YOU WERE

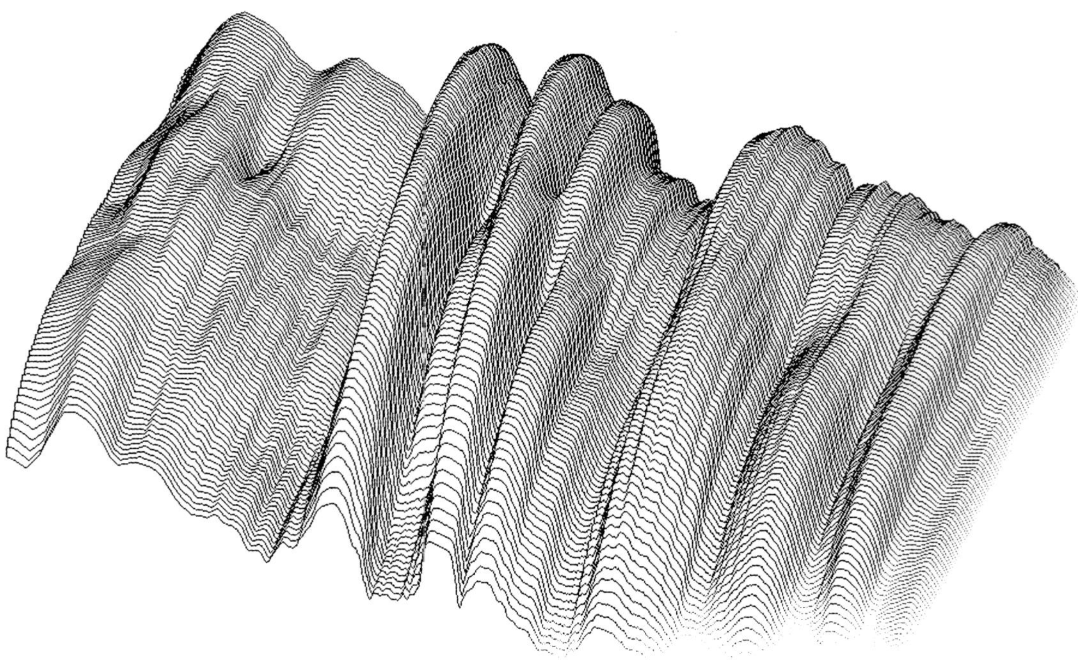

Everton

gɛɾ ˈɪjə

Up here you learn that back of the throat tension –
the back of the throat is really quite active in
sounds like 'wachh'. You haven't got that western 'drive'
but here, you could say, people almost have a slightly
harder skin at the back of their tongues
because it's in use all the time.

FROM UP THERE, YOU TALK A BIT MORE DELICATE.' OLD SWAN 'EH, I'M ASKING

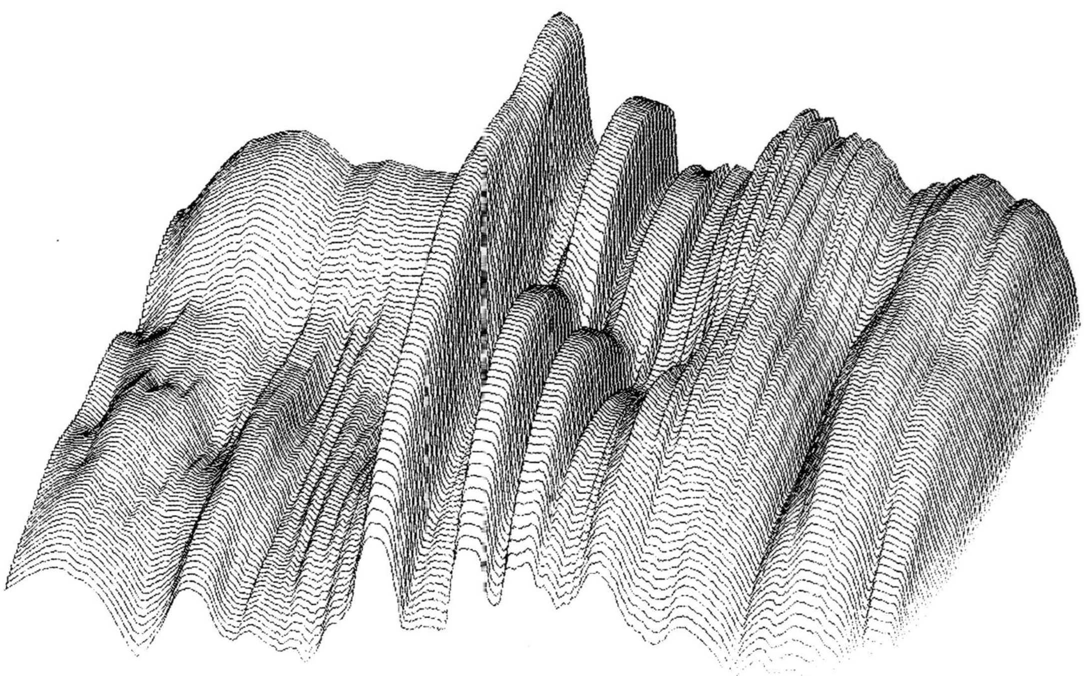

Norris Green

ˈgɛ·ɾ i·ə

It's the uvular rather than the velar fricative,
so instead of 'can't' you'll get 'khants, khhants'; 'back' – 'bakh';
'neck' – 'nekh'. In terms of resonators, they're in the head,
chest, body – lower sounds in the chest and body, high
sounds in the chest and head. It tends to be squeaky – it goes up
into the head, and women much more so than men.
High pitched girls...

YOU.' DINGLE **'IT'S THE POWER, IT'S THE CONTROL.'** EDGE HILL **'IF YOU YELL IT**

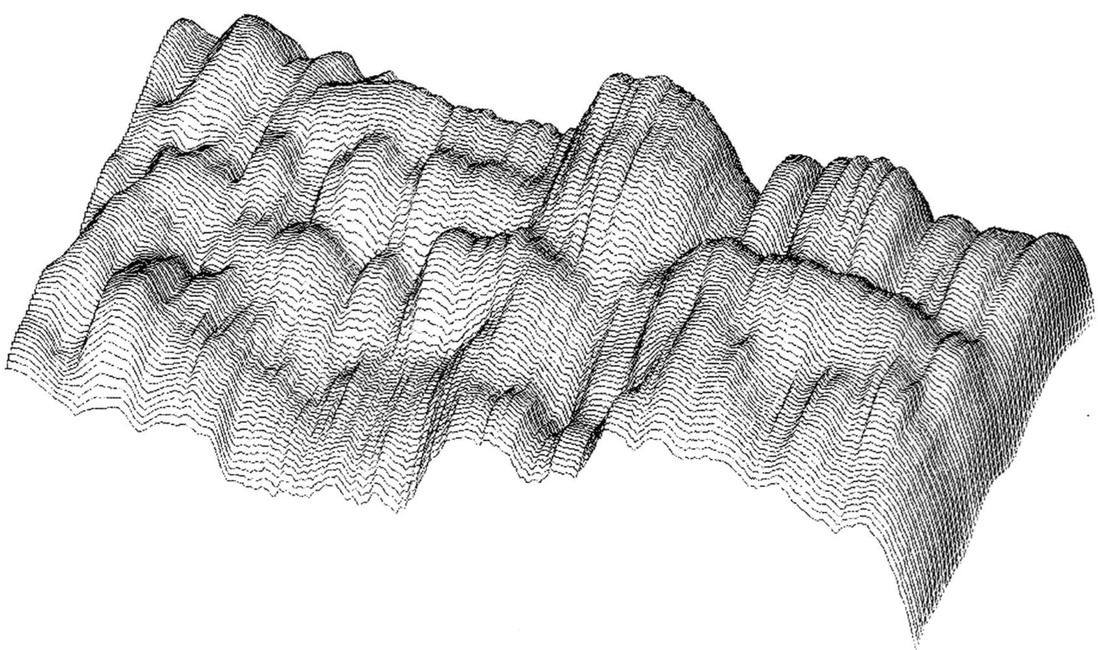

Edge Hill

{W oˑ ˈgɛɹ iə W}

The energy in the vowels, it works like a little punch.
The 'a' in 'dance' – it'll be the 'a' a Southerner would use in 'apple', rather than 'darns' or 'daft'. The posh version holds onto the 'h'; 'r's and 'l's are quite strong. The 't's are used to really press the point, because the consonants stop the
vowel sounds so the message really gets cut when you hit a vowel – they tend to use them like spitting peas.

YOU'RE LOSING IT AND WHEN YOU'VE LOST IT, YOU'RE GONE.' SCOTLAND ROAD

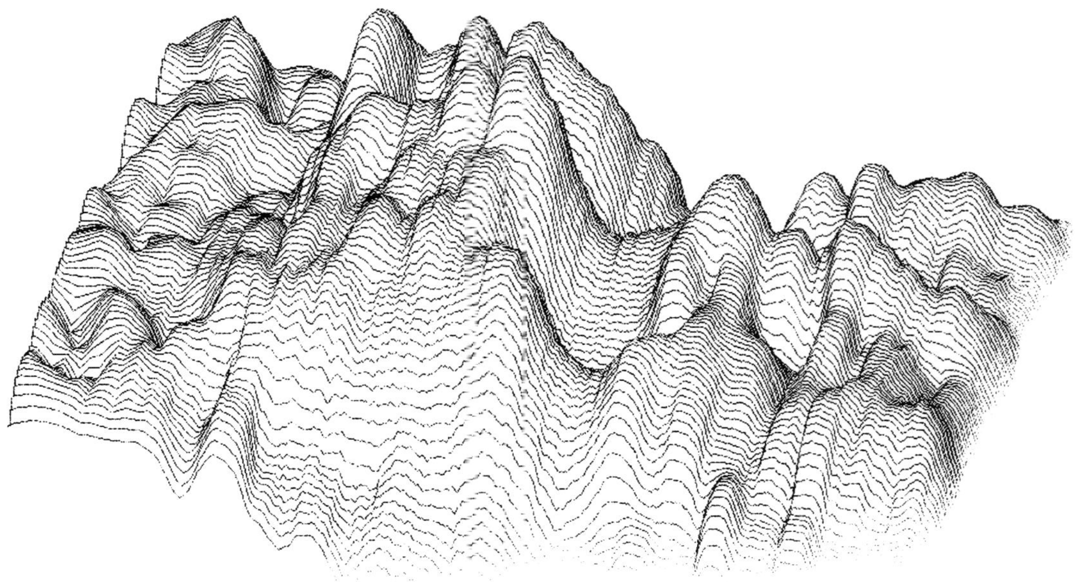

Toxteth, whispered

oʊ ˈgɛɹ ↘iˑə

It's very musically led in terms of where you put the stress in a line, and so on – and the breath's important. There are busy tongue movements which have their roots further to the east. You get that tapped 'ɾ' and that combines with the sing-song southern sound to give you quite a tense back of throat and back of tongue and quite a high back of tongue.

'HEY YOU! WHAT THE HELL YOU DOING?' WELSH STREETS **'WHEN YOU SAY IT IN A**

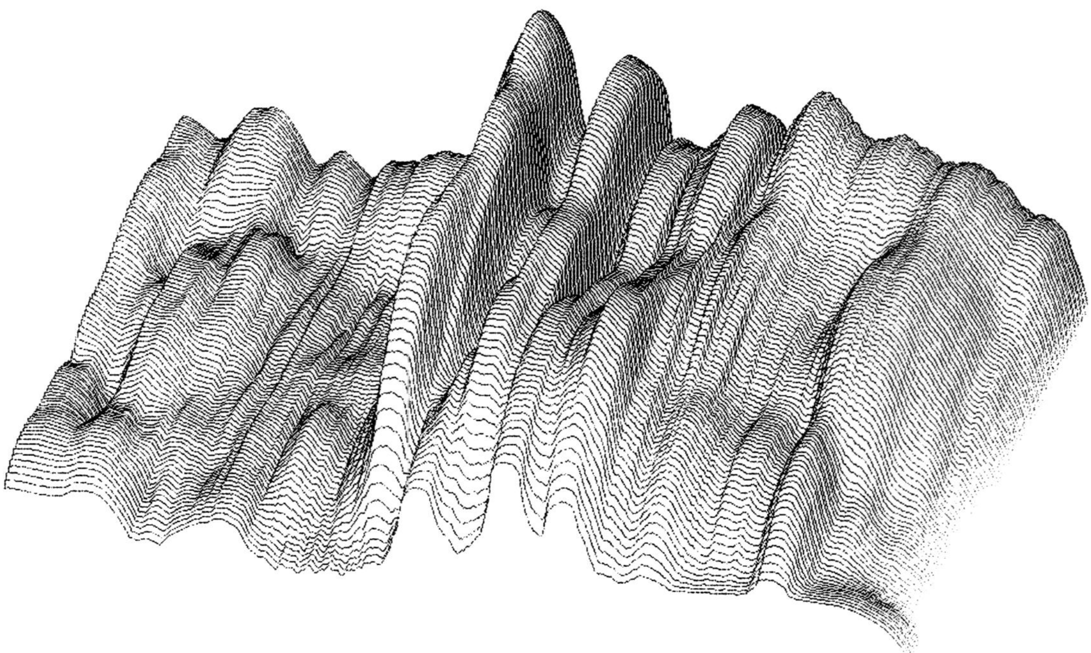

Kensington

ˈgɛɾ ɪə ↘ ˌna̰

There's a sort of coming and going of energy
in the sound, coming from our antecedents, if you like,
'de-dah de de de dah de de, de dah de de de dah de de…',
and it's how the musicians who couldn't read music
used to put tunes to each other:
'Ai de diddly diddly ai de die, de diddly diddly ai de dai…'

QUIET VOICE, IT'S MUCH MORE EFFECTIVE THAN SHOUTING.' SCOTLAND ROAD

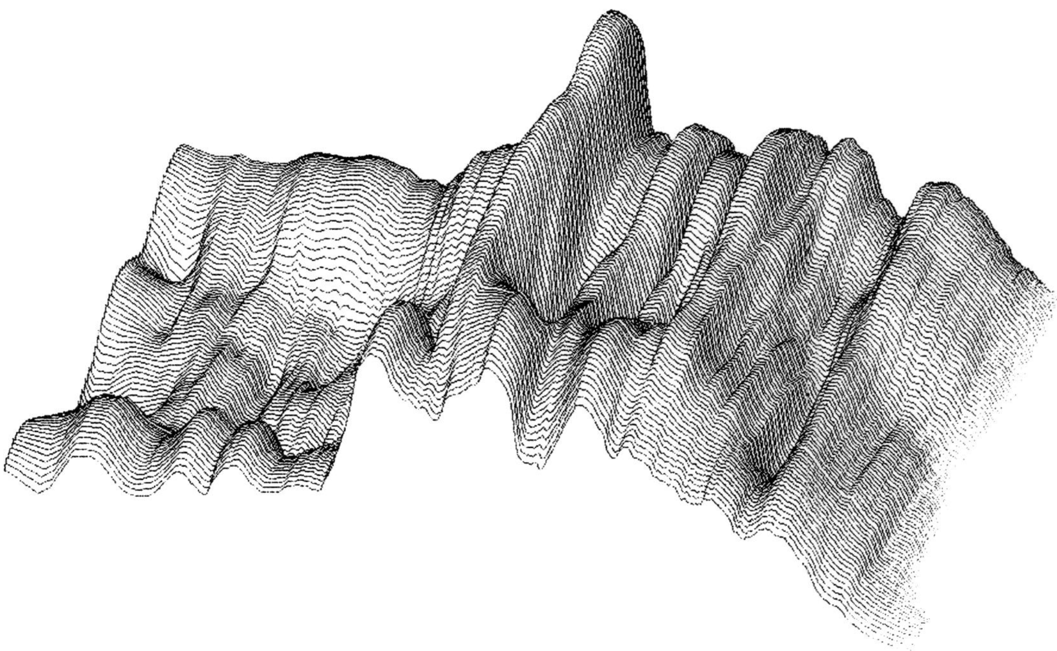

Actress mimicking

ˈgjɛɹ ↘i ˑ↗ə

So you're going along like this in the rhythm,
and every now and again you sort of stretch it, just to make
something happen. The sounds are almost being
pulled out of your mouth in a continuous stream, like a
stream of consciousness...

'THAT ACCENT WE GOT DOWN THERE, I THINK IT'S GOT ALOT TO DO WITH THE

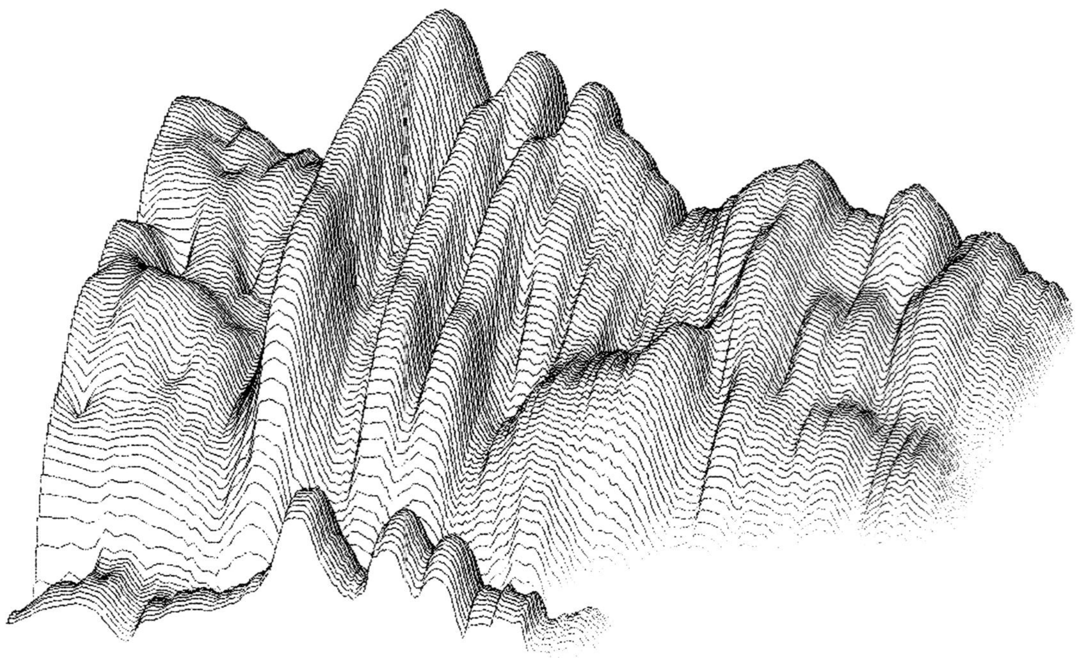

Huyton

{Vh ˈgɛɹ ↘ɪə naʊ Vh}

There's the female thing, it goes in and out of your nose
because the soft palate's slightly open, and you get what we call 'nasal
bleed' – and it's in a minor key, so you get that sinusy whine.
You'll get 't's replaced by glottal stops except when you want
to emphasise – 'Be*tt*er ge*t* on' – that 't' is really like a
finger in the chest and it really means '*Get on*!'.

IMMIGRATION.' TOXTETH **'WELL I ALWAYS THOUGHT I WAS COMMON AND YET WHEN**

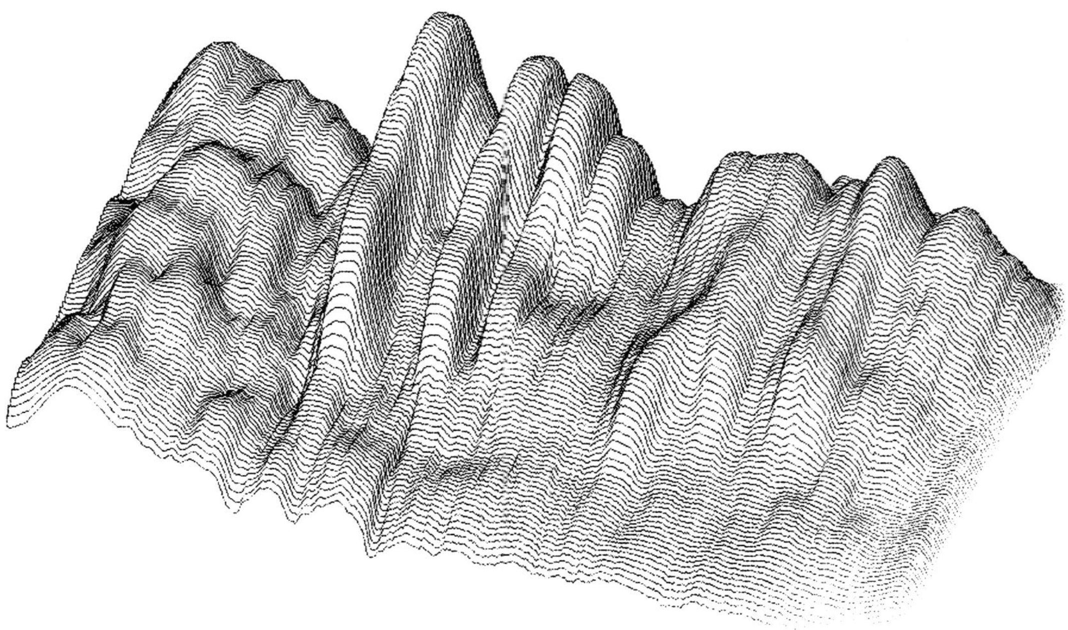

Vauxhall

{Vh ˈgɛɹ ɪjə Vh}

Everyone I know, they'll put in the 'f' word,
but not the whole 'f' word – so it's like 'Foch'n'. It's not held in your
throat, it sort of bounces around your throat.
One of the theatre students came in late the other day and he said,
'Ah 'm foch'n sorry Terry, bu' the foch'n buzzies foch'n stopped me cos
thee won' me foch'n road tax, an' ah'm no' fochin' 'avin i'.'

MOVED UP TO THE NORTH END, THEY CALLED ME THE POSH ONE.' EVERTON 'IT

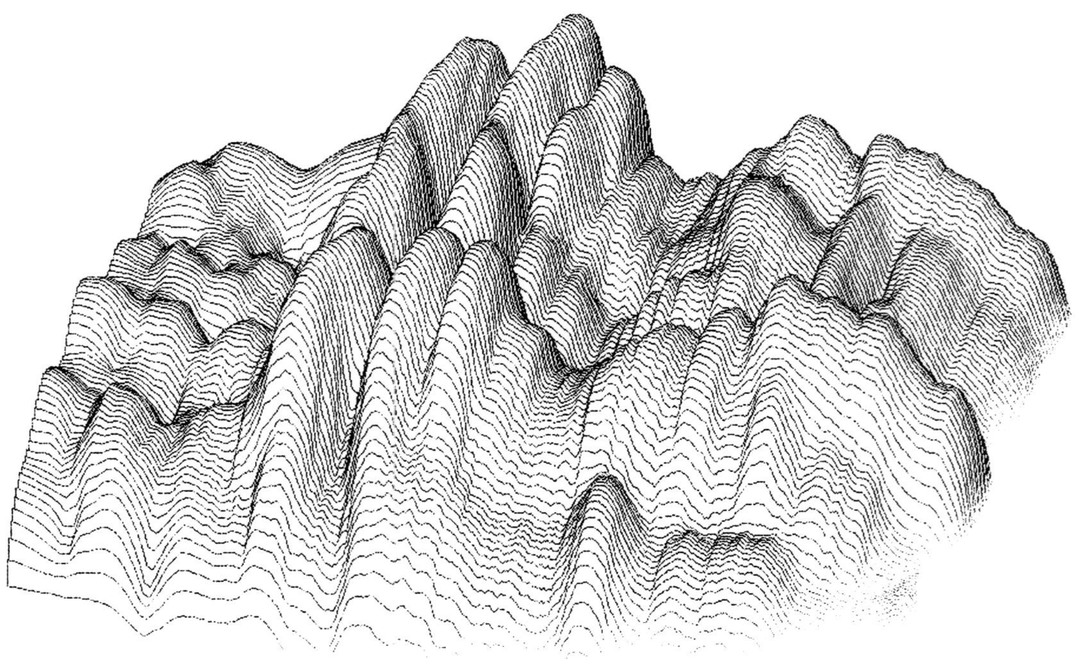

Dingle

ˈgɛɾ ɪə ˈju ˌtʉ

'H' is generally dropped – 'Ah'm goin' 'ome' –
'ome' – and there's a standard deviation between north, south, east
and west on the 'air' sounds. Over the water you'll get the deep 'urr'
sounds – 'Ave yer gorrenny spur cash?'.
It's much more over here that you'll hear a smiley one,
and they'll really lean on that vowel – 'spair cash' –
and they just don't mix.

BRINGS BACK THE BIG UNION PEOPLE AND THE DOCKERS.' EDGE HILL 'WILL YOU

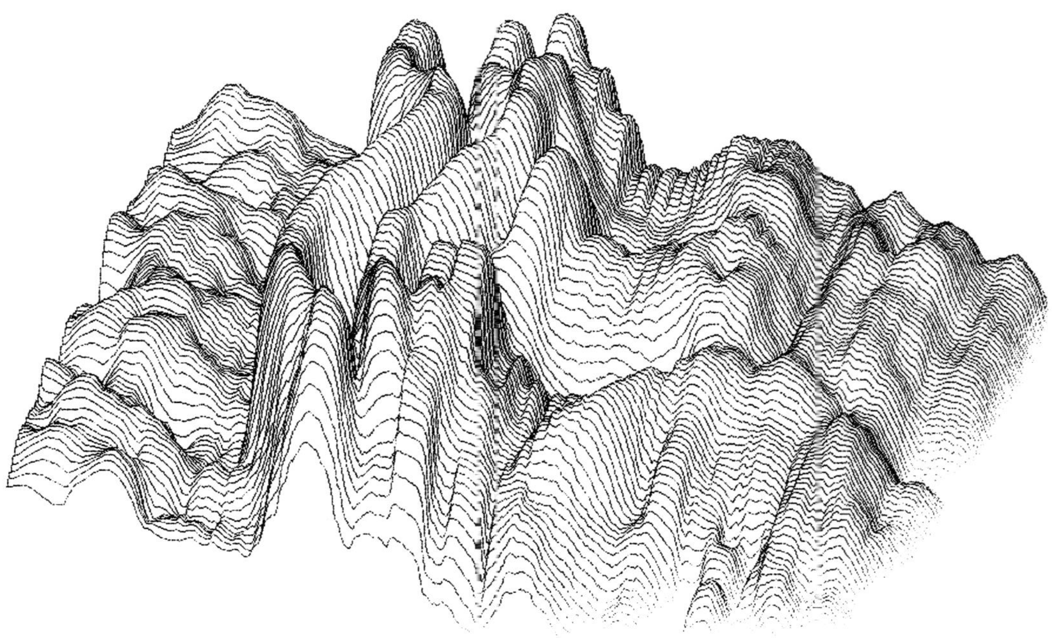

Scotland Road

gɛɹ ↗ˈi↘ə ↗ˌjuː

There's a pulling back of the corners
and a tight smile. The lips are drawn back wide –
– that's why you tend to see these creases come up in younger people.
And there's a point of tension in the jaw,
it doesn't move very much so you have to spread the
hole of the mouth as wide as possible to let the sound out."

SPEAK PROPER!' EVERTON **'YES, I'M HERE! WHAT YOU WANT FROM ME?'** GRANBY

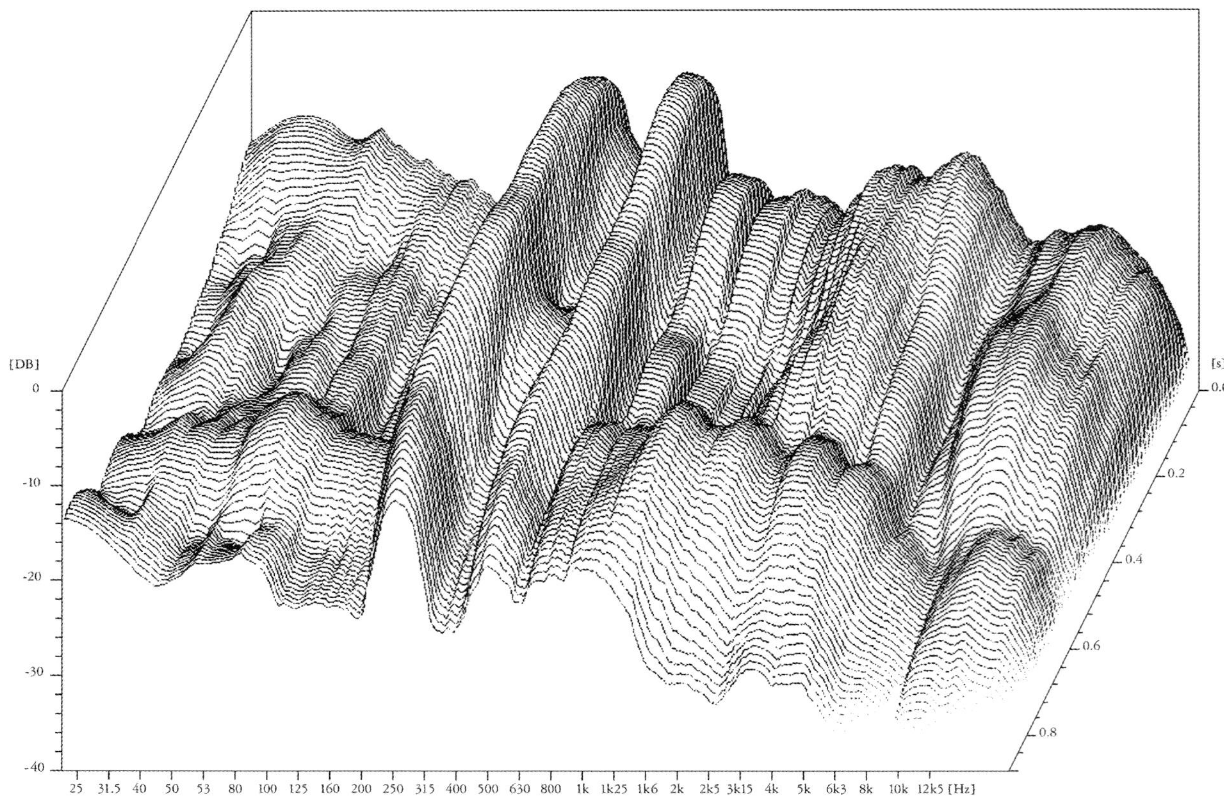

Topography of a Voice asks: how to describe an accent? Like all accents, Scouse, spoken in Liverpool in the UK, is associated with certain characteristics, figures and images in popular culture, and specific and economic conditions – the basis for a character profile is built up. Recordings of the Scouse phrase 'Get here!' (meaning come here, and spoken almost exclusively by women – a legacy of child-care), which were made in different neighbourhoods in the city, are submitted to various forms of transcription and translation. The voices include those of local people whose families have lived here for generations, actresses in training, who are working on an authentic Scouse accent, and recent immigrants from Somalia, for whom mastering the local slang is key to local acceptance. The words of a voice coach and dialect specialist provide an explanation of the physiological production of the Scouse sound, which runs as a central narrative through the pages. Each of these transcriptions and translations is partial, both grounded and limited by its particular terms: phonetics (IPA), comments about the accent by Scouse speakers, and 'waterfall plots' – digital visualisations produced by a sound analysis programme, which charts decibels, wavelength and duration.

(The audio samples in *Topography of a Voice* are part of a larger collection made for *Get Here*, a 10.2 surround sound installation, 2006).

MLADEN DOLAR / THE PHONETIC BURROW

I propose to examine the notion of phonetic skin through one of the most striking of Kafka's stories, "The Burrow". It was written in the winter of 1923/24, shortly before his death, not quite the last piece he wrote, but it seems to have been the one before last, the last one being notoriously "Josephine the Singer". If we look at these two stories together, as forming a strange diptych, then there is the astounding and inscrutable fact that Kafka, on the brink of death, took the problem of sound and voice as the last most tenuous and tenacious red thread of his pursuit, something that goes perhaps most straight to the core of his work, and something that has the value of a testament.[1]

The story describes an animal, usually taken to be a badger, although it is never named in the story itself. It goes around in its elaborate and convoluted underground burrow, its subterranean castle, the underground counterpart of the other Castle and its labyrinths, and this citadel was meticulously designed in such a way that it would keep all possible enemies at bay. This took a superb effort of craftsmanship underpinned by a magnificent streak of paranoia. In order to make this underground bastion safe and unassailable, the animal had to carefully scrutinize all possible strategies of all imaginable enemies and devise ways to counteract them. All eventualities had to be considered and seen to, but no matter how scrupulous the efforts, no measures seem to be thorough enough. The more 'the badger' exerts itself, the more there remains to be done. Paranoia has the structure of a self-fulfilling prophecy, it is self-propelling, engendering ever more paranoia, the more enemies one imagines the more they lurk around the corner.

The burrow is a retreat, the secret hideaway most carefully protected against all outer threats. It is the inside which should be clearly separated from the outside – there is a topological problem at the heart of this story, the problem of a division of space, a line of demarcation. Obviously, the biggest and the most immediate problem is that of the entry/exit, the neuralgic spot of transition between the inside and the outside of the burrow and which presents the most vulnerable point. The first part of the story deals with this at some length.

No matter how much the entry is hidden and overlaid by moss, whenever 'the badger' has to emerge from his burrow or go back inside this involves the moment of greatest danger, it requires a series of anguished strategic maneuvers, but the moment of transition is always the moment of exposure to risk which cannot be avoided. The first peep outside has to be accomplished by trusting the luck, and when re-entering one has to examine the surroundings at length to make sure that one is unobserved by the enemy eye. There has to be the point of transition and communication between the inside and the outside, but this is the point of incalculable risk, the moment of the unforeseeable and the uncontrollable.

But this vulnerable point of entry/exit/transition is only a condensation in one point of something which is massively present overall. The burrow in its whole is far from being a safe-haven, it is at all points the space of total exposure to the Other. The complex architecture of meandering labyrinths has been entirely dictated by the invisible enemy and its possible stratagems, by its omnipresent invisible threat. Quite literally, the inner safe space of 'the badger' is the space shaped by the Other, by the supposition of the external menacing Other, it is like the supposition turned into space, the inner abode coinciding with the spatialized supposed Other. The safer it is, the more it is imbued with the Other. The burrow is the spatialized paranoia, entirely shaped by the scenario of the Other. It is the literal embodiment of the opposition,

[1] The story was first published in 1931 (by Max Brod and Hans Joachim Schoeps) in the first collection of his unpublished stories. The title (provided by the editors, but this is the keyword of the piece) already presents a problem, for the German word can mean the burrow (also the dungeon, the cell), which is the self-evident assumption, as well as a construction, an edifice, with the oscillation between an underground cavity and a building erected above the ground; furthermore it can mean the process of construction, of building, and a structure or a texture of a material (or a plant or a novel). The vacillation of meaning has some relevance.

and the coincidence in the very opposition, that Freud was so fond of, *heimlich/unheimlich*, homely/uncanny, the home being at all points haunted by the uncanny and coinciding with it. There is no inside that could escape the outside, and 'the badger' occupies the space of the constantly shifting lag between the two, the very principle of spatialization in which it tries to find its abode at the interstice of the inner and the outer. The inside and the outside communicate and there is an overlap, yet the lag is essential, it prevents the smooth transition, the simple passage of the one into the other/Other. The outside is present as the constant crack of the inside which cannot be filled in, healed and recuperated.

At almost the precise middle of the story (the story is not finished, but probably close enough) there is a shift which brings the problem to a pinnacle, providing a very good entry into our problem of the phonetic skin, the phonetic appearing precisely at the point of partition inside/outside:

> "I must have slept for a long time. I was only wakened when I had reached the last light sleep which dissolves of itself, and it must have been very light, for it was an almost inaudible whistling noise [*ein an sich kaum hörbares Zischen*] that wakened me. I recognized what it was immediately; the small fry, whom I had allowed far too much latitude, had burrowed a new channel somewhere during my absence, this channel must have chanced to intersect an older one, the air was caught there, and that produced the whistling noise [*das zischende Geräusch*]. What an indefatigably busy lot these small fry are, and what a nuisance their diligence can be! First I shall have to listen at the walls of my passages and locate the place of disturbance by experimental excavations, and only then will I be able to get rid of the noise."[2]

So there is a sound, a noise, which appears at the edge, most significantly at the edge of sleep and wakefulness and on the edge of the inside and the outside, the intrusion of the outside into the inside. Its first interpretation seems to be easy enough: this must have been caused by some tiny animals ('the small fry', *das Kleinzeug*) which must have dug some channel intersecting with other channels, there was some tiny passage of air which must have caused the whistling noise. It is a nuisance, but it shouldn't be too difficult to locate it and fill it in. "I must have silence in my passages." (Ibid.) To be the master is to be the master over sound and its emission. – Curiously, it never occurs to 'the badger' that the sound may be a phenomenon of inorganic origin, caused by a draught, a change of pressure, etc. The assumption is that the sound is always alive, it comes from animation, a rustling movement of life. Where there is sound something budges, the edge between the inanimate and the animate is blurred, the sound is like becoming animate of the inanimate. But this attempt at simple explanation comes to nothing.

> "I don't seem to be getting any nearer to the place where the noise is, it goes on always on the same thin note, with regular pauses, now a sort of whistling, but again like a kind of piping. [...] But whether trifling or important, I can find nothing, no matter how hard I search, or it may be that I find too much. [...] Sometimes I think that nobody but myself would hear it; it is true, I hear it now more and more distinctly, for my ear has grown keener through practice; though in reality it is exactly the same noise wherever I may hear it, as I have convinced myself by comparing my impressions." (p. 344, 345)

The mysterious noise immediately poses the question of its cause and location, as any sound does. The sound is an enigma, it is structurally mysterious, one hears it, i.e. one perceives it by its having made its passage inside, and the moment one hears it, it places one in the position of having to figure out what causes it, there is an enigma pertaining to causality. The sound, at its minimal, is always a rupture of causality that one has to re-establish and straighten out. And the first step to determine its cause is to try to pin down its spatial location, and hence its source, that is, to pin it to a point outside and thus solve its riddle. If hearing a sound pertains to time, then it is the time which insistently demands its translation into space. The conundrum of sound has a temporality which can only find its solution in spatiality. It requires a partition of space (far/close), more than that, its singularization, the singling out of a separate and discrete location within indeterminate and continuous space. But for the poor 'badger' this spot recedes, there are no clues or too many clues, which amounts to the same, and the even distribution of clues makes them useless. ("... wherever I listen, high or low, at the roof or the floor, at the entrance or in the corners, everywhere, everywhere, I hear the same noise." p. 347) The temporal fluidity of the sound calls for the spatial fixation, and there is a movement of subjectivity that is placed in this loop, between time and space, between fluidity and fixation, between the free-floating non-fixity of the sound and its attachment. There is a hermeneutics of cause and space which precedes the hermeneutics of meaning, of making sense of sounds.

[2] Franz Kafka, *The Complete Stories* (New York: Schocken Books, 1983), 343. This story was translated by Willa and Edwin Muir. For the original cf. *Die Erzählungen. Originalfassung* (Frankfurt/Main: Fischer, 1996).

Furthermore, there is an eerie quality to sound – can it be that only I can hear it? Does it have an 'objective' status at all? Is it in my head or does it come from outside? Its spatial location poses the problem of whether there is a spatial location at all. There is a moment of phantasmagoria when the sound wavers, if ever so minimally, between its reality and unreality. One has to make sound tests to ascertain that this is indeed a sound to be located outside and not a sound imagined or dreamed up – and remember, 'the badger' was just awakening from light slumber, this may be a strange continuation of a dream that refuses to be dissipated. The sound is a test – of being awake, alert and conscious, of being in possession of one's senses – but is one ever? The ability to locate the sound is like the test of sanity, for if one can't situate it one stands on the brink of delusion, hearing voices, incapacity to make sense of the world at large. One stands on the verge of an abyss, where the temporal is suspended and fails to converge into space. The tiny sound which wouldn't go away and resists being assigned a place and a cause is like an interminable prolongation of a tiny vacillation inherent in every sound. It is the extension of the enigma that it poses from the outset, its temporal protraction which, unplaceable and implacable, infests all parts of space.

The interstice of time and space in sound also makes for a slide between the sound and the gaze. The one has the propensity to translate into the other.

> "I go once more the long road to the Castle Keep, all my surroundings seem filled with agitation, seem to be looking at me, and then look away again so as not to disturb me, yet cannot refrain the very next moment from trying to read the saving solution from my expression." (p. 357)

The sound has the aptitude to return the gaze. It doesn't merely originate from anywhere and everywhere, but also imbues the space with exposure to visibility. The impossibility to escape hearing the sound is transposed into the impossibility of evading the gaze. One is being looked at, with no hiding place, without a hideout in this huge and meticulously designed hideout of the burrow. One cannot close one's ears, as opposed to the eyes that one can always close, one is always open and available for the sound, but this impossibility to cut short the influx of sounds comes to equal the impossibility for the omnipresent gaze to close its eyes. The gaze is reading me, and I cannot read it.

How many sounds are there?

> "There still remains the possibility that there are two noises, that up to now I have been listening at a good distance from the two centers, and that while its noise increases, when I draw nearer to one of them, the total result remains approximately the same for the ear in consequence of the lessening volume of sound from the other center." (p. 345)

What is the number of the sound? Can it be submitted to count? Again there is a structural problem, for even the sound at its minimum, a thin whistling noise remaining persistently 'the same', poses the constant question of 'one dividing into two' and hence into an ineradicable multiplicity. There is a thesis in this which one could spell out as follows: the sound is never one, it resists oneness by its very nature, it poses a problem of an inherent multiplicity by its mere being a sound. And the enigma it presents is not only the enigma of its cause, location and source, but through all this the attempt to render it one, to submit its multiplicity to oneness. Again, can one ever? And can one ever decompose it into discrete countable traits? There is again a movement of subjectivity caught in the turmoil between the multiple and the one, the imposition of one on something that seems to be by its nature uncountable, something that seems to be constantly doomed to failure.[3]

Then there is the question of its intermittency, the tricks played upon its duration.

> "Simply as a rest and a means to regain my composure I often make this experiment, listen intently and am overjoyed when I hear nothing. But the question still remains, what can have happened? [...] Sometimes I fancy that the noise has stopped, for it makes long pauses; sometimes such a faint whistling escapes one, one's own blood is pounding all too loudly in one's ears; then two pauses come one after another, and for a while one thinks that the whistling has stopped forever. I listen no longer, I jump up, all life is transfigured; it is as if the fountains from which flows the silence of the burrow were unsealed." (p. 347, 350)

The sound is essentially temporal, but its temporality is punctuated. In order for there to be a sound, it has to be intermittent, that is, there has to be the possibility of there being a non-sound, a silence against the backdrop of which the sound can emerge at all. But the demarcation line between the two is uncertain – can one ever be sure of hearing nothing? Of perceiving pure silence, the

[3] Read in this way, this could invoke like 'the primary scene' of Badiouean philosophy. One can recall Badiou insisting on the first pages of *Being and Event* that being is a multiplicity, indeed a multiplicity of multiplicities, and that 'one' is an operation performed on this irreducible multiplicity. Is the badger a prototype of a Badiouean philosopher?

absence of any sound? For silence itself is always populated by infinitesimal sounds, there is the heart and the pounding of blood, there is the sounding presence of one's own body whose limits stretch into the ambiance, if ever so little, and this produces the incapacity to be fully assured and confident. Silence is not the absence of sounds, but quite the opposite, the state of the greatest alertness in which sub-sounds emerge, the minimal thumps of both one's body and the ambient surroundings, slightly overlapping on the verge. Silence is the condition of sound, its interpunction, the punctuation of its flow, its frame, but also an elusive line of division which has to be drawn by an uncertain decision. Just as the sudden emergence of the sound had the power to transform the already nightmarish life of 'the badger' into a far worse nightmare,[4] so the silence has the capacity to transfigure it instantly into bliss, albeit short-lived. ("I listen, but the most perfunctory listening shows at once that I was shamefully deceived: away there in the distance the whistling still remains unshaken." p. 351) The intermittency of the duration of sound, shaping its rhythm, overlapping with the elusive boundary between sound and silence, translates into the oscillation between nightmare and bliss. The excitation on the elusive line pushes into two extremes, the movement of subjectivity being caught in the exchange between the two. One's damnation and salvation depend on figuring out the sound and its treacherous absence.

The opposition between the threatening outside and the safe inside can be reversed:

> "I push my way up and listen. Deep stillness; how lovely it is here, outside there nobody troubles about my burrow, everybody has his own affairs, which have no connection with me; how have I managed to achieve this? [...] A complete reversal of things in the burrow; what was once the place of danger has become a place of tranquility." (p. 352)

The home, this tentative safe-haven achieved by so much effort, has been de-homed (if I can venture this expression) by the mere presence of the sound, embodying all threats, condensing them under a single heading, so the external space of constant threats can now turn into the refuge from the refuge, the asylum from the contaminated asylum, the outer threat offering a relief from the unfathomable inner peril. So the oscillation introduced by the sound can further translate into a reversal of inside/outside, refuge/danger. Where could one find one's proper place of safety?

There is further the question of volume.

> "The noise seems to have become louder, not much louder, of course – here it is always a matter of the subtlest shades – but all the same sufficiently louder for the ear to recognize it clearly. And this growing-louder is like a coming-nearer; still more distinctly than you hear the increasing loudness of the noise, you can literally see the step that brings it closer to you. You leap back from the wall, you try to grasp at once all the possible consequences that this discovery will bring with it." (p. 351)

What makes the sound the same? Is it ever? Its volume and its pitch? Its volume (and its pitch) is constantly subject to fluctuation once one concentrates on it. The volume is the subtle difference of volume, it increases/decreases, if ever so slightly, it can only remain 'the same' if one doesn't pay attention to it. The moment one isolates the single sound and fully concentrates on it, its mode can only be crescendo. And in the strange loop which binds together time and space in sound, it comes ever nearer. The sound is getting you, it is gaining ground on you, it is winning, you feel your defenses crumbling, all your weapons are of no avail. The sound 'means' getting louder and nearer, closer to the bone. And one never hears merely with the ears, the bones are involved, starting with the tiny ones in the ear.

The attempt to squeeze the inherent multiplicity of the sound into the mold of one leads to a further expansion, indeed a crescendo of oneness.

> "But what avail all exhortations to be calm; my imagination will not rest, and I have actually come to believe – it is useless to deny it to myself – that the whistling is made by some beast [*ein Tier*], and moreover not by a great many small ones, but by a single big one. [...] it has a plan in view whose purpose I cannot decipher; I merely assume that the beast – and I make no claim whatever that it knows of my existence – is encircling me; it has probably made several circles around my burrow already since I began to observe it." (p. 353, 354)

If there is to be a common denominator to this intriguing and vacillating multiple sound, then it must have a single cause, one should be able to account for it by a single big creature as its unitary origin. The sound is the sound of a beast. It is a beastly sound. There is something in its nature, or its counter-nature, its super-nature and un-nature,

[4] In retrospect all the previous nightmares seem but a trifle compared to this one. "I have had a great deal of luck all those years, luck has spoiled me; I have had anxieties, but anxiety leads to nothing when you have luck to back you." (p. 351) Luck is the retroactive product of calamity, one's luck never coincides with one.

that implies a beast. The beast not as a part of the natural animal kingdom, but its excrescence, an excess of animality, the animality turned monstrous, the specter of Animal as such. If there is a search for cause and spatial location necessarily called for by every sound, then this is the next stage, seemingly impossible to avoid: imputing the cause to a ghost. The impossibility to pin down the cause to a locus and to unravel its source, to discern the indiscernible, offers a crack where fantasy comes in. If the sound cannot be quite counted for one, then fantasy can take the relay of oneness and give it a spectral existence. There is a beast in the machine. And the beast is encircling me – despite its being One, the unitary agent pulling the multiple strings of sound, it is also all around, everywhere, unplaceable, encompassing. Being is a beast. It is a creature of assumption and imagination (Kafka's words), yet overwhelming. Its purpose cannot be deciphered, and this is what makes it intractable and inscrutable. It is the supposed One which is all over, ubiquitous, the monstrous underside of *hen kai pan*, the old philosophical adage of conceiving being, in all its diversity, as 'one and all'.

The hermeneutics of cause and location precedes the hermeneutics of meaning, which is the required next step, but there is a gap between the two where fantasy sneaks in. Isolating the source of the sound is like a deflation of meaning – so this is where it has been coming from, this is what has been producing it, there is nothing to worry about and nothing further to interpret. The sound would thus be put in place, neatly allocated. And the possibility of doing this at least roughly and for practical purposes is no doubt what keeps us from the paranoia lurking implicitly in every sound. It is only when the sound quavers and lingers in suspense for some moments, or minutes or agonizing hours, unplaceable and unfathomable, that one is suddenly aware of the tiny gap which divorces the sound from its source, the lag which prevents it from ever being simply collapsed on its source, the fissure which thwarts the proper placement of its time into a spatial slot and makes it irreducible to it. This gap is the entry point of fantasy which necessarily gets hold of meaning once this gap is kept open for any length. The meaning of a sound, the assumption one necessarily makes, is placed in the very impossibility of its univocal placement, deracinating, if slightly, its firm roots. The spatial anchorage would make it univocal, i.e. sounding *una voce*, with one single voice. If there is a meaning to be sought for and figured out, this stems from a dislocation of natural causality, the failed allotment of sound to a spatial point. Fantasy equally intervenes in the gap between multiplicity and oneness, the irreducibility of sound to one, and it proposes an assumed specter of One as the solution of this predicament. One is One of the beast. There is something ghostly and beastly in making sense of sound, that is, in making sense *tout court*. In the pursuit of sense there is always a beastly moment, the elusive beast intervenes that doesn't quite vanish in sense but rather conditions it.

The beast behind the sound is all-powerful, but its omnipotence only gives shape and substance to what is overpowering and invasive in the sound itself. It gathers in its bosom the eeriness, the mystery, the intrusive force of the sound, it draws its strength from sound and it provides it with strength in return. It unifies the absent cause of sounds into a single beastly creature. Once the beast is given life by the assumption one makes in this predicament, then all sounds become manifestations of the hidden beast. And if the beast seems to have suddenly appeared as lurking behind them, then it can only follow that it had been there all the time without our noticing.

"Now I could not have foreseen such an opponent. But apart altogether from the beast's peculiar characteristics, what is happening now is only something which I should really have feared all the time, something against which I should have been constantly prepared: the fact that someone would come." (p. 354)

The sound implies the beast that can jeopardize the whole life, and retrospectively the whole life has been a long wait for this jeopardy. It is not that it has suddenly emerged from nowhere, one was foolish and naïve not to have anticipated its coming, one has been deluding oneself. The peaceful life without the beast was based on blindness, or rather deafness, actually both. The whistling sound was a surprise, totally unexpected, but it was bound to come, it had a destination to fulfill by its coming out, it was secretly lurking behind all sounds and waiting for its moment, its sudden emergence was just a materialization of its virtuality in every sound, in the crack involved in the world of sounds.

Can one come to terms with the beast, reach an understanding with it?

"If it should really break through to the burrow I shall give it some of my stores and it will go on its way again. It will go its way again, a fine story! Lying in my heap of earth I can naturally dream of all sorts of things, even of an understanding with the beast, though I know well enough that no such thing can happen, and that at the instant when we see each other, more, at the moment when we merely guess at each other's presence, we shall both blindly bare our claws and teeth, neither of us a second before or after the other ..." (p. 358)

The world is not big enough for 'the badger' and the beast, there is no room for a friendly coexistence, for a division of space and goods, it's an either-or, a life and death struggle. The beast grew out of the tiniest of sounds, a mere whistling, and it grew to spectacular proportions, out of all proportion, taking over being at large. It has imbued being with an excessive presence, a presence too much, the too-muchness of presence (to use the excellent word proposed by Eric Santner), pinned to a mere sound. The beast of being has come too close by merely emitting a sound, but this pertains to the very nature of the sound: the hazard of its coming too close, the impossibility to keep it at bay. What would be the proper distance of the sound, between its closeness and remoteness? Can it ever be at an appropriate distance? Not too far, not too close? And can one ever keep being at a proper distance? The beast of being, a mere creature of sound, the slightest and the most immaterial of substances, is nevertheless endowed with claws and teeth, it can rip one apart should it appear in flesh, yet despite its unbearable closeness, the unbearable closeness of being, it pertains to its nature that it keeps in retreat, a retreat within the retreat, never stepping into the full brightness of noon, in line with the nature of the sound which immediately imposes itself, piercing all protection, but at the same time never quite discloses its source and location. It dwells in the dislocation. The sound is an advent of presence, compellingly inflicting itself, but simultaneously a truncated presence, resisting to be revealed, posing an enigma, a retreat in its very disclosure.

Kafka's burrow is a sound laboratory. It isolates a single sound and scrutinizes very carefully and most lucidly all its implications, all the subject positions in relation to it. It operates with the absolutely minimum. It places the sound on the edge, on many crucial and decisive edges. First of all, there is most conspicuously the edge between the inside and the outside, both the inside of an intimate retreat in relation to its threatening outside, and the inside of one's head, one's perception and psyche in relation to external world, the edge of sanity and insanity. Then there is the edge of a derailment of causality, where the sound presents a quirk that cannot be easily dispensed with, the normal causal link cannot be easily reestablished; further, the edge of space and time; the edge of floating and fixation, location and dislocation, of detachment and attachment of sounds; the edge of the one and the multiple, where every sound presents a hybrid multiplicity recalcitrant to unity and to decomposition into discrete countable traits; the edge of duration and intermittency, placing the sound against the backdrop of elusive silence. Then, in a broader scope, there is the edge of the relation between the subject and the Other, where the otherness, by mere sound, pierces its way straight into the intimacy; the edge between reality and fantasy, where the fantasy sneaks into the gap of sound's dislocation, permeating everything and imbuing the very process of making sense. Furthermore, there is the edge between the sound and the voice, the inanimate and the animate, implying the blurred demarcation line between the senseless and the meaningful. Finally, there is the edge between on the one hand wakefulness, consciousness, alertness and on the other hand sleep – and one can point out that quite commonly one is awoken by a sound which has become too intrusive, so that the sound is quite literally, in common experience, something that embodies that line, the bridge between the two but which is always cracked. And one could say that the sound that wakes up 'the badger' in that burrow is like a parable of a wake-up call – but not admonishing us to wake up to the fully constituted given reality, but rather to wake up to the awareness of something that appears on its edge, a reality with a crack, like an ontological opening to something that we usually dismiss by being asleep in our very wakefulness. – It may seem that Kafka's parable is atemporal and ahistorical – and what could be more ahistorical than an animal in its burrow? But there is something in it that pertains very intimately to its historical moment, for the ontological opening it examines, the barely perceptible ontological crack which emits a sound, announces the new experience of modernity, it is its wake-up call. The very notion of phonetic skin is a way of spelling out the modern experience. On the one hand it presupposes the neat division into an inside and an outside, with the skin separating the two, but on the other hand the moment one posits the skin as the clear demarcation line one posits it as a question mark, an edge which implies its permeability, its porousness, its untenability, and it is this quality that conditions the experience, a new experience on which so much modern art and philosophy is premised. Something has come too close for us to reach, and this is what makes us modern subjects. In this sense Kafka's phonetic burrow has the emblematic value of a modern parable, our version of the Platonic cave.

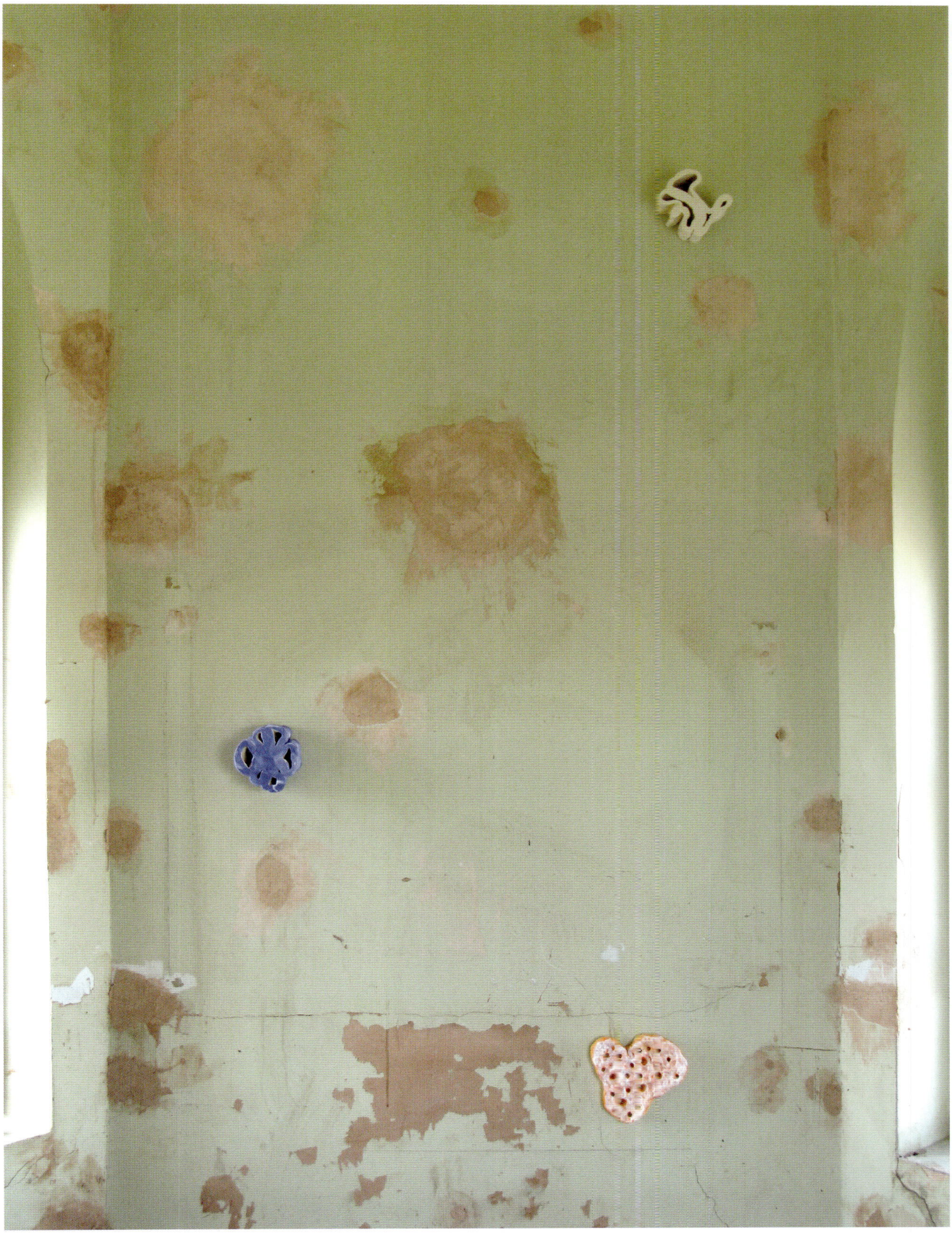

Fig. 1

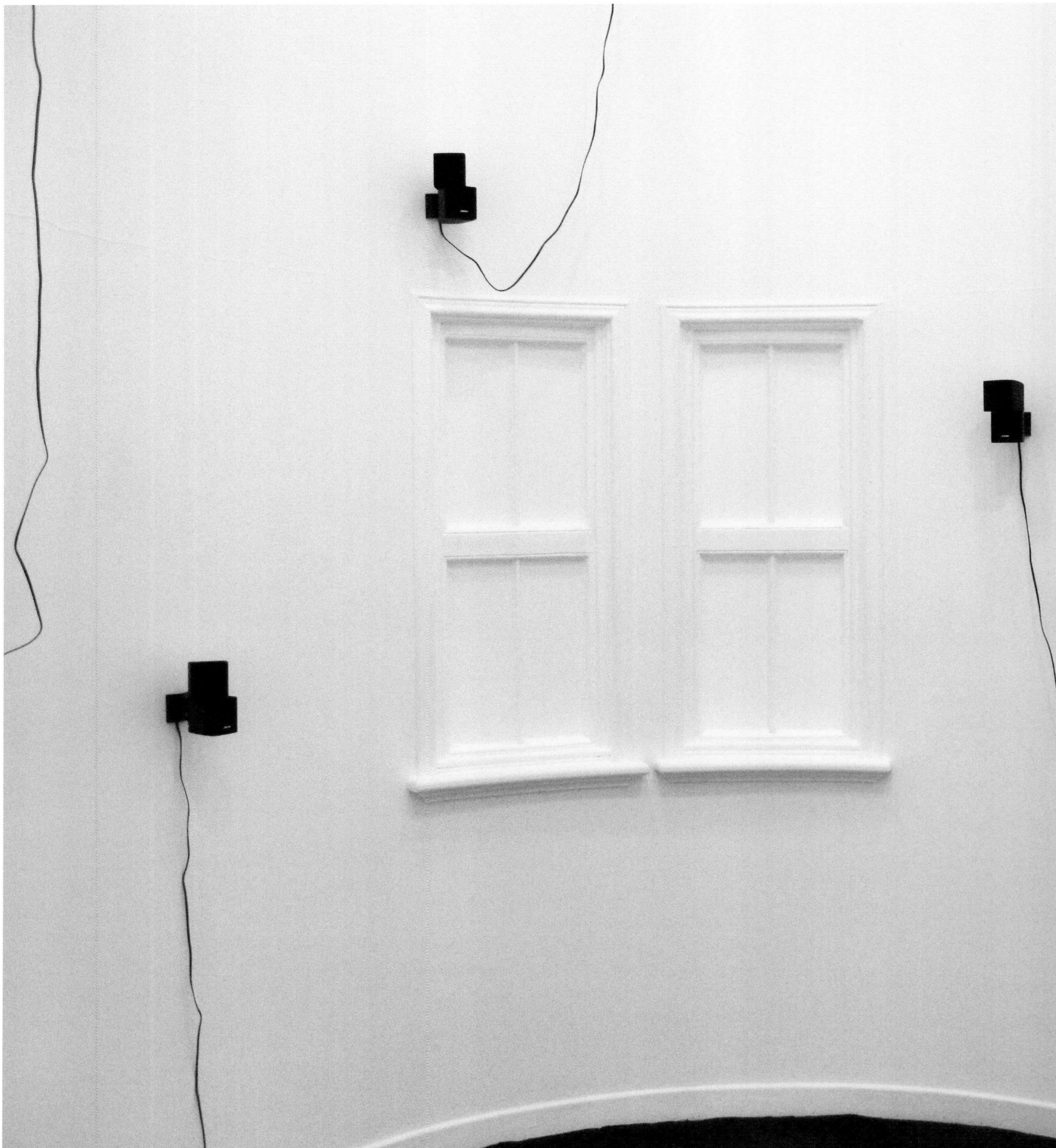

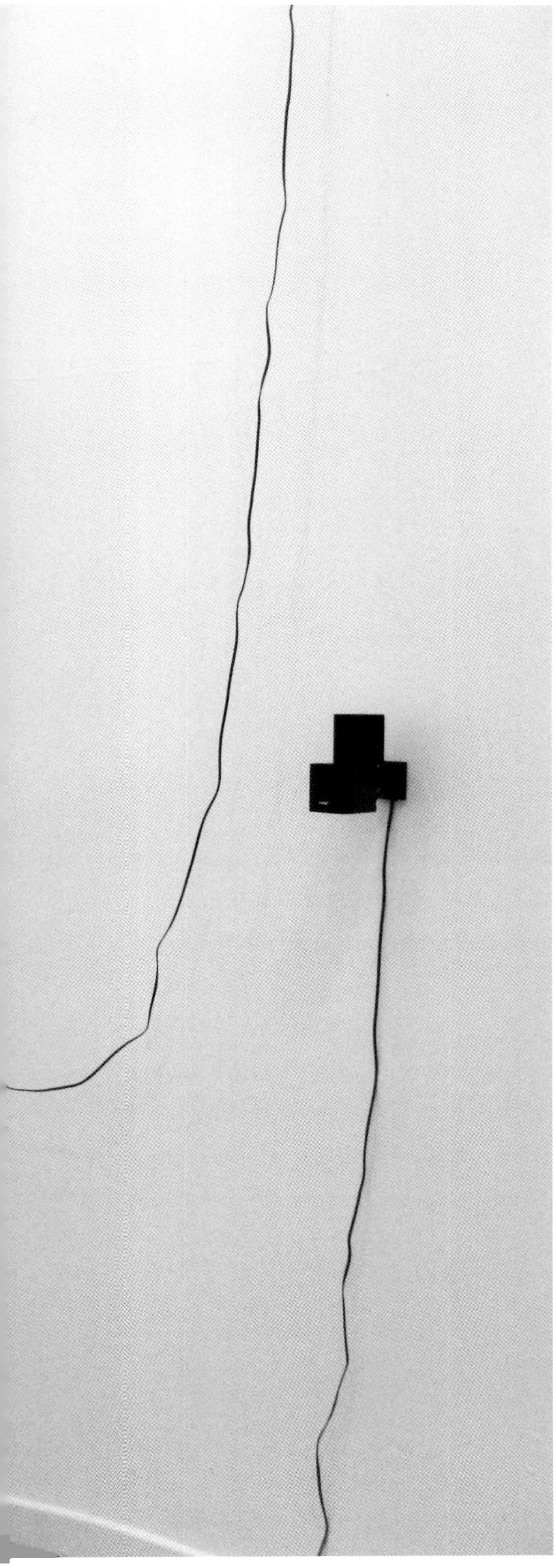

Der fühllose Hintergrund des Glücks. Stille Weite tiefer Zerstreutheit, die zu Wachsamkeit führt. Eine Art von Verdammung, eine Art Gleichmut, eine Art unsteter Ruhe, eine Art verlorenen Vergessens, in dem das Warten innehält.

The imperceptive background of happiness. A silent vastness of profound abstraction approaches alertness. A kind of curse, a kind of serenity, a kind of uncertain calm, a kind of forlorn oblivion where waiting comes to a halt.

Fig. 1 (page 37): JÜRGEN PARTENHEIMER, *Small Bodies [Particle Zoo I – III]*, 2006, IKON Gallery – Perrot's Folly, Birmingham, 2008.
Fig. 2: JÜRGEN PARTENHEIMER, *Copan [Voices]*, IKON Gallery, Birmingham, 2008.

„Ich gebe dir meine Haut." Ich schenke dir diese Linien, ihr Geflecht, ihre Räume.
Alles verbindet sie über das Denken hinaus in das Schattenwerk der Tage und Stunden ...
Jedes Blatt ist eine Welt, jede Zeichnung ein Text jenseits der euklidischen Vektoren,
jeder Text ein metaphorisches Instrument, jedes Instrument eine Zeichnung.

"I give you my skin." I present these lines to you, their web and their rooms.
Beyond thought everything is connected with the act of the shadow from days and hours ...
Every page is a world, every drawing a text beyond Euclidean vectors,
every text a metaphoric instrument, every instrument a drawing.

Fig. 3: JÜRGEN PARTENHEIMER, *ICH-Räume [phonetic skin], #68*, 2010,
pencil, ink on paper, 41 x 31 cm.

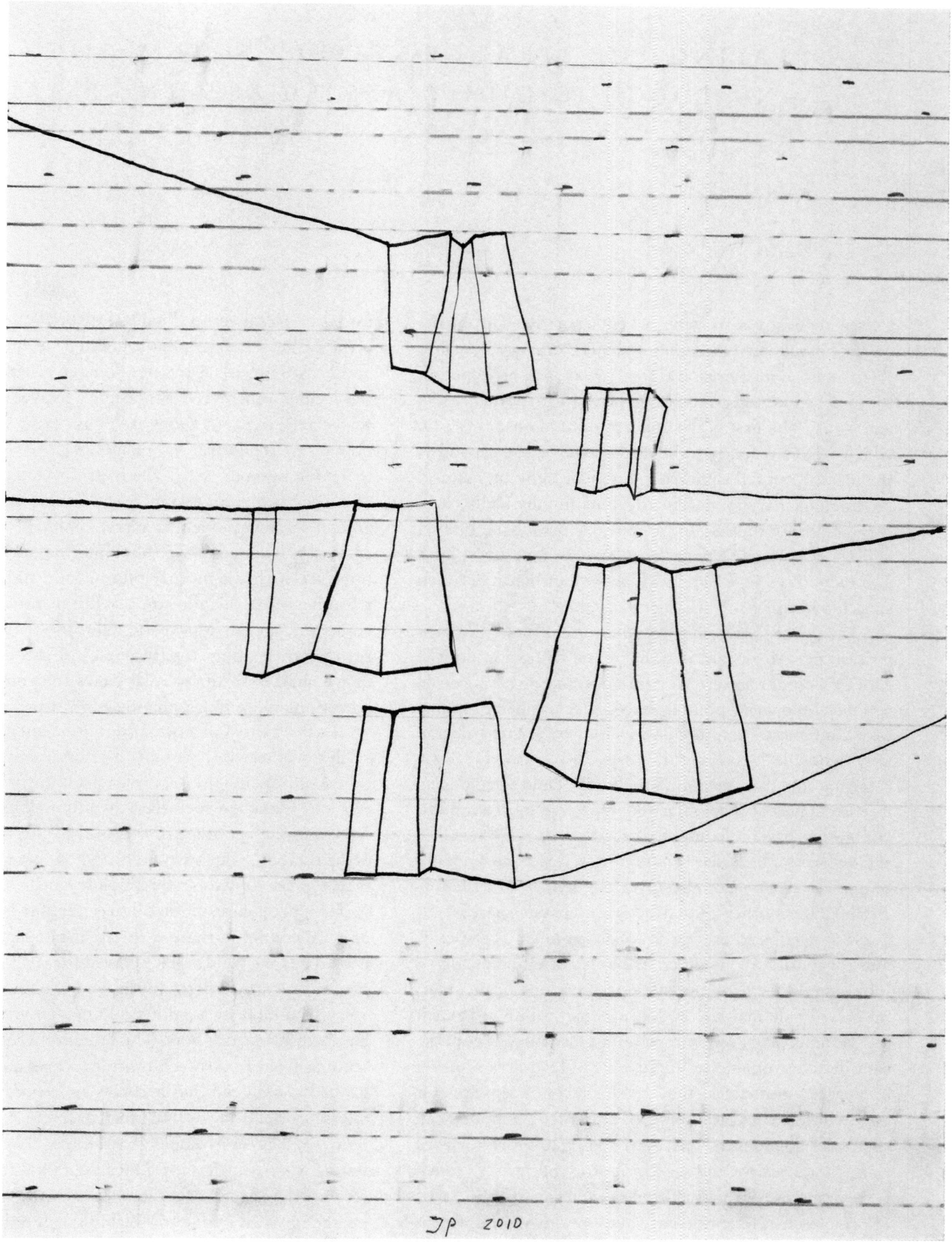

Fig. 3

NAOMI SEGAL / 'PLAYING THE STRANGE STATUE': SOUND, SILENCE AND TOUCH IN DIDIER ANZIEU AND *THE PIANO*

I want to begin with two concepts borrowed from the work of psychoanalyst Didier Anzieu (1923–1999), whose theory of the *moi-peau* [skin-ego] was first broached in the mid-1970s, and published in book form twice, in 1985 and 1995. The first is the concept of 'consensuality', on which I have recently published a study;[1] the second is the idea of 'formal signifiers', a way of thinking cultural phenomena psychoanalytically and linguistically, in a turn of phrase that is also a gestural turn of the body. I will bring both these aspects to bear on Jane Campion's *The Piano* (1993), a film in which love mediates between speech and touch.

The skin-ego is both a metaphor and a reality; Anzieu writes: 'par Moi-peau, je désigne une figuration dont le Moi de l'enfant se sert au cours des phases précoces de son développement pour se représenter lui-même comme Moi contenant les contenus psychiques, à partir de son expérience de la surface du corps' [by 'Skin-ego' I am referring to a configuration used by the child's ego during its early stages of development to represent itself as an ego containing psychic contents, based on its experience of the surface of the body].[2] In its earliest days, the baby not only receives care but also gives out signals to its family circle. In the mother-child dyad it is no passive partner: by a sort of 'feedback' process, it solicits as much as responds and can withdraw as much as be neglected: exchanging looks, smiles, noises and sense-impressions, it 'acquiert un pouvoir de maîtrise endogène qui va d'un sentiment de confiance dans ses entreprises à un sentiment euphorisant de toute-puissance illimitée' (80) [acquires a power of endogenous mastery that develops from a sense of confidence into a euphoric feeling of unlimited omnipotence]; such over-confidence is necessary for it to move forward to further affective and sensori-motor enterprises. Touch is the first sense-faculty to develop embryonically and thus 'la peau est le référent de base auquel sont spontanément rapportées les diverses données sensorielles' (83) [the skin is the basic reference-point for all the various sense data]; and because touch is the only reflexive sense – I feel myself feeling, touch myself touching – it gives rise gradually to the reflexivity of thought. Thus 'avoir un Moi, c'est pouvoir se replier sur soi-même' (84) [to have an ego is to fold in upon oneself]. The baby develops the phantasy of a 'peau commune à la mère et à l'enfant, interface d'un côté de laquelle se tient la mère, l'enfant étant de l'autre côté' (85) [skin common to the mother and the child, an interface with the mother on one side and the child on the other]. But this illusion can fail in various ways: the common skin can appear too tight, too loose or violently torn away, leading to pathologies of the skin-ego; later, as we shall see, Anzieu also views the common skin as something more like a phantasy of reciprocal inclusion.

In the course of normal development, as Anzieu describes it, there is a 'double interdit de toucher' [double taboo on touching] (161–79), which every child encounters and without which there is no possibility of moving from the skin-ego stage to that of thought; it precedes the oedipal taboo, which would be impossible without it. 'Le tactile n'est fondateur qu'à condition de se trouver, au moment nécessaire, interdit' (165) [tactility is fundamental only on condition that, at the right moment, it is forbidden]. Thus the child is not allowed to touch itself or other people on certain parts of the body, is required to keep away from fires or windows and made to hold an adult's hand when out of doors. The taboo on touching is what sends us from an early echo-tactile form of communication towards a skin-ego that becomes an 'espace d'inscription intersensorielle' (178) [the space of inter-sensorial inscription] – and as for psychoanalysis, it uses the circumscribed setting where touch is forbidden but talk is free-flowing to recreate the effects of tactile contact by the work of replacing the physical by the psychical (I shall return to this).

A dual surface turned both inwards and outwards, the skin-ego has a number of 'functions' including containment, holding, protection against excitation, sexuality, toning – and 'consensualité' (AMP 250, 253, 261, 264) [consensuality]. This term is used by Anzieu for the fifth function of the skin-ego, which brings together the perception of all the senses in one place – all our senses are sited somewhere on our skin – and thus stands for the coherence, coincidence or co-presence of perceptions.[3] Interestingly, Anzieu often also uses other terms: 'intersensorialité' (127), [intersensoriality] or 'sens commun' [common sense], 'concordance',[4] 'correspondance' [correspondence], 'convergence' (AP 15, 56), 'consensus' (35) or 'complémentarité (65) [complementarity]. The qualities of the sense of touch serve as the 'toile de fond sur laquelle les autres qualités sensibles émergent comme figures' (35) [backcloth on which other sense qualities stand out as figures].

The word was borrowed from Donald Meltzer, who observes of a child's imaginative play: 'we are envisaging attention as the strings which hold the senses together in consensuality'.[5] It is from him that Anzieu takes the term for what can go wrong with this function: the consensual convergence may fall apart or, as Meltzer puts it, be passively 'dismantled' by an autistic child when, 'somewhat akin to allowing a brick wall to fall to pieces by the action of the weather, moss, fungi and insects' (12), the senses are made to attach singly and separately to the internal or external object that is 'the most stimulating at that moment'. But when consensuality works well and the skin-ego is in place, it can lead towards an ability to '[être] en quête de concordances, de convergence' (AP 104) [seek out concordances and convergence] and forms of thought that emphasise analogy, the microcosm and 'systèmes de correspondance entre mots, choses et pensées' [systems of correspondence between words, things and thoughts].

I borrowed this term as the title of my book not only because, as these citations show, it is central to psychoanalytic thinking about the sense of touch, but also because both the book and this essay are intended as exercises in convergence, bringing together cultural processes, objects and theories so that they can work together consensually. For of course the most obvious meaning of the term – in both French and English – is to do with consensus and consent. Etymologically, as Anzieu notes, the idea of consensus derives from the 'accord des sensations entre elles' (35) [mutual agreement of the senses] and the idea of a 'common sense' brings the body together with the mind to create a basis for thought:

'[S]ens' a surtout un sens double. 'Le sens', c'est la 'signification', laquelle trouve dans le langage son organisation la plus étendue. 'Les sens', ce sont les organes du corps par lesquels l'être humain entre en contact avec ce qui l'entoure et en premier lieu avec sa mère. Le travail par lequel s'élabore, chez le tout-petit, l'appareil psychique et, chez le patient et son psychanalyste, l'interprétation, ce travail consiste à articuler le sens aux sens. Les mots valent et portent par leur poids de chair. L'inconscient n'est pas langage ; il est le corps, [...] l'intelligence du corps.[6]

[The word 'sense' has a double meaning. 'Sense' means 'signification', which finds its most extensive organisation in language. 'The senses' are the body organs by which the human being makes contact with its surroundings and in the first place with its mother. The work by which the infant creates its psychic apparatus, and by which the patient and analyst create interpretation, consists of articulating 'sense' with 'the senses'. Words have value and bear meaning through their weight of flesh. The unconscious is not language; it is the body, [...] the intelligence of the body.]

If the intelligence of the body is the basis of both sense and consent, the question of consensuality is also to do with human relations based on the sense of touch, most particularly the mother-child couple and the relation of desire. As Merleau-Ponty argues in *Le Visible et l'invisible*, every touch is double: it involves both an active and a passive experience; I feel myself feeling and felt.[7] Thus, when I touch a sculpture or a piano, I am also dwelling on the surface of the body of the other. If pleasure is a tactical, tangential experience, is it also contagion? What are the limits of consent between bodies? If love is intrinsically mediate, can it ever be mutual?

That is the first concept I want to carry to my reading of *The Piano*. The second is one that Anzieu proposes in *Les Enveloppes psychiques [Psychic Envelopes]*: that of the 'signifiant formel' [formal signifier].[8] These signifiers are characterised by their dynamic nature; they are concerned with 'changements de forme' (AEP 1) [changes of form]; they are spatial, capturing the 'propriétés psychiques [de l'espace]' (6) [psychic properties of space], and represent not psychic contents but psychic containers. My interest in them is based on their potential as a way of reading cultural objects, including human figures, in terms of a linguistically perceived spatial image that embodies (this term is not casual) their particular style, manner or significance. Introduced late in Anzieu's theory almost as a taken-for-granted, the formal signifiers focus his own 'literary' perspective on human behaviour and motive and I borrow them as another reader of the shapes and patterns that culture thinks in.

Each individual's fundamental formal signifier derives from a time when they were not yet capable of repression, still tied in psychically to the closeness to the mother that Anzieu calls the 'common skin'. Its structure is different from that of phantasy. It takes the form of a sentence that has a subject and a verb but no object-complement; often the verb (in French) is reflexive; and the subject is a part of the body or an isolated physical form, never a whole person. It is not a scene or an enactment but the 'transformation d'une caractéristique géométrique ou physique d'un corps (au sens général d'une portion de l'espace), transformation qui entraîne une déformation, voire une destruction de la forme' (15) [geometrical or physical transformation of a body (in the general sense of a portion of space) which entails a deformation or destruction of form]; the space in which it appears is two-dimensional, and the individual senses it as external to themselves. Anzieu gives examples: 'un axe vertical s'inverse, un appui s'effondre [...], un trou aspire [...] un corps solide est traversé, un corps gazeux explose [...] un orifice s'ouvre et se ferme [...] une limite s'interpose [...] des perspectives différentes se juxtaposent [...] mon double me quitte ou me contrôle [...] un objet qui s'éloigne m'abandonne' (15--16) [a vertical axis is reversed, a support collapses [...] a hole sucks in [...] a solid body is crossed, a gaseous body explodes [...] an orifice opens and closes [...] a limit interposes [...] different perspectives are juxtaposed [...] my double leaves or controls me; [...] an object goes away, abandoning me' (15–16). I suggest that we can discern, in cultural figures and artefacts,[9] a set of formal signifiers that allow us to think metaphorically and psychoanalytically. The characteristic formal signifier of Gide's desire, for instance, is twofold: 'a compulsion to empty the body of its fluid content', and 'a straight line that ends in a swerve',[10] that of the public figure of Princess Diana 'a circle around, into and out of, the surface-point of the skin' (SC 101–18), that of certain recent films 'desiring from inside the body of another' (SC 143–68) and that of the mode of love in *The Piano* 'the caress of the back of the hand'. What Anzieu's theory offers to such cultural readings is a structure and vocabulary that may be able, consensually, to contain them without preempting them.

A last preliminary point. Here are two descriptions of the physical experience of being in love. This is how Anzieu describes the young couple in love:

> Pour ma part, je préfère me représenter les deux amoureux imaginairement reliés par le fantasme d'une peau commune, reduplication [*sic*] de la peau commune à la mère et à l'enfant : n'éprouvent-ils pas le besoin, en se touchant, en se serrant, en s'accolant sans cesse, d'avoir un même morceau de surface cutanée en partage ? Cette interface, en position de diamètre intérieur de leur couple, est une surface d'inscription des signes, un organe de communication directe, sans médiation, censé procurer à chacun la connaissance immédiate des pensées, des impressions, des affects de l'autre. Par ailleurs, le couple amoureux s'enferme à l'intérieur d'une bulle, cherchant à fonctionner en système fermé, en huis clos, coupé le plus possible des exigences, des intrusions de la réalité extérieure. Il s'agit là d'un type d'enveloppe psychique différent de la surface d'inscription, d'une enveloppe pare-excitation globale, totale et, à mon sens, double afin qu'elle soit plus résistante : les amoureux la constituent avec les peaux imaginaires de leurs mères respectives (ou de leurs tenant-lieu) qu'ils ont emportées avec eux en se séparant de celles-ci.[11]
>
> [I prefer to think of the two lovers as linked in imagination by the fantasy of a common skin, a duplication of the common skin between the mother and the child – touching, holding or embracing each other all the time, aren't they expressing the need to share a single piece of cutaneous surface between them? This interface, in the position of a diameter internal to their couple, is a surface for the inscription of signs, an organ of direct communication, without mediation, which supposedly lets each of them know immediately the thoughts, impressions and affects of the other. In addition, the couple in love shut themselves inside a bubble, trying to function in a closed system, in camera, cut off as far as they can be from the demands and intrusions of the outside world. That is a different kind of psychic envelope from the surface of inscription, an envelope of protection against stimuli that is total, global and, in my view, double so that it can be more resistant: the lovers make it out of the imaginary skins of their respective mothers (or primary carers) which they took away when they separated from them.]

And in an otherwise rather different section of 'L'entrelacs – le chiasme', Merleau-Ponty writes this:

> Pour la première fois, le corps ne s'accouple plus au monde, il enlace un autre corps, [s'y] appliquant soigneusement de toute son étendue, dessinant inlassablement de ses mains l'étrange statue qui donne à son tour tout ce qu'elle reçoit, perdu hors du monde et des buts, fasciné par l'unique occupation de flotter dans l'Être avec une autre vie, de se faire le dehors de son dedans et le dedans de son dehors. Et dès lors, mouvement, toucher, vision, s'appliquant à l'autre et à eux-mêmes, remontent vers leur source et, dans le travail patient et silencieux du désir, commence le paradoxe de l'expression. (187)
>
> [For the first time, the body no longer couples with the world, it intertwines with another body, applying itself carefully to it with its whole expanse, tirelessly outlining with its hands the strange statue which, in its turn, gives everything it receives, cut off from the world and from ordinary aims, occupied with the sole

fascination of floating in Being together with another life, making itself the outside of its inside and the inside of its outside. And then at once, movement, touch and vision, applied to the other and to themselves, head back to their source and, in the patient, silent work of desire, commence the paradox of expression.]

In terms of the skin-ego, then, to love is the wish to reproduce the other's original common skin, as a reciprocal inclusion, holding and being held. But it is also, following Merleau-Ponty, an aesthetic act, the mutual and careful creation of a 'strange statue' out of what is also 'another life', leading to something akin to silent expression. How is love represented in *The Piano*?

Ada chose to stop speaking at about the time that she began playing the piano. In many languages the word for piano-keys is directly connected to the sense of touch – French *touches*, German *Tasten*. In an interview, Anzieu describes the way the psychoanalyst may avoid the demand of touch in the analytic setting by saying: 'on peut toucher de la voix' [one can touch with the voice].[12] He goes on:

On dit, dans le langage courant: 'prendre contact avec quelqu'un' ou 'avoir un bon contact avec une personne'. Cela montre bien que l'origine première du contact étant tactile, le contact devient métaphoriquement transposé aux autres organes des sens, aux autres domaines sensoriels. Ce qui me semble spécifiquement analytique, c'est de trouver, en s'appuyant sur diverses organes des sens, sur divers champs sensoriels, des équivalents verbaux de ces échanges primitifs qui introduisent le nourrisson au monde des signifiants, mais qui demandent ensuite d'être abandonné pour que l'être évolue.

[In everyday language we talk of 'getting in touch with someone' or 'having good contact' with them. This shows that the earliest version of contact was actually tactile, and then it was metaphorically transposed to the other sense organs and sensorial fields. What seems to me specifically analytical is to draw on these sense organs and sensorial fields in order to find verbal equivalents of those primal exchanges that introduce the nursling to the world of signifiers, but which have to be abandoned afterwards if the child is to develop.]

By reversing this principle, *The Piano* shows us what happens when touch stands in for the voice. As in Merleau-Ponty, the caress in this film is an aestheticizing act, but one that changes the 'strange statue' that Ada has been, along with her piano, into human flesh. This pygmalionesque process comes about, I want to suggest, not so much by her being caressed but by her own caressing.

At the beginning of *The Piano* we see fingers. A high-pitched woman's voice speaks lines that we sense are audible only to her and us. 'The voice you hear is not my speaking voice but my mind's voice', she says; 'I have not spoken since I was six years old'. It is not clear that the hazy vertical stripes of reddish light are fingers until we see the reverse shot: a wedding-ringed hand with one dark eye looking out. Red tints are rare in the film, the most striking being the lacy cloth Baines uses to divide his hut, creating a feminized flavour in his male space. Aside from this, shades of sub-aqueous blue predominate, and flesh is very white. Preparing to leave Scotland, the protagonist tends to her sleeping daughter, from whom she cuts a roller-skate (echoed later in the shoe she looses off to save herself from drowning) and then turns to her piano:

in the dim light she begins to play strongly. Her face strains, she is utterly involved, unaware of her own strange guttural sounds that form an eerie accompaniment to the music.

An old maid in night-dress looks in. Abruptly the woman stops playing. The emotion leaves her face, it whitens and seems solid like a wall.[13]

The guttural noises are omitted in the film, but the air of concentration and the 'wall' are very clear. That wall is Ada's psychic skin. Anzieu's wife and colleague Annie Anzieu describes such silence in autistic mutes: 'La situation apparente du mutique est telle que rien ne sort de lui, mais rien n'y pénètre non plus; son corps est un peu comme un œuf en mouvement. Il semble que sa coquille imaginaire lui serve à protéger un noyau intérieur essentiel' [nothing emerges from [them] but nothing goes in either; their body is rather like an egg in motion. It seems as though they use this imaginary shell to protect an essential inner core].[14] Ada is not autistic but she has made an autistic choice, 'not a handicap but a strategy'.[15] All the characters think of her silence in the Victorian terms of an exorbitant 'will'. We are told when it began but not why or how. Later we hear that she has played the piano since she was 'five or six', but which came first and which may have caused or encouraged the other is never suggested.

If the voice is a normalizing emissary, Ada chooses two ways to replace its function. The first is her daughter, the second is the piano; both are also objects of intense intimacy and both are mediated by the hand. As we have already seen, when we watch Ada playing her piano we witness something that is inward-turned, involving all her senses together. Baines inherits this fascination with the piano as something that must be touched as well as heard; the blind piano-tuner also reads it with his fingers and his nose. It sends and refuses messages; it is awkward and beautiful. Thus it stands in for its owner's body and is an image of her relation to something of herself that does not form words. It is all the more essential as a means of communication between Ada and Baines because he cannot read so she cannot write.

Hands feature in most of the scenes of *The Piano*, not only when we hear the music. They flail and catch as Ada and Flora are uncomfortably transported onto the beach. They play, inseparably stroking and communicating, as the mother tells her daughter a story. They hold a portrait, a message, they need scrubbing, they dress and undress, they dictate rebuffs; they shadow-mime threat and carry out violence; they cover a mouth to indicate shock or frame a face viewing itself; they measure out a bargain or turn pages; a hand held in an audience may suggest marital intimacy (though Ada removes her ring to play the piano but not to make love); hands touch and caress.

What I am most interested in is the formal signifier I pointed to earlier: a particular use of the hand that occurs at a number of significant points in *The Piano*: the use of the back of the hand to caress a human or inanimate object. Ada's key objects are four: the piano, the child, the man and the sea. Before taking each of these in turn, I want to discuss the importance of the back of the hand. Rilke complained to Gide that

> la langue allemande avait bien un mot pour désigner le dos de la main, mais aucun pour en désigner l'intérieur.
>
> – Tout au plus, peut-on dire *Handflächen* : la plaine de la main. L'intérieur de la main, une plaine ! s'écria-t-il. Par contre, *Handrücken* est d'emploi constant. Ainsi, ce qu'ils considèrent c'est le dos de la main, cette surface sans intérêt, sans personnalité, sans sensualité, sans douceur, cette surface qui s'oppose de préférence à la paume tiède, caressante, douce, où se raconte tout le mystère de l'individu ![16]

> [the German language has a word for the back of the hand but no word for the palm.
>
> 'At the most, we can say 'Handflächen': the flat [*plaine*] of the hand', he cried. 'Imagine calling the inside of the hand a 'plain'! Whereas 'Handrücken' is used all the time. That's what they think about, the back of the hand, a surface with no interest, no personality, no sensuality, no softness, by contrast to the palm, which is warm, caressive, soft, and expresses all the mystery of the individual!']

From the point of view of this film, he is entirely wrong. In 2003, Eve Sedgwick wrote: 'to touch is always already to reach out, to fondle, to heft, to tap or to enfold',[17] but I disagree with her too. The touch of the back of a hand suggests the fingers in their least haptic, most patient mode; it is the obverse of grasping and very much what Sartre has in mind when he writes:

> mon corps se fait chair pour toucher [le corps d'autrui] avec sa propre passivité, c'est-à-dire en se caressant à lui plutôt qu'en le caressant. C'est pourquoi les gestes amoureux ont une langueur qu'on pourrait presque dire étudiée : il ne s'agit pas tant de *prendre* une partie du corps de l'autre que de *porter* son propre corps contre le corps de l'autre. Non pas tant de pousser ou de toucher, au sens actif, mais de *poser contre*.[18]

> [my body becomes flesh in order to touch their body with its own passivity – in caressing itself against it rather than caressing it. This is why the gestures of lovemaking have a languor that one might almost call studied: it is not so much that we *take hold* of a part of the other's body but that we *bring* our own body up against the body of the other. Not so much pushing or touching, in an active sense, but *placing up against*.]

This is what he calls, in terms that echo the passages from Merleau-Ponty and Anzieu quoted above, a '*double reciprocal incarnation*'.

When Baines first asks Ada to come half-clothed to his bed, she lies face down, looking away, as though to protect herself against either his or her own desire. Later, as we shall see, Stewart feels more rather than less under threat when she makes him lie on his front. But between Ada and Baines her back has been the object of attention from the start; this has been his way to reach the woman making music who turns away towards her own playing, whose consensuality is self-directed – not, I think, because this is what refuses him nor because it exposes her 'vulnerable spine',[19] but because this inward-turning gesture is what is most fascinating about her. Thus he touches, kisses, gazes at the nape of her neck; but when he caresses it with the back of his hand, she scents danger and 'changes the music to something brisk, almost comical' (Campion 60).

When, with the return of the piano, Ada loses this scenario, she discovers it is something she cannot do without. We see the changeover from her exclusive libidinous attachment to the instrument to a wish to be observed again by her lover when she sits down to play:

> She starts with wholehearted feeling, her eyes closed, but before long she is surprised by a moving reflection across the piano and she starts, glancing over her shoulder. She stops and begins again. But once more a reflex has her glance across her left shoulder and she pauses in her playing. Disquieted, she starts again and again she looks away. She stops, confused, unable to go on, unable to get up, one hand on the lid and one on the piano keys. (80)

At this point, then, she perceives that it is not enough to enjoy consensuality without the participation of another; she needs to be the object of a desiring gaze. This scene of playing is briefer in the film. We see Ada gaze without warmth at the piano while chewing a forkful of food; go over to it; place her napkin carelessly on it, and then pass the back of her hand across the keys, first one way and then the other. She starts to play, looks behind her, again runs the back of her fingers over the unsatisfying keys. This gesture has occurred once earlier on. With Baines kissing her shoulders and neck as she lies warily beside him, we watch her expression change from the backward-consciousness of him to a forward concern with the piano. He stops, she gets up, goes to the piano and runs the back of her hand along the keys – then he shuts the lid so that she has to pull her hand away, and with tears in her eyes, puts on her jacket and leaves.

In these scenes, the non-haptic, non-active relation of the fingers' back to the piano stands at the turning-point between two ways of living for Ada. The piano, like Baines, always faces her, offering itself front-on. By touching it through the back of her hand, she moves away from its prosthetic role in her address to herself and begins, uncertainly, to address herself to the other.

The second object that Ada touches with the back of her hand is her daughter. We see the girl take this initiative first, lying in bed laughing, caressing her mother's cheek with the back of her fingers while the latter signs to her the story of her relationship with Flora's father. Once, we see the back of Ada's hand on Flora: barricaded in Stewart's house, they are asleep together and the mother, apparently dreaming of her lover, passes the back of her hand across the child's night-dress and hair until this wakes her, shocked, and she moves on to her husband, in the scene we shall look at in a moment. The same placing, mother and daughter with hand-backs on each other's chest and neck, finds them asleep on the morning that Stewart decides to take down the planks. If it stands for anything, I suppose it is for innocence – which is the challenge we also take into the next example, Ada's caressing of her husband's body.

This is perhaps the most curious moment in *The Piano*, and one that Campion added as a supplement to the basic adultery tale. Her producer Jan Chapman comments: 'I think this is the thing that makes the film modern actually, and not sentimental' (Campion 138) and Campion goes on:

> Ada actually uses her husband Stewart as a sexual object – this is the outrageous morality of the film – which seems very innocent but in fact has its power to be very surprising. I think many women have had the experience of feeling like a sexual object, and that's exactly what happens to Stewart. [...] to see a woman actually doing it, especially a Victorian woman, is somehow shocking – and to see a man so vulnerable. It becomes a relationship of power, the power of those that care and those that don't care. I'm very very interested in the brutal innocence of that. (138–39)

Sam Neill, who plays Stewart, several times the agent of a simpler brutal innocence, has this to add: 'What happens to him, I think, is that this shell – a carapace that Victorian men could assume – is cracked and disintegrated by the power of his feelings for Ada, leaving him very exposed. I think of him as being a man who has lost all his skin' (147).

Yet when an almost sleepwalking Ada comes to his bed to caress him (having been, we surmise, shocked to find herself reaching for Flora while dreaming of Baines), it is his skin that she focuses on, caressing it carefully and seemingly tenderly, running the back of her hand across and around his face, turning it in his open palm. Bruzzi notes 'the use of a luscious golden light and a fluid camera that (ironically in Stewart's case) intensifies the attraction of the male skin',[20] and infers from it that Ada 'has discovered a more abstract desire for closeness'. Campion's stage-directions focus more on a strange equivalence of childlike qualities: Stewart 'looks up into her face like a child after a bad dream, fearful and trusting' (89) but then 'childlike she stops and kisses the soft skin of his belly. [...] Ada seems removed from Stewart as if she had a separate curiosity of her own' (89–90).

In the second scene, he is lying on his front. Ada has her eyes closed. She places first the front, then the back of her hand on his buttocks. When he leaps up, saying 'I want to touch you. Why can't I touch you? Don't you like me?', she just 'looks back, moved by his helplessness, but distanced, as if it has nothing to do with her' (93). What is interesting here is the dedication and glow of this desire redirected onto an unloved body and simply 'curious' and detached. It is as much a surprise to see Stewart bathed in golden light as to see Baines draping a pink lace cloth in his hut, so dominant have the shades of blue been in this film.

It is with these shades of blue that my last example is concerned. The endgame has been played out, Stewart has 'heard' Ada's voice telling him to release her and he has 'returned' her to Baines. She is seated in the long-boat that is carrying her, her lover, daughter, possessions and piano to Nelson. Suddenly she signs to the child that the piano must be thrown in the sea: 'she doesn't want it; she says it's spoiled'. At Ada's insistence Baines agrees. She strokes the water with the back of her hand – once, twice, as if preparing it or herself; then gazes at it. A moment later, she steps into the coiled rope and is pulled down with the piano.

Once again the director attributes her protagonist's action to 'curiosity' (121), this time 'fatal [...], odd and undisciplined'. Moments later, of course, Ada chooses life and enters into the unexpected happy ending that many viewers cannot forgive. But my question is: why the back-of-the-hand caress at exactly this point? Is it because she is bidding a complicated and ambivalent farewell to the whole skin of that world in which she was consensual with herself, the 'egg in motion' of her autistic enclosure, which is no longer in season now that missing parts can be connectives rather than only lacks?

NOTES

All translations into English, unless otherwise attributed, are my own and reference is given to the original text. Further references to a cited text will appear after quotations; passages without page reference are from the last-cited page and page-numbers without specified text are similarly from the one last named. Unless otherwise stated, all italics are the authors'.

[1] Naomi Segal, *Consensuality: Didier Anzieu, Gender and the Sense of Touch* (Amsterdam and New York: Rodopi, 2009), hereafter abbreviated SC.

[2] Didier Anzieu, *Le Moi-peau* (Paris: Dunod, [1985] 1995), 61; hereafter abbreviated AMP.

[3] See also Michel Serres, *Les cinq sens [The Five Senses]* (Paris: Grasset, 1985), 53, 59 and 83.

[4] See Didier Anzieu, *Le Penser [Thought]* (Paris: Dunod, 1994); hereafter AP, 15 and 39.

[5] Donald Meltzer et al., *Explorations in Autism* (Strath Tay: Clunie, 1975), 12–13.

[6] Didier Anzieu, 'La psychanalyse, encore' ['Still psychoanalysis'] in *Psychanalyser [To Psychoanalyse]* (Paris: Dunod, 2000), hereafter APs, 268.

[7] Maurice Merleau-Ponty, 'L'entrelacs – le chiasme' [The intertwining – the chiasmus] in *Le Visible et l'invisible [The Visible and the Invisible]* (Paris: Gallimard, 1964), 174, 179–80.

[8] Didier Anzieu, *Les Enveloppes psychiques* (Paris: Dunod, [1987] 1996), hereafter AEP, 1–22.

[9] In a project running as an ESF-COST Synergy in 2009–11 for the European Science Foundation Standing Committee for the Humanities and the European Cooperation in Science and Technology Domain on the Individual, Society, Culture and Health, a definition was agreed for the objects of researchers in literary and cultural studies [LCS] who apply literary thinking to a variety of cultural material: 'No longer restricted to the study of printed books or other fictional genres, LCS researchers focus on cultural objects or "text-like structured artefacts" which have one or more of the following elements in common: textuality, rhetoricity, fictionality and historicity'.

[10] For the former, see SC 79–100, and for the latter, my *André Gide: Pederasty and Pedagogy* (Oxford: Oxford University Press, 1998), 342–64.

[11] Didier Anzieu, *Créer Détruire* (Paris: Dunod, 1996), hereafter ACD, 254.

[12] Didier Anzieu, *Une Peau pour les pensées: Entretiens avec Gilbert Tarrab [A Skin for Thought: Interviews with Gilbert Tarrab]* (Paris: Apsygée, 1991), 75.

[13] Jane Campion, *The Piano screenplay* (London: Bloomsbury, 1993), 10. All quotations without page-reference are from the DVD of the film: Jane Campion (dir.), *The Piano* (CiBy 2000).

[14] Annie Anzieu, 'De la chair au verbe' [From flesh to the word], in *Didier Anzieu* et al., *Psychanalyse et langage [Psychoanalysis and Language]* (Paris: Dunod, [1977] 1989), 129.

[15] Jane Campion in interview with Ian Pryor, *Onfilm 10* (9 October 1993), 25.

[16] André Gide, *Incidences* (Paris: Gallimard, 1924), 63.

[17] Eve Kosofsky Sedgwick, *Touching Feeling* (Durham & London: Duke University Press, 2003), 14.

[18] Jean-Paul Sartre, *L'Être et le néant [Being and Nothingness]* (Paris: Gallimard, 1943), 431.

[19] Lynda Dyson, 'The return of the repressed? Whiteness, femininity and colonialism in *The Piano*', *Screen,* 36: 3 (1995), 271.

[20] Stella Bruzzi, 'Tempestuous petticoats: costume and desire in *The Piano*', *Screen,* 36: 3 (1995), 261.

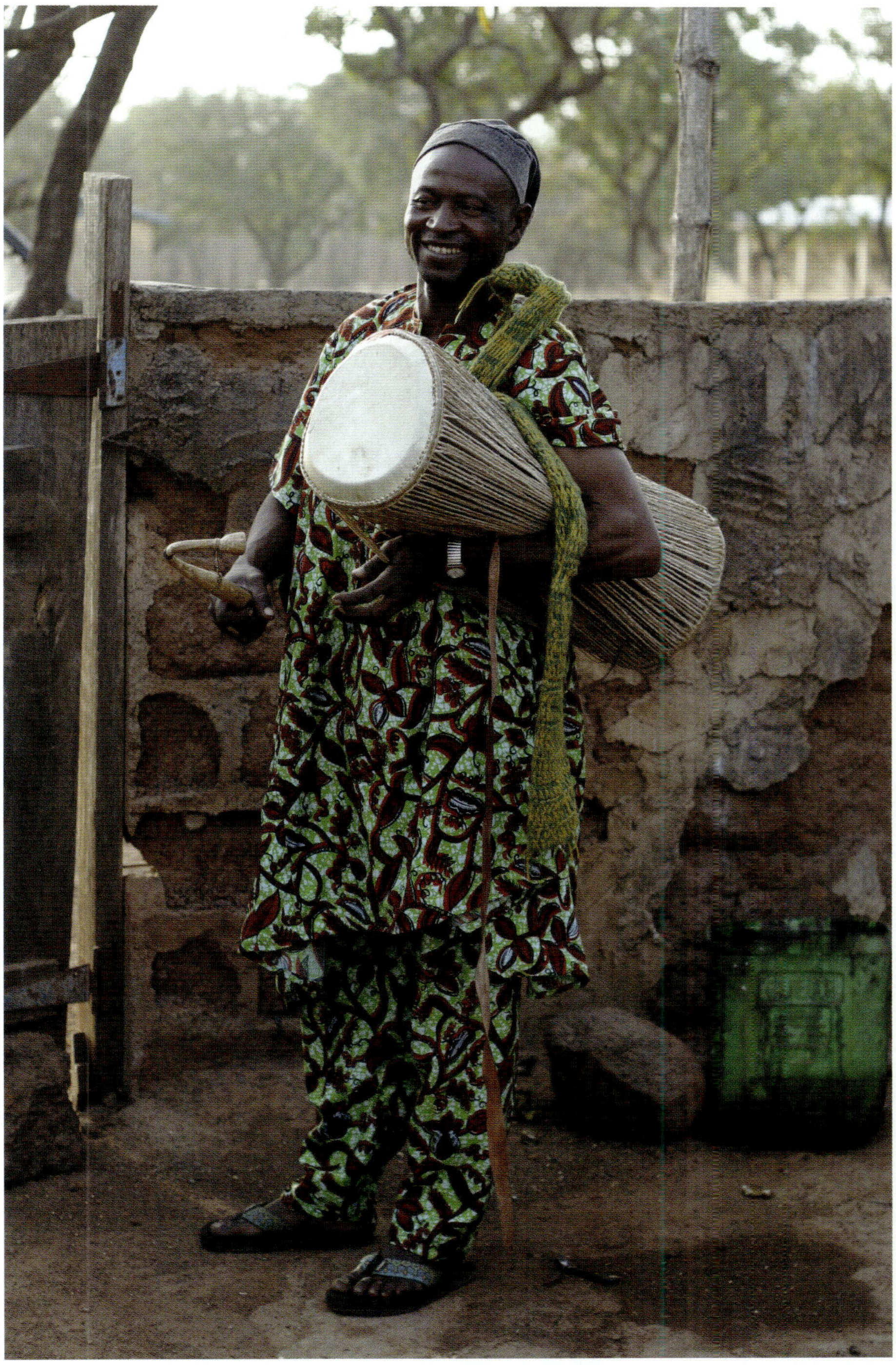

Amidu Abubakari (son of Alhaji Abubakari) standing with luŋa. Photo: Katharine Stuffelbeam.

DAVID LOCKE / SKIN AS A METAPHOR FOR ETHNOMUSICOLOGICAL INQUIRY ABOUT DAGOMBA DRUMMING

Skin describes the boundary between within and without, and is simultaneously a sensitive instrument for communication, directing external information inwards, and outwardly expressing inner states.

This paper uses the skin metaphor to discuss my ethnomusicological work on Dagomba dance drumming, which has produced a large body of information presented on a wiki website hosted by Tufts University titled simply, "Dagomba Dance Drumming" (http://Dagomba.uit.tufts.edu). The DDD site enables users to study in mediated fashion, with late Alhaji Abubakari Lunna, acclaimed expert on Dagomba performing arts and culture. Alhaji, as I will refer to him, was my teacher and research colleague from 1975 until his death in 2009. Users can hear him teach the music part-by-part, listen to him perform the music, and read his accounts of the history of each piece. Alhaji and I developed this material together, working both as master-apprentice and also as informant-scholar. Musicians are our primary audience. Through transcripts of interviews with Alhaji, the site also provides detailed information about the cultural history of Dagomba dance drumming and the life story of one of its leading exponents in the 20th century.

What features of this project fit within the skin metaphor, with its implication of a permeable membrane that filters the in-and-out flow of information? I understand "skin" as a metaphor for mediation, boundary, and contact between things on either side of the covering membrane.

* Dagomba drumming, which loudly proclaims implicit texts, is a skin between the Dagbani language and its manifestation in sound.
* Within the domain of drumming, chanted vocables, an oral notation for instrumental music, are a surface that links the conceptual image of drumming with the actual performance on the instruments.
* Alhaji Abubakari, an insider within the society of drummers, mediates between the Dagomba luŋa tradition and those of us outsiders who are seeking knowledge of it.
* My work, informed by ethnomusicological theory and method, connects what I have learned from Alhaji Abubakari about Dagomba culture to the outside world. I mediate between the "writing-free" world of Dagomba drummers and the "writing-constrained" world of the literate cosmopolitans.
* DDD wiki brings users into mediated contact with Alhaji Abubakari.
* Writing bridges the language and sound of Dagomba dance drumming with its representation in text and notation. The ephemeral experience of music, known its own moment-by-moment time, rubs against the extended time of analytic and aesthetic contemplation.

This paper begins with a quick introduction to Dagomba drumming, which exists within its own skin. Then I provide examples of my work on vocables, drum language, staff notation, and music theory. Finally, I give examples of specific "works" of Dagomba music.

Dagomba Dance Drumming

All Dagomba members of the drumming family trace descent from one man, *Bizuŋ*, who gave up the chance to be chief in favor of becoming a musician. If your father was born into this family line, then you also are a member. The word for drum and drummer are the same, *luŋa* (plural, *lunsi*). Through speech, song and drumming the lunsi recount the history of the Dagomba kingdom, called *Dagbon,* and the genealogy of the royal families. Among the lunsi of Dagbon, highest prestige goes to those who chant the epic narrative of the nation in all-night performances called *Sambaŋluŋa*. Lunsi also play music for dance at social events, which is the type of music featured on the DDD site.

Dagomba drumming is based on words in the Dagbani language, the mother tongue of the Dagomba people. Every note of music has meaning in drum language or "drum talks," as Alhaji called them. A core tenet of Alhaji's teaching is that players should know the language that is the music's foundation.

Drumming energizes people to dance at social functions. Music may be for individuals to dance solo or for groups to do traditional choreography. Every musical work has a place in the social life of the Dagomba people, as outlined below.

* **Invocations:** When a drummer first shoulders a drum, custom dictates that an invocation be played. Invocations align drummers with their history and with spiritual forces. Invocations also are a method of tuning up and alerting other musicians that you are ready to play.
* **Praise Name Dances:** Praise Name Dances or appellations, called *salma* (story) in Dagbani, are for people to dance one-by-one to drumming that honors famous chiefs from the past. There is a strong association linking the music to the person who is the subject of the drum language. Often, the dancer is in the family lineage of the historical chief being saluted by the drummers.

* **Occupational Lineage Dances:** In Dagomba society certain jobs, including drumming, are assigned by birth to members of special lineages. Drummers play special items of repertory for the occupational lineages of blacksmiths and butchers. Alhaji's accounts of the origin of these items of repertory are particularly rich sources of information about Dagomba society and culture.
* **Group Dances:** Drummers play for people to dance in group formation. The dancers are united by a shared factor, for example, gender, social status, age or place of residence. Sometimes the dance group becomes a formal association that is hired to perform at social functions. The history of these Group Dances sheds light on the origin of the polity of Dagbon and character of the social world of the Dagomba people in "the old days."
* **Festival Dances:** In Dagbon, the annual progression of the lunar months is marked by a cycle of festivals, each with its characteristic music and dance. Most well known is the *Damba* Festival, celebrated on the occasion of the birthday of the Prophet Mohammed.

The Drums

The lunsi play drums of two kinds – *luŋa* and *guŋ-gɔŋ*. The luŋa drum has two-heads that are connected by leather ropes over an hourglass-shaped wooden body. Held close into the player's armpit with a long scarf, the ropes are pressed and released to change the tension of the drumhead, thus changing its pitch. Alhaji points out that the pressure actually pulls on the drum's cane rims, whose subtle movement affects the tension of the goatskin. A curved wooden stick with a flattened knob on the end is the drumbeater. Using precisely intoned pitches, the luŋa drummer sets implicit texts, or drum language, to melodies that closely resemble the sound of speech. In music for dance, the luŋa drums have two roles – the lead luŋa, which directs the drumming and presents many drum language texts, and the answer luŋa, a part played by many drummers that provides a recurring melo-rhythmic theme in counterpoint to the lead luŋa part.

Complementing the melodic sound of the two luŋa roles is the guŋ-gɔŋ, a double-headed drum with a cylindrical wooden body. A snare-like cord, called *chahira*, tied across the upper portion of each drumhead divides the drumhead into two playing areas, enabling the drummer to play interactive figures in call-and-response relationship. Players use the bare hand to modulate the sound of center strokes and also to play finger strokes in the chahira zone of the drumhead. Dancers groove to the booming bass sound made by two guŋ-gɔŋ drummers. Some items of repertory call for interlocking phrases for lead guŋ-gɔŋ and answer guŋ-gɔŋ. In these cases, the lead guŋ-gɔŋ part features variations and leeway for improvisation. In other items of repertory, the two drums play in unison.

The ensemble for Dagomba dance drumming has, at minimum one leading luŋa drum, three answer luŋa drums, and two guŋ-gɔŋ drums. Since there is no upper limit on duplication, the answer luŋa part might be played by dozens of drummers on festival days. The lead luŋa calls the ensemble to begin, signals endings, and plays the drum talks that are associated with each item of repertory. The answer luŋa drummers respond to the calls of the lead luŋa by playing the phrase that is appropriate for the item of repertory. The musical back-and-forth between lead and answer luŋa parts is an essential feature of Dagomba dance drumming. In comparison to the variety of phrases sounded by lead luŋa and the guŋ-gɔŋ players, the answer luŋa drummers repeat the same phrase over-and-over with only modest leeway for change.

The luŋa drum is melodic as well as rhythmic. Alhaji Abubakari taught that every luŋa drum has "its own voice." In other words, each instrument has its own proper resonance and range of pitches. Alhaji explained the Dagomba conception with reference to conversation – the sound of each person's voice is unique but everyone is speaking the same language. Drummers control a luŋa's pitches by squeezing and releasing the cords that run between its two drumheads. Changes in pressure on the cords affect the tension on the drumheads and thus the pitch made by a drum stroke. The melodic intervals of the luŋa are easy to sing but difficult to play on an actual drum. This technical challenge is one reason why chanting the vocables is such a wonderful way to learn this music.

Crucial Music Phenomena

Dagomba dance drumming has two kinds of musical rhythm – quaternary or ternary – according to the internal design of "beats," i.e., the steady flow in musical time of moments marked for musical consciousness. In quaternary time, beats contain four faster temporal units or time-points; I write this music with the quarter note as the beat, making sixteenth notes represent the quick units. In ternary time, beats contain three faster temporal units; I write this music with the dotted quarter note as the beat, making eighth notes represent the quick units. Because Dagomba rhythm does not fully conform to the nature of Western music in so-called "simple" and "compound" time, I do not show time signatures in the staff notation.

Dagomba music that uses quaternary time has two main rhythmic features – (1) tempo can be felt at different durations in a 1:2 ratio (akin to "double-time" and "cut-time"), and (2) offbeat accentuation, especially of the fourth time-point within the first beat of the first measure in the temporal cycle. Dagomba music that uses ternary time has two main rhythmic features – (1) cross rhythm, and (2) permanently offset main beats. I employ the term "cross rhythm" to indicate rhythms with 3:2, 2:3, and 4:3 patterning. These patterns arise when music combines binary and ternary temporal values, that is, quarter notes with dotted quarter notes over a span of two ternary beats (3:2), dotted eighth notes with eight notes over a span of one ternary beat (2:3), or dotted eighth notes with quarter notes over two ternary beats (4:3). This sort of rhythmic organization is pervasive in ternary time. Less ubiquitous is the phenomenon of offset beats. In this situation, the lead luŋa part consistently accentuates a flow of beats that is displaced from the onbeats accents of the dancers and other drums in the ensemble. This rhythmic condition is not common in other ethnic traditions in Africa, in my experience, and certainly is alien to most other musical traditions of the world.

Vocables

Vocables are a way to "play drum with mouth." The sounds have no lexical meaning in language, but to call them "nonsense syllables" would be misleading since they precisely symbolize the drumming music. Vocables are a verbal notation system that captures the pitch, timbre, melody, rhythm, dynamics, and articulation of notes in a drum phrase.

When he teaches a new drum phrase, Alhaji usually has students begin with vocables. After they learn to chant the drumming phrase, he instructs, "Now make the exact same sound on the drum." Memory is a key attribute for drummers in Dagbon. Alhaji reports that a drummer with "good hand" but weak memory would never be considered a top-flight lead drummer. Another drummer might have "good head" for drum language but be physically uncoordinated on luŋa. The best drummers are those who can do both: recall the appropriate proverbs and put them nicely into drumming music. Fluency with vocables is crucial to becoming a good drummer.

For the luŋa drum, the three pitch classes are distinguished by vowel sound: "a" for low-pitch, "e" for mid-pitch, and "i" for high-pitch. The way the drumstick hits the skin is indicated by the consonant at the beginning of the vocable: in most musical settings the vocable for bounce strokes starts with "d." In special musical situations, such as a relatively soft-sounding initial note in a figure, Alhaji uses "z." When Alhaji verbalizes a two-stroke press role, which he usually plays with turned-stick technique, he uses the sound "gr." Vocables also represent the duration of a note and the way it ends. Notes of longer than normal duration end with the nasal consonant "n." The "n" sound also occurs on the final note in a motive.

In addition to drum strokes, vocables also indicate notes produced by pressure on the luŋa ropes. The sound "h" indicates notes produced by increased pressure. Thus, the two-syllable vocable "dahin" represents a low-pitched bounce stroke followed by a high-pitched note that is the result of increasing the pressure on the luŋa ropes. The sound "y" indicates notes produced by decreasing the pressure on the luŋa ropes. The vocable "diyen" represents a short high-pitch note followed by a long mid-pitched note produced by decreasing the pressure on the luŋa ropes.

Subtle upward and downward pitch bends are an important yet subtle aspect of luŋa drumming. Notes of low- and mid-pitch may be approached either from above or below, but high-pitched notes only are approached from below. Alhaji's systematic use of vocables includes this nuance. "Neighbor pitches" retain the vowel of the main pitch; in performance the drummer simply intones the neighbor pitch a major or minor second below or above the main pitch. The vocable "dihin" indicates a high-pitch stroke approached from its lower neighbor. The vocable "deyen" indicates a mid-pitch stroke approached from its upper neighbor.

Just as the musical phrases and drum language of guŋ-gɔŋ are less complex than luŋa, so its system of vocables is simpler, too. "Ka" stands for bounce stick-strokes in the center of the drum. "Ki" stands for press stick-strokes in the center of the drum. "Zi" stands for bounce stick-strokes at the edge of the drum (chahira zone). "Gi" stands for bounce finger-strokes at the edge of the drum (chahira zone). As on luŋa, the nasal "n" finishes a vocable for a center stick-stroke of long duration or those positioned at the end of a motive. By carefully listening to the way Alhaji sings the motives played in the chahira zone of the drumhead, you can know the sticking pattern. For example, the phrase "kan kakan zi zigizi" represents three center strokes with long-short-long time values, followed by four chahira strokes played stick stick / hand / stick.

Staff Notation

Notation is a means to study the melody and rhythm of these drum talks. The notation indicates features of drumming technique, including the squeeze-and-release of the pressure ropes on the luŋa drums and the "handedness" of chahira strokes on the guŋ-gɔŋ drum. The lyrics line beneath the staff associates the musical sound of Alhaji's voice to the vocables that he chants and the Dagbani drum language that is implicit to his drumming. Although I believe that repeated listening is the most valuable way to learn this music, contemplative consideration of the staff notation also is an important method of inquiry.

Staff notation is not "natural" to Dagomba drumming, which before now has existed in an unwritten condition. Dagomba dance drumming is a "writing-free" tradition that has been passed from person to person over generations. Confining it within a written form entails risk. For example, oral transmission insures an interpersonal relationship between teacher and student within a social context shaped by cultural history. I am cautious that writing Dagomba music in staff notation may facilitate the wrongful appropriation of African cultural achievements by strangers. But I have come to the conclusion that Dagomba dance drumming should be regarded as a wonderful human heritage that can provide artistic edification to everyone, not just members of Dagomba society. In addition to issues of post-colonial politics and morality in globalized culture, there are musical problems inherent in using staff notation, as well. Scholars of African music especially flag problems with staff notation's conventions of accentuation within measures and the one-dimensional image of rhythmic grouping for notes connected by a beam. I believe that providing the audio material on which the notation is based mitigates this problem. Once the music becomes familiar through repeated listening, the staff notation can be "heard" with the sound of Alhaji's performance in mind.

On the luŋa drum, there are three main pitch classes: low, mid, and high. These pitch classes are represented on a 5-line staff in G clef (lowered an octave) with notes B, D and E. Spectacularly accurate intonation of these pitch classes was a mark of Alhaji's mastery of the luŋa. Through vocables we all can accurately sing the luŋa part, but being able to control the pitch of an actual drum takes years of practice.

In order to make the drum sound like the Dagbani language, Alhaji supplements the low-pitch and mid-pitch primary pitches classes with "neighbor notes" – (1a) below-low, (1b) above-low, (2a) below-mid, and (2b) above-mid. In notation, neighbor notes to low-pitch are A-sharp and

C; neighbors for mid-pitch are C and E. The written note that represents the actual drum stroke receives an accent mark; the written note that represents the pitch made by pressure technique is tied to the accented note and is marked as unaccented.

The neighbor pitch resolves towards the primary pitch. Typically, Alhaji would strike the luŋa drum skin with the ropes set to the neighbor pitch and then increase or decrease pressure so that the drum's pitch rose or fell toward the main pitch class. These auxiliary pitches enable the drum to imitate long vowels and nasal sounds, thus more closely imitating the sound of speech.

To facilitate comparison among pieces, I have written the music with 6/8 (ternary duple) or 2/4 (quaternary duple) time signatures. By deliberately hiding the Western time signature, however, I wish to encourage users to interpret the notation according to the nature of Dagomba dance drumming. I intend to discourage readers from glibly assuming that the music "is in 6/8" or "in 2/4," so to speak. It is not. Instead, its temporal organization is approximately equivalent to 6/8 or 2/4. As a practical matter, time signatures must be specified for music software to work efficiently.

Staff notation allows the scribe – me, in this case – many options for joining notes together with beams. For many musicians who would notate African music, this flexibility has proved problematic because you must chose one option among many. In its unwritten form, the temporal relationship of notes to implicit beats is a matter of internal feeling for players and listeners. Written music, on the other hand, demands that notes be related to the beats of only one metric groove. But, as I show in detail in my music analysis of each piece, Dagomba dance drumming conforms to multiple patterns of rhythmic accentuation. Selecting one system of beaming, or even using any beaming at all, inevitably presents a simplified graphic picture of a complex sonic world. Nevertheless, I think the advantages outweigh the drawbacks.

In ternary-duple time, three-in-the-time-of-two patterns of accentuation are endemic. In the terms of staff notation, we can say that 3/4 accentuation patterns are omnipresent in music written in 6/8. Beats with binary internal structure, i.e., quarter notes, co-exist with ternary beats that contain three faster time-points. Accentuation of the 3:2 type time, for example, three quarters in the duration of two dotted quarters or three eighths in the duration of two dotted eighths, forces a choice on the scribe: do you show the notes in relationship to an invariant series of unsounded beats, or do you beam to call attention to the pattern of accentuation created by the sounded notes? In most cases, I beam to the primary ternary schema. But musical common sense and notational elegance sometimes take precedence over theoretical rigidity. When the "phenomenal surface" of the music, so to speak, clearly establishes a 3:2 pattern, I simply go with it.

A very important dimension of Dagomba tension drum technique is the way drummers make notes not only by striking the drum skin, but also by releasing or squeezing the pressure cords that join the rims of the drumhead fixed on each end of the drum's body. Without these relatively quiet "pressure notes" the luŋa drum will not sound like the Dagbani drum language texts that underlie the music. Gliding between notes – portamento or glissando in Italianate lingo – is not ornamental, in other words, but essential. This was among the most important realizations that emerged from my study of this tradition with Alhaji Abubakari. Although graphically representing this dimension of drumming makes the staff notation more difficult to read, pressure technique is essential to make the luŋa "talk."

Ties and accent marks indicate the gliding dimension of luŋa technique. The sound produced by a drum stroke is shown with an accented note head, while the sound produced by pressure technique is shown with an unaccented note head. Ties join an unaccented "pressure" note to an accented note. In other words, an unaccented note that is tied to a prior accented note is showing a sound that has been created by pressure technique on the luŋa ropes rather than a hit on the drum.

Music Analysis

As African music, Dagomba dance drumming has musical features that are quite unlike music from other regions of the world. Even within the domain of African music, Dagomba dance drumming has distinctive qualities, such as the melodic nature of the drumming, the nuances of technique on the luŋa drum that enable it to "talk," and the rhythmic sense of several streams of offset onbeats happening simultaneously. In the music analysis, I interpret the drumming as a style of music that can be appreciated by a universal, global audience. In my conception of the DDD wiki, the most important information I myself have created is the staff notation of the Part-by-Part Sessions. This graphic display of information is loaded with important detail. In particular, this notation shows the pressure technique on the luŋa drums that is crucial to making them sound like the spoken Dagbani language. The notation also shows phrasing, multi-stroke technique, and nuances of dynamics. Ironically, the Part-by-Part notation obscures the first thing most non-Dagomba musicians want to know – the timing of drum strokes. Further, breaking the musical texture of the drum ensemble into its many parts does not address the overall unity of the music. To remedy these issues, each item of repertory gets a musical example that shows only the rhythm of drum strokes.

My analyses clarify musical nuances that likely are obscure in the Part-by-Part notation examples. For example, although Dagomba dance drumming uses temporal cycles that are longer than two beats in duration, the notation is written in two-beat measures. The musical analyses discuss the various cyclic forms, making ample use brackets above the staff to convey vital information about musical meter. Furthermore, beaming to the beats obscures 3:2 patterning, which becomes another important topic for analysis. Although staff notation is an elegant, flexible method of communication, Dagomba music is not easily reconciled to this system.

ANALYSIS EXAMPLES

This section of the paper excerpts selected material from the longer analytic discussions of each item of repertory found on the DDD site. The written and graphic material illustrates the "skins" of drumming:language, vocables:drumming, notation:sound, scholar:teacher, and writing:experience.

Music in Quaternary Time
Nantoo Nimdi

Nantoo Nimdi, which means "poisoned meat," is the appellation for Naa Yakubu, king of Dagbon in the mid-1800s and progenitor of all subsequent kings. Alhaji Abubakari's history story tells of how Naa Yakubu became king because of the efforts of his zealous and powerful nephew, Idantoma. Because he had Idantoma as an ally, it would have been dangerous for someone to threaten Naa Yakubu, which is why he likens himself to poisoned meat (see Table 1).

Nantoo Nimdi provides a very clear instance of rhythm in quaternary time (see Figure 1). Its groove is characterized by the dotted rhythm of the response theme, which moves 3 + 3 + 2 through the quaternary temporal grid. The interlock of the offbeat drum strokes in the response parts with the implicitly felt onbeats generates the basic groove. Answer luŋa stroke one is right on beat one, stroke two is just before beat two, and stroke three is midway between beat two and the downbeat of measure 2. The unaccented tones created by pressure on the luŋa ropes enable the drum to imitate the sound of speech. The rhythm of the guŋ-gɔŋ is very similar to the answer luŋa rhythm because they both express the same drum talk. Lacking the luŋa's ability to change pitch, however, the guŋ-gɔŋ player uses "ki," the turned-stick press stroke, to convey the upward direction of the melody.

Response Drums	*Kaɣili sulisi*	Vultures disturb.
Lead Luŋa Talk 1	*Akul 'dapal' Nantoo Nimdi,*	Son of the fearless one,
	To Nimdi Nantoo Nimdi.	Nantoo Nimdi.

Table 1: Drum Language – Nantoo Nimdi

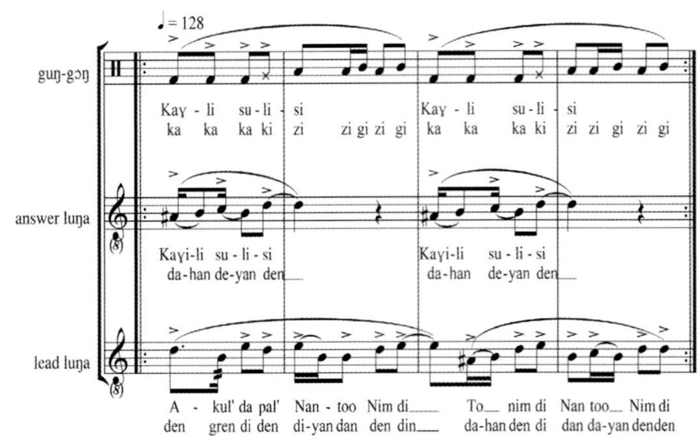

Figure 1: Staff notation – Nantoo Nimdi

Although Alhaji seldom uses the essential format without elaboration, the essence of the lead luŋa part is to fill the silence in the response parts. Lead luŋa phrases in Nantoo Nimdi are relatively short in comparison to many other items of Praise Name drumming. The basic framework is four beats per phrase. The principal talk for lead luŋa is "Akul 'dapal' Nantoo Nimdi." Alhaji uses a press roll (marked with tremolo bars) to render the Dagbani "-kul," thus effectively mimicking with the drum the tongue-rolling "l" sound of the spoken language.

Suligu

Suligu is the appellation for Diari-lana Bukali. The History Story is set during the time of the last war between the Dagombas and the Gonjas, whose territory is located to southwest of Dagbon. The Gonja chief, Kumpatia, was advancing on Yendi, the capital of Dagbon. Naa Zanjina, the Dagomba king, could not get any support from his brothers, so he sent the chief of Diari to convince a strong warrior, Andani Siɣli, to lead the fight. The word "suligu" means hawk, a tribute to Diari-lana Bukali's formidable strength (see Table 2).

Suligu has a majestic, regal musical feeling (see Figure 2). In the response theme, motives separated by pauses create a spacious quality. The rhythm begins and ends with compelling offbeat syncopation balanced by solid onbeat accents in the middle portion of the theme. Gaps in the response theme are dramatically filled by lead luŋa, giving Suligu a very effective back-and-forth quality between the two sections of the ensemble.

The crucial feature of the response theme is the timing of the first stroke. Coming just before an onbeat, it imparts tremendous rhythmic propulsion to the motive. Three notes follow on the midpoint between successive beats. A fifth note placed on the beat brings closure to the motive. The first of the two linking motives is simply one note (den). This stark single hit echoes the final note of the opening motive, serving to slow down the rhythmic pace. The busier second linking motive (den den dedan din) ends with high-pitch on a backbeat, giving the rhythm an unresolved quality that nicely sets up the return of the "mani mini o n-kpoi" theme.

Response Drums	*Mani mini o n-kpoi,*	I think he took [it].
	Hoi!	Hey!
	Buyli noo ku o kpoi.	[It is] the land god's fowl he took and killed.
	Zami kpemba la.	[It is] against the ancestors.
Lead Luŋa Talk 1	*Man' mini-mini ŋun kpuri.*	I am thinking he took it.
	Man' mini-mini,	I am thinking,
	Ti buyli noo ku o ku gba.	He killed the god's fowl.
Lead Luŋa Talk 2	*Baa ku nyɔmsi nɔŋa.*	Dog can never smell scorpion.
	baa ku nyɔmsi nɔŋa	Dog can never smell scorpion.
	Nyɔm ka nya	Smell it and see!
Lead Luŋa Talk 2	*Bi yeri ma jɔyujɔyu.*	People gossip a lot about me.
	Ku kari ma.	That cannot sack me.
	Tiŋ ni ka m-beni.	I will be there in town.

Table 2: Drum Language – Suligu

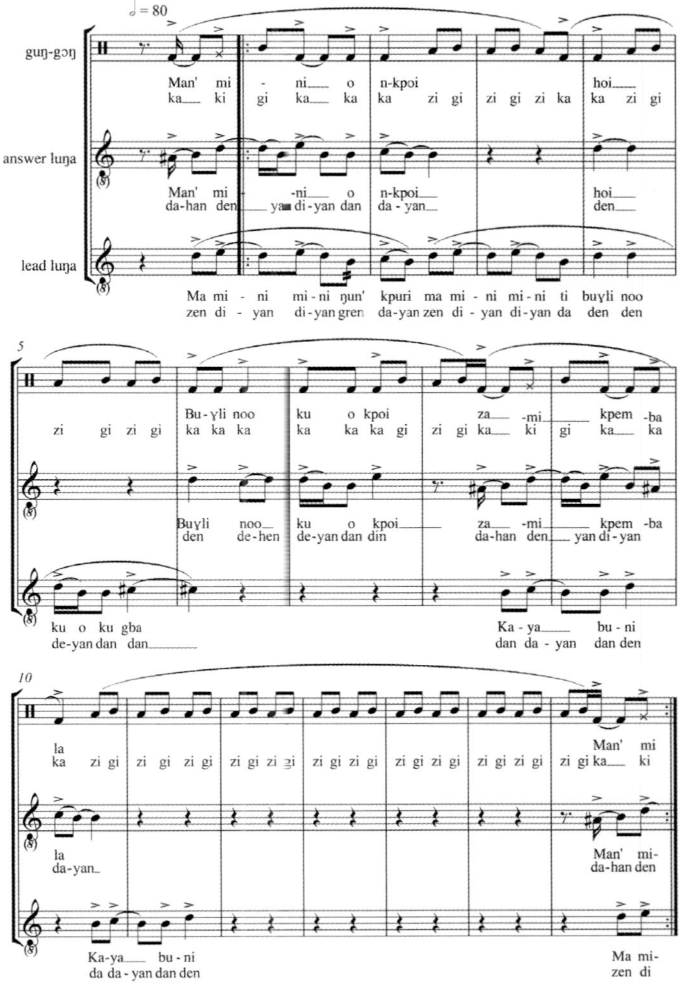

Figure 2: Staff notation – Suligu

Suligu's lead and response phrases are unequal in duration (12 beats + 20 beats = 32 beats). With more time to play with, so to speak, the lead luŋa part has more underlying texts set to more complex melodies. The rhythm of the drum talks presents a metric situation that may prove challenging to non-Dagombas – "flipping" the beat.

The Dagbani phrase, "Ma mini mini ŋuni kpuri," underlies the main lead drum phrase in Suligu (see Figure 2; for other lead luŋa drum talks please go to Dagomba Dance Drumming website http://Dagomba.uit.tufts.edu). This phrase requires controlled release of pressure on the luŋa ropes from high- to mid-pitch, a difficult technique happens twice in rapid succession. The drum talk "Bi yɛri ma jɔɣujɔɣu" also needs advanced drumming technique. To sound the word "ma," the drummer must strike a low note and then immediately squeeze the luŋa ropes so that the listener hears high-pitch. Then, the drummer must release the ropes back to low-pitch and twice play two-note rolls to pronounce the word "jɔɣujɔɣu." To make the word "tiŋa" the high note must be strongly struck and then released from high to low. Finally, "Baa ku nyɔmsi nɔŋa" really challenges a listener's musical ability to maintain steady sense of metric orientation. By starting strongly on the backbeat, this drum talk seems to shift the bar line, so to speak, by one beat. If one is not focused, the whole gestalt of the rhythm can appear to shift. Thus, Suligu has two types of strong accentuation – (1) on the "ands" of the main beats, and (2) on the "backbeat," that is the second count in a duple measure.

Damba

The answer luŋa theme of Damba generates terrifically powerful forward motion through musical time (Figure 3). The phrase has five events: four strokes followed by a strongly felt silence at the end (16 = 3 + 4 + 4 + 2 + 3). Four offbeat strokes fit within four quaternary beats: stroke one is on the fourth time-point within beat one, while strokes two, three, and four are on the third time-point, or upbeat, of beats two, three, and four. In other words, the phrase begins on an extreme offbeat moment and then stabilizes on three upbeats. Stroke four, however, feels rhythmically unresolved, as if hanging in musical space like an unanswered question. Guŋ-gɔŋ provides the answer with its powerful "ka" stroke on beat one.

As revealed in Alahji's presentation of vocables and on drum, pressure on the luŋa ropes is an important feature of the phrase's rhythm and melody. Strokes one and two approach low-pitch from the lower neighbor; the final two strokes have no such squeeze-release effect, which makes them sound strong and powerful. Pressure technique thus reinforces the "two pairs" structure of the phrase. Strokes two, three and four also share an important characteristic – upbeats accentuation. Players sometimes omit stroke one, which highlights the rhythmic similarity of these three strokes. A three note phrase that marks the upbeats of beats two, three and four is a widespread timeline pattern for quaternary music in the forest and coastal regions of West Africa.

The rhythm of the answer luŋa phrase in Damba is deeply engrained in Dagomba dance drumming. With different sequence of pitches, the answer luŋa phrase of Damba reappears in the Group Dance *Kondaliya*; with different pitches and metric setting it occurs in the Group Dance *Takai*. As revealed in the discussion of other pieces in quaternary time, above, many items of dance drumming share the timing of its notes and their positioning within meter. Its musical design is a profoundly generative cultural trope, so to speak. I would go so far as to say that the rhythm is imprinted on the musical being of a Dagomba person during his or her period of childhood enculturation. It is a feature of entrainment that contributes to the cultural identity of the ethnic group.

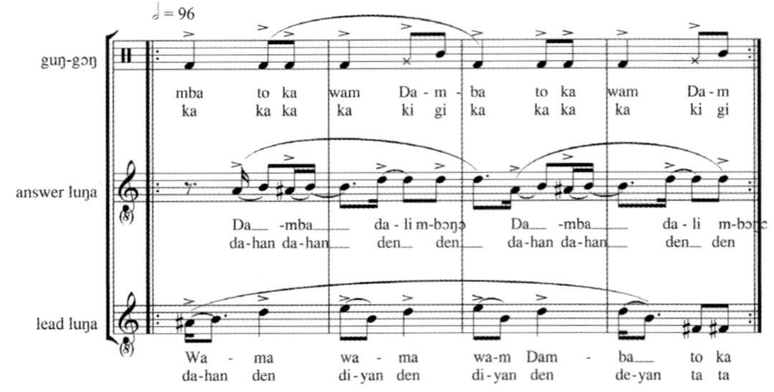

Figure 3: Staff notation – Damba

Music in Ternary Time
Dambobugo

Dambobugo praises Savelugu-naa Bukali Kantamparum, a son of Naa Yakubu, as a generous provider to his family, telling them to "Eat and be satisfied." When Bukali was maneuvering to rise from being the chief of a smaller town, many people tried in vain to prevent him from being promoted to Savelugu, a higher post. After he had gained the chieftaincy, the weather was particularly good for farming and the harvest was plentiful. The drum language for Dambobugo says he has defeated his enemies but continues to think good of everyone. God has rewarded his generous spirit by bringing rain so that big families can eat well and be satisfied (see Table 3).

Response Drums	*Dambobugo din tayi.*	Big family, eat and be satisfied.
	To to,	Yes, yes,
	Dambobugo din tayi.	Big family, eat and be satisfied.

Table 3: Drum Language – Dambobugo

Like other Praise Names in ternary time with this sort of formal structure, three-in-the-time-of-two (3:2) features prominently (Figure 4). The morphology of the response theme in Dambobugo is ABA – an opening motive (A), followed by two figures that simply mark downbeats (B), and then a return of the opening motive (A). In motive A the strokes move in two duplets from one downbeat to the next. The melodic contour is LLLML but in order to properly represent the implicit Dagbani text the drummer must be clever with the pressure technique after striking the drum. The A motive has five notes: note one – "Dam-" – begins on below-low-pitch and is squeezed up to low; note two –"-bobu-" – begins on above-low-pitch and is released down to low; note three – "-go" – is virtually identical to stroke one; on note four – "din" – the drum plays a plain mid-pitch stroke that carries strong accentuation because it is not modified with after-bend; after the fifth stroke the drummer should release the pressure cords as quickly as possible to make the luŋa's sound match the glottal fricative in the Dagbani, written with the symbol "ɣ." The rhythmic impact of this complex pressure technique is to separate the duplet accents of drum strokes into short-long figures – notated sixteenth-eighth – that speed up the temporal motion and increase the density of the motive's texture.

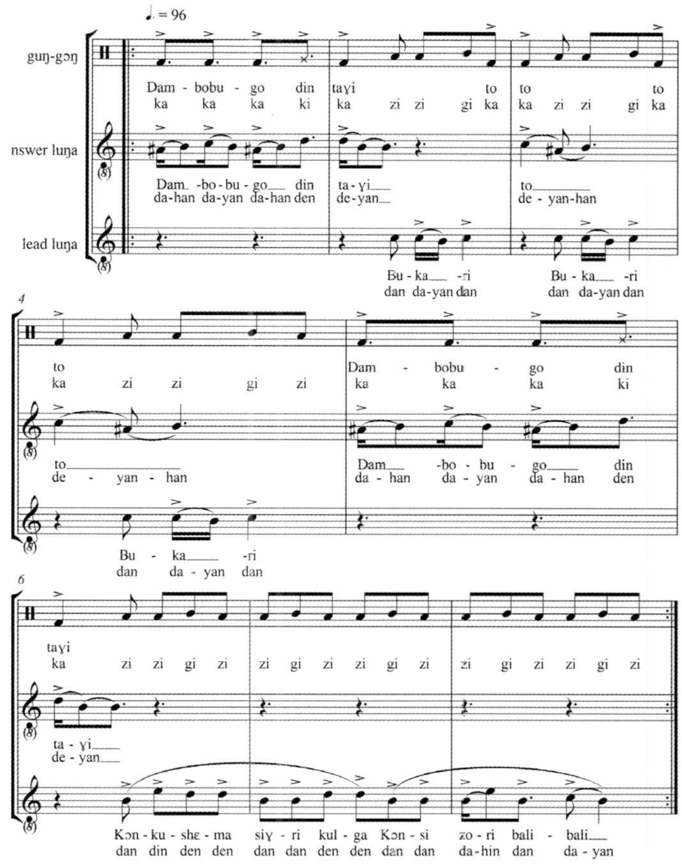

Figure 4: Staff notation – Dambobugo

Dɔɣu Maŋgli

Dɔɣu is the appellation of Tuɣu-lana Yemusa. Yemusa, son of Naa Andani Siɣli (see Suligu), was born on the same day that Naa Siɣli killed Kumpatia, king of the Gonjas. Yemusa was made the regent when his father died. In a town called Baɣli, another person named Yemusa, who was also made regent at his father's funeral, chose one of Tuɣu-lana Yemusa's appellations for himself. When Tuɣu-lana Yemusa found out that another Yemusa was using his appellation, he went to Baɣli to challenge him. Tuɣu-lana's warriors tortured Baɣli Yemusa in an effort to make him stop using the appellation, but he refused. Eventually, Tuɣu-lana ordered him killed. The drum language for Dɔɣu means "he killed him because of a name." A proud prince would rather be tortured to death than relinquish his appellation to an archrival. In contemporary practice, Dɔɣu is played for individuals who have the title and social role of "regent," that is, the eldest son of a deceased chief (see Table 4).

Response Drums	*Chɛli yuli, taɣi yuli!*	Leave title, change title!

Table 4: Drum Language – Dɔɣu Maŋgli

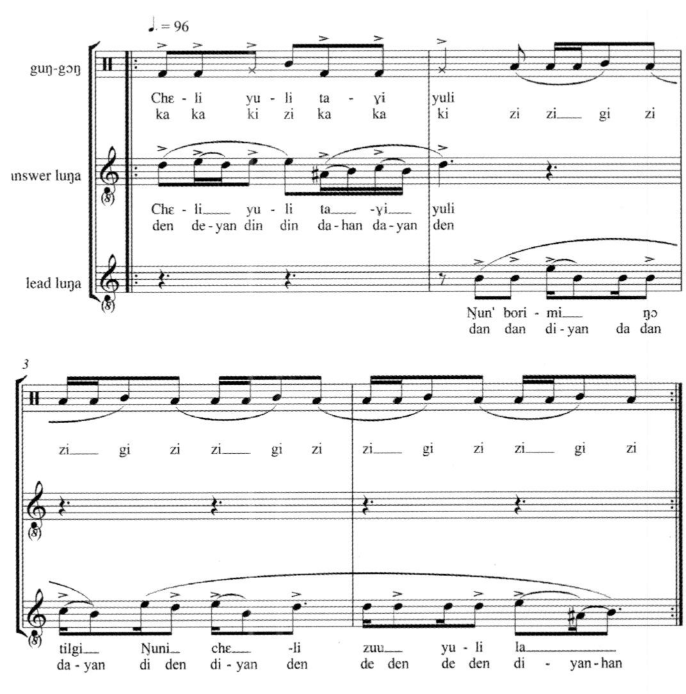

Figure 5: Staff notation – Dɔɣu Maŋgli

As music, Dɔɣu is two separate pieces distinguished by tempo. The slow-paced music is designated in Dagbani as "maŋgli" or the main piece; the fast-paced music is termed "tuli" or the hot piece. Dɔɣu Maŋgli has a regal quality, as befits a piece that is played for regents. The music's grandeur comes from its stately tempo and the decorous manner by which the call-and-response is handed off between the drums. The double-time rhythm of the leading luŋa suggests power percolating beneath a smooth surface – a musical metaphor for the latent force of the regent should his authority be challenged. Both pieces may be singled out for the prominent way that 3:2 in the built into the design of the response theme.

Dɔɣu Maŋgli has classic, straightforward call-and-response – the lead luŋa plays a "call" theme that receives response from answer luŋa and guŋ-gɔŋ (see Figure 5). The balance between call and response is weighted strongly toward the call. In other words, the lead luŋa phrases are much longer than the reply from answer luŋa and guŋ-gɔŋ. As notated in eighth notes the sum is 24 = 17 + 7.

The response theme of Dɔɣu Maŋgli is completely built on three-in-the-time-of-two. The answer luŋa plays seven even strokes that move from the downbeat of measure four to the downbeat of the entire temporal cycle in measure one. Although the implicit beats are ternary, these strokes get a binary rhythmic grouping from drum language, dynamic accents and melodic contour. This is a clear case of 3:2 between quarter notes and dotted quarter notes, phrased "one two three one." In order for the drum to closely resemble the sound of the underlying Dagbani text, Alhaji taught his students to use pressure technique on the cords that connect the luŋa's two drumheads. With proper release and increase in pressure, the rhythm of the answer luŋa phrase acquires a more articulated shape.

Zim Taai Kulga

Zim Taai Kulga is the appellation for Naa Alaasani, grandson of Naa Yakubu. When his predecessor died, the kingmakers of Dagbon chose Naa Alaasani to be king but disagreement led to a stalemate that lasted several years. One of Naa Alaasani's relatives got help from British troops to make way for Naa Alaasani to become Yaa Naa. In drum language the response drums compare Naa Alaasani to an elusive fish that avoids capture (see Table 5 and Figure 6).

Response Drums	*Kulpalnim' wɔlim jɛ.*	Fishermen fished [for him] in vain.
	Kulpalnim' wɔlim jɛ.	Fishermen fished [for him] in vain.
Lead Luŋa Short Call	*To to to,*	Listen
	Abulai dapal', Alaasani.	Son of Abudulai, Alaasani.
Lead Luŋa Talk 1	*Nyɛma nyɛma zim pali kulga ni.*	See, see, many fish are in the river.
	Nyɛma nyɛma zim pali kulga ni.	See, see, many fish are in the river.
Lead Luŋa Talk 2	*Tipariga Tipariga, Alaasani.*	Tipariga, Alaasani.
	Tipariga Tipariga, Alaasani.	Tipariga, Alaasani.
Lead Luŋa Talk 3	*Katini dapal', Tipariga.*	Son of Katini, Tipariga.
	Katini dapal', Tipariga.	Son of Katini, Tipariga.

Table 5: Drum Language – Zim Taai Kulga

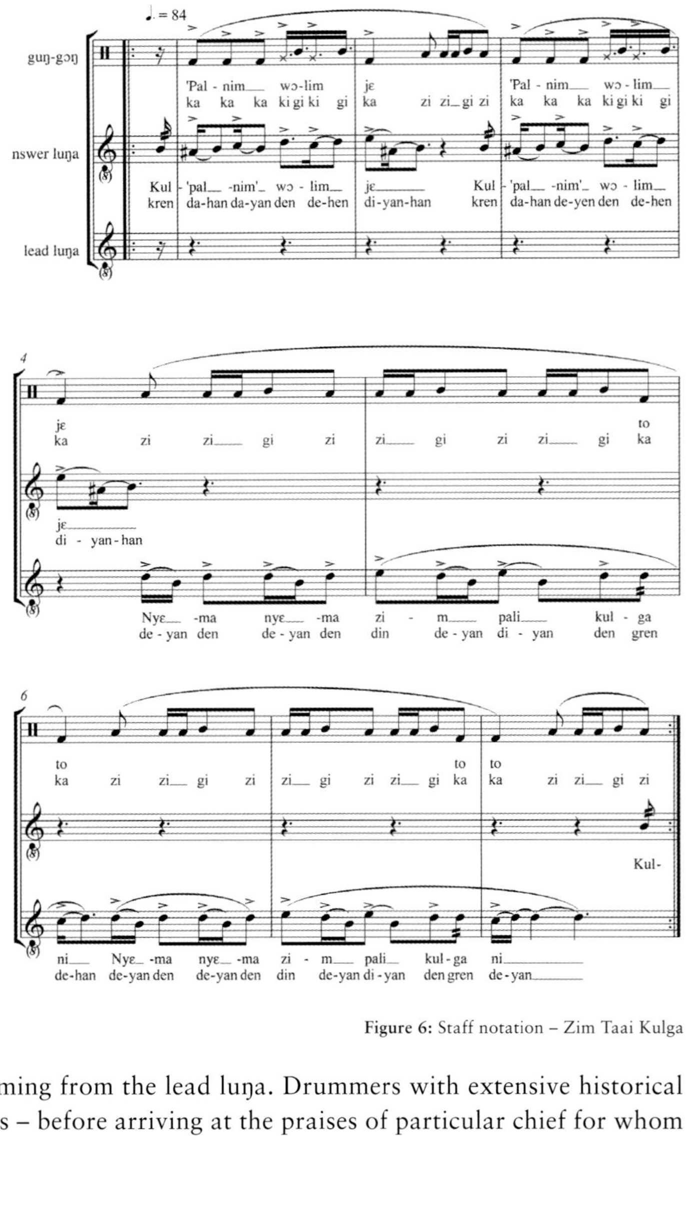

Figure 6: Staff notation – Zim Taai Kulga

Like all Praise Names, Zim Taai Kulga begins with solo drumming from the lead luŋa. Drummers with extensive historical knowledge play for a long time – calling the names of ancestors – before arriving at the praises of particular chief for whom the piece is played.

However, in these demonstrations, Alhaji reduced the opening call to its essential minimum, what he called "short play." For Zim Taai Kulga, he simply said in drumming, "Son of Naa Abudu, Alhassan" and then went directly to the first praise proverb. In Dagbon, a drummer of Alhaji's reputation who never perform Zim Taai Kulga without calling the names of Naa Alhassan's forbearers at least back as far as his four grandparents.

In Zim Taai Kulga, drummers use the image of fish in the river to praise Naa Alhassan for rising above his competitors to claim the title of Yaa Naa. They also compare him to a rare tree that is prized for its fine wood by naming him "Tipariga." Finally, they say that he is "Son of Katini," referring both the room in the palace compound where the incoming Yaa Naa must spend a night as part of the investiture process and the female royal who is in charge of that space.

The first drum talk says, "Nyɛma nyɛma zim pali kulga ni," "See, see many fish are in the river" (see Figure 7). Alhaji's demonstration of this phrase in vocables and drumming exemplifies many essential characteristics of lead luŋa playing. Without melodic nuances of pressure technique, a simplified version of the melody would move in two- or three-stroke units between low-mid and high-mid-pitches before ending with three consecutive mid-pitch tones – LM LM HMH MMM, LM LM HMH MMM. The phrase's rhythmic accentuation moves in quarter note time values that are in 3:2 with the flow of implicit ternary beats. Re-beaming the notes from a flow of ternary beats (dotted quarters) to a flow of binary beats would show the flow of quarter note accents clearly – 2 3 1, 2 3 1, 2 3 1, 2 3 1. (Readers are invited to re-write Drum Talk 1 from 6/8 to 3/4 time signature.) Alhaji would accept this style of performance from his students but he himself always played with sophisticated pressure releases that enabled his drum to have a very full breath-like sound. When releasing the drum's cords for the "-m" sound of the word "zim" (fish, pl.), he achieved an amazingly full bass sound.

A very similar 3:2 rhythmic structure occurs in the drum talk "Tipariga." The pattern of accentuation in this theme bears an interesting relationship to what we can term the "linear" manifestation of 3:2 between quarters and dotted quarters. Commonly in West African music, a time span of four ternary beats is felt according to a rhythmic pattern that can be nicknamed "one two three, one two," i.e., one set of three quarters – 1-a-2-a-3-a – followed by one set of two dotted quarters – 1-y-a-2-y-a (see Table 6, row A). The drum phrase "Tipariga" accentuates a displaced position of this widespread metric rhythm, as shown below (see Table 6, rows B and C).

The third talk for lead luŋa uses the linear 3:2 rhythm just mentioned, above, but with faster time values (eighths and dotted eighths). The rhythmic pattern is located so that the "1 2 3" falls in beat two and the "1 2" comes on beat one.

A.	1	a	2	a	3	a	1	y	a	2	y	a	1	a
B.			one		two		three		one			two		
C.			Ti-	pari-	ga		Ti-	pari-	ga		A-	laa-	sa-	ni

Table 6: Rhythmic Displacement in Zim Taai Kulga Drum Talk

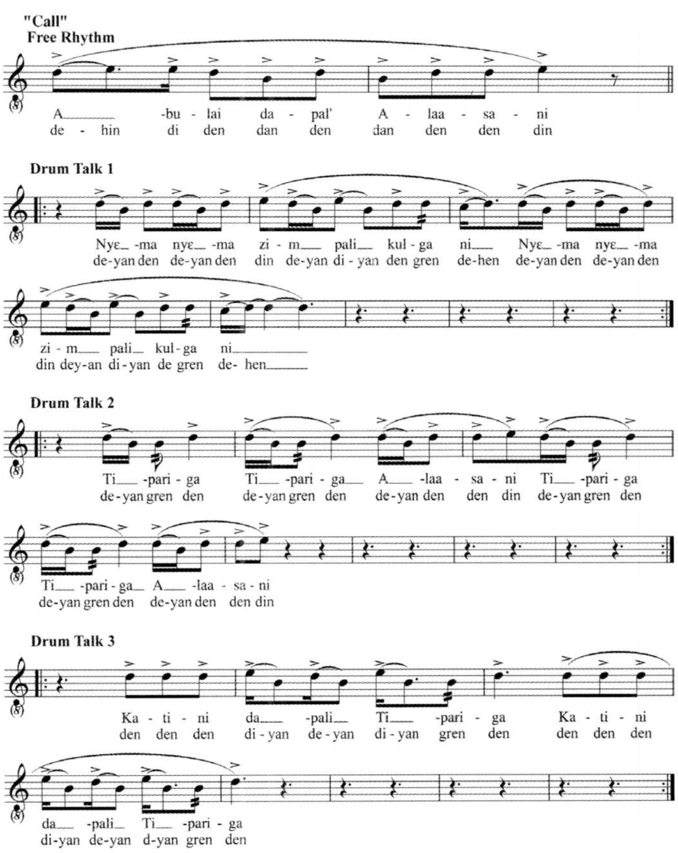

Figure 7: Staff notation – Lead Drum Talks for Zim Taai Kulga

Conclusion

The paper has illustrated ethnomusicological scholarship, which inevitably operates on the border between different music-cultures. Living on the edge, so to speak, ethnomusicologists mediate between musical traditions. We not only negotiate the "skins" established by our informants and research associates, but also participate with our scholarly colleagues in perpetuating and sometimes challenging the "skins" found in the academy.

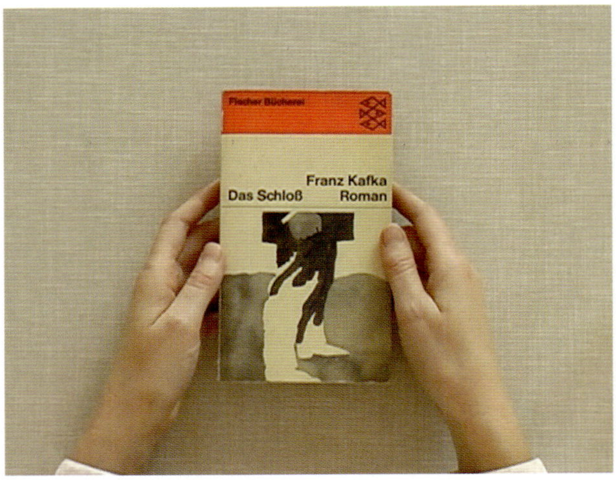
Fischer Bücherei
Franz Kafka
Das Schloß
Roman

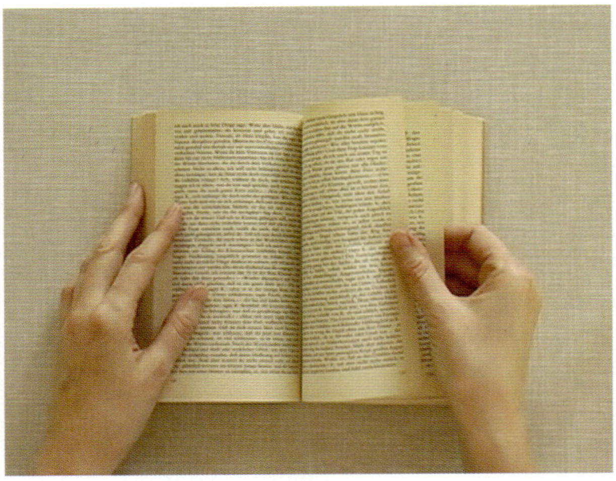

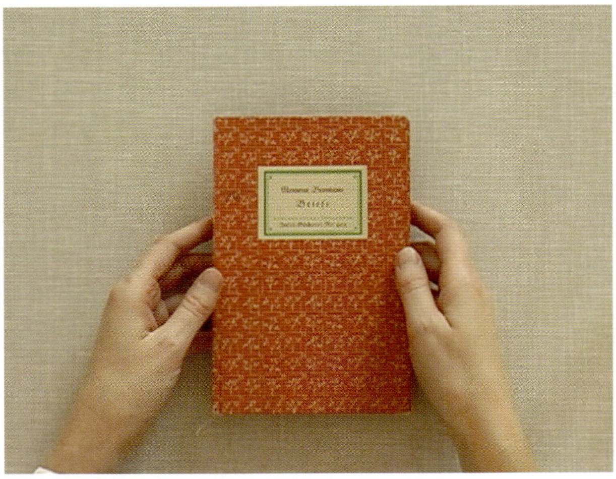

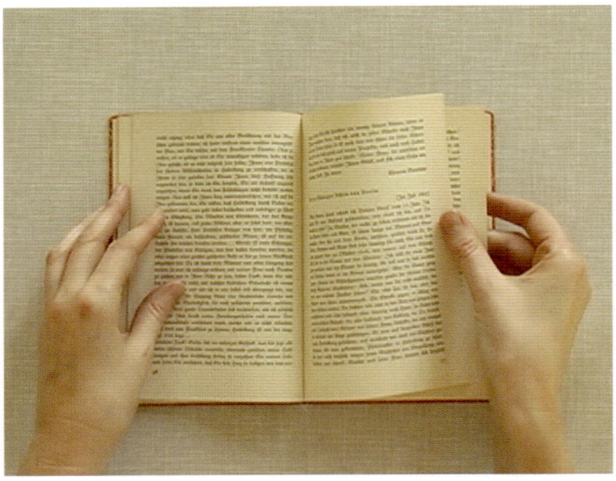

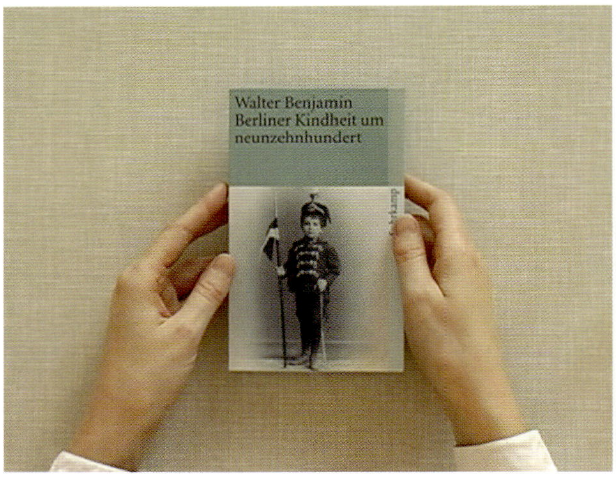
Walter Benjamin
Berliner Kindheit um
neunzehnhundert
suhrkamp

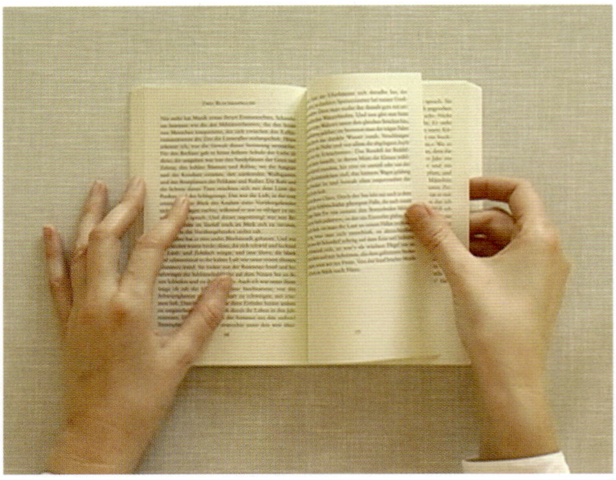

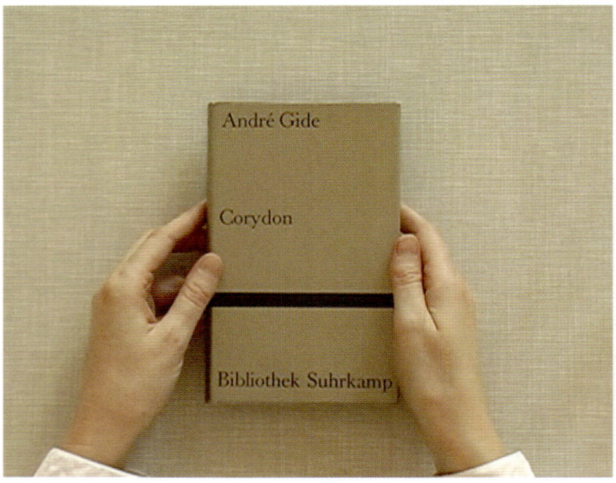
André Gide
Corydon
Bibliothek Suhrkamp

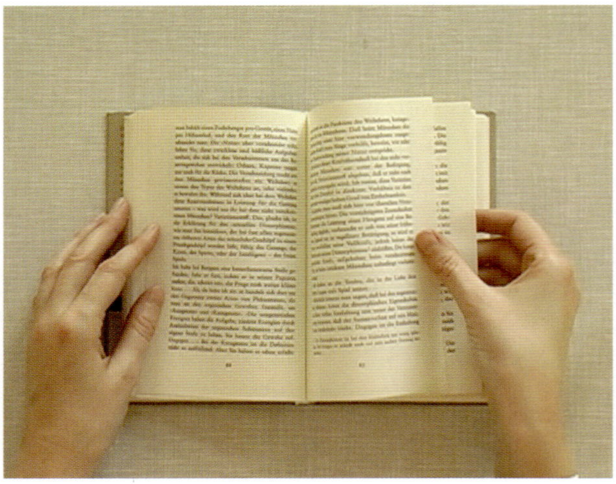

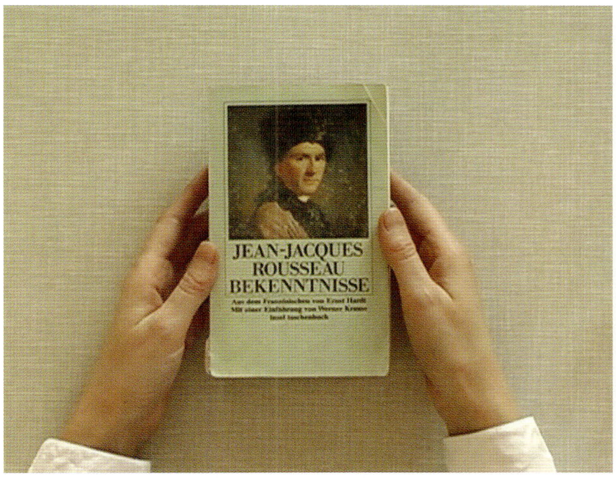
JEAN-JACQUES
ROUSSEAU
BEKENNTNISSE

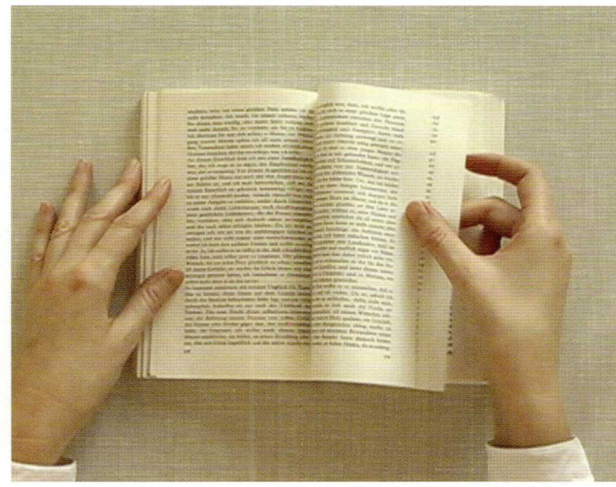

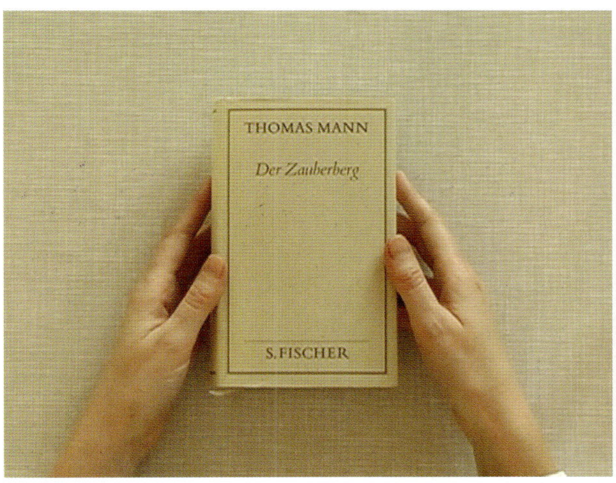
THOMAS MANN
Der Zauberberg
S. FISCHER

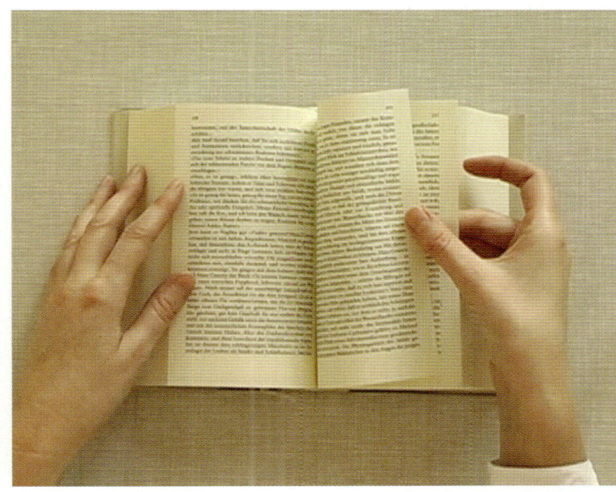

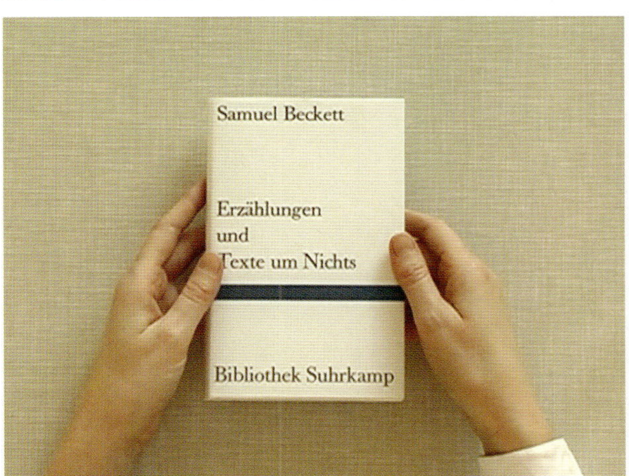
Samuel Beckett
Erzählungen
und
Texte um Nichts
Bibliothek Suhrkamp

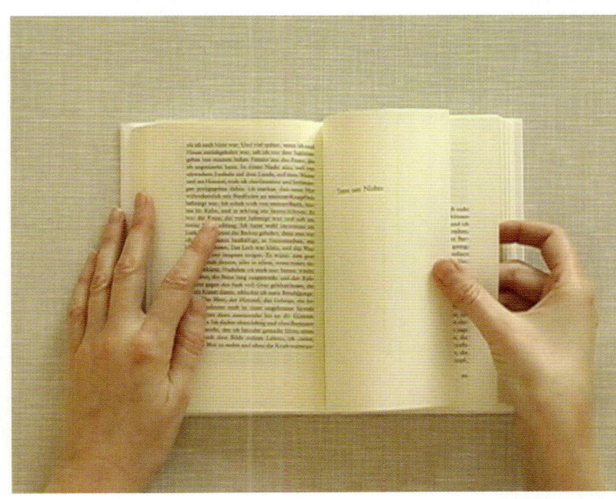

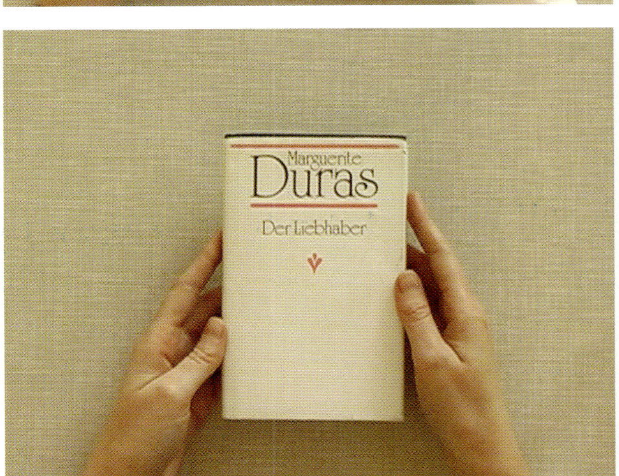
Marguerite
Duras
Der Liebhaber

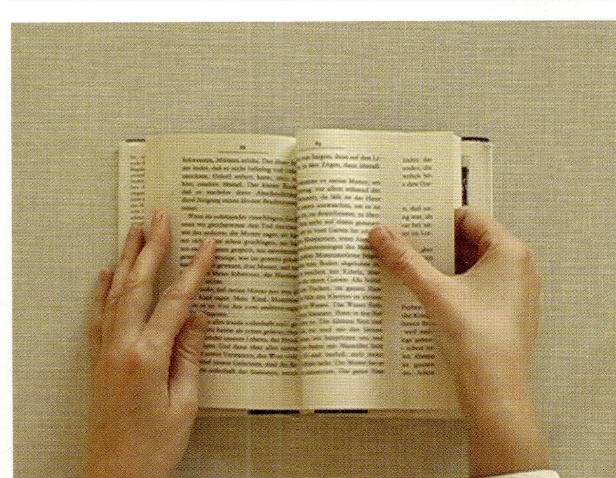

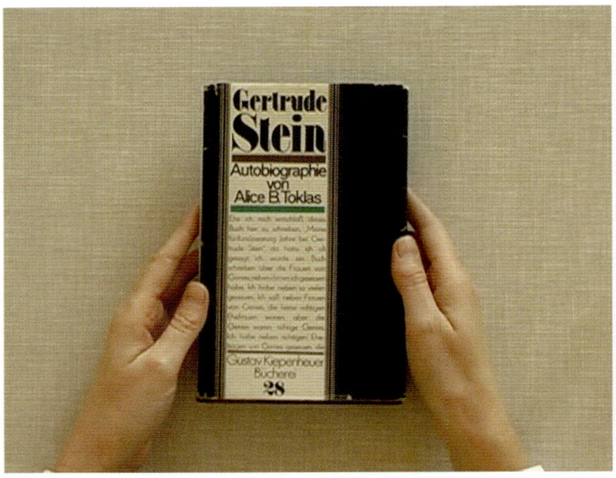
Gertrude
Stein
Autobiographie
von
Alice B. Toklas
Gustav Kiepenheuer
Bücherei
28

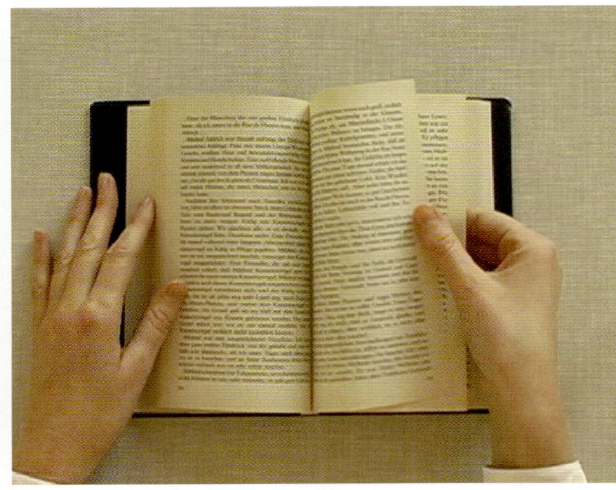

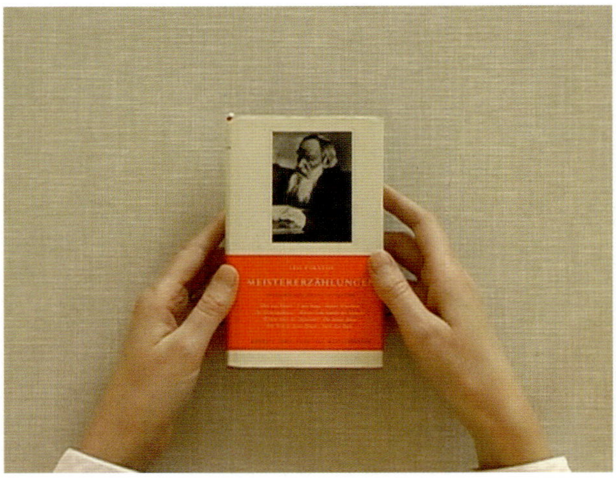

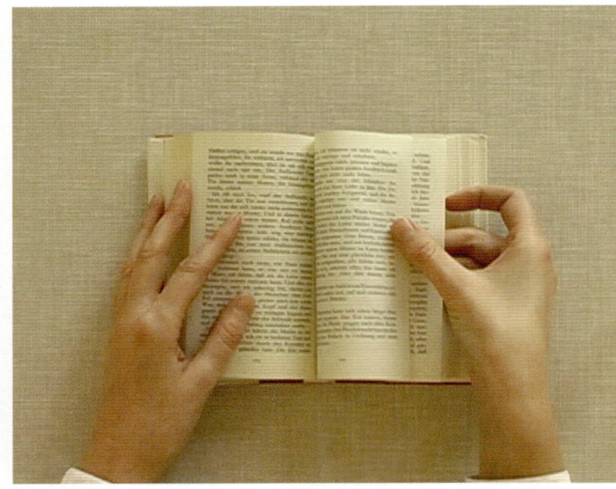

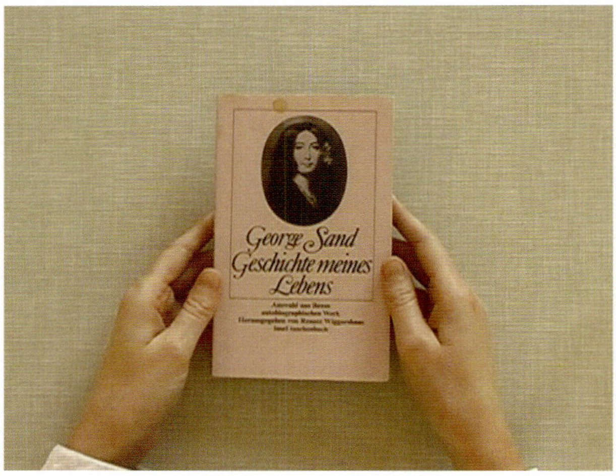
George Sand
Geschichte meines
Lebens

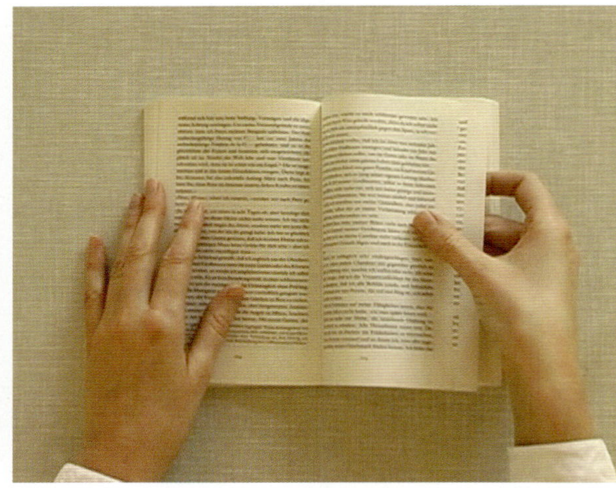

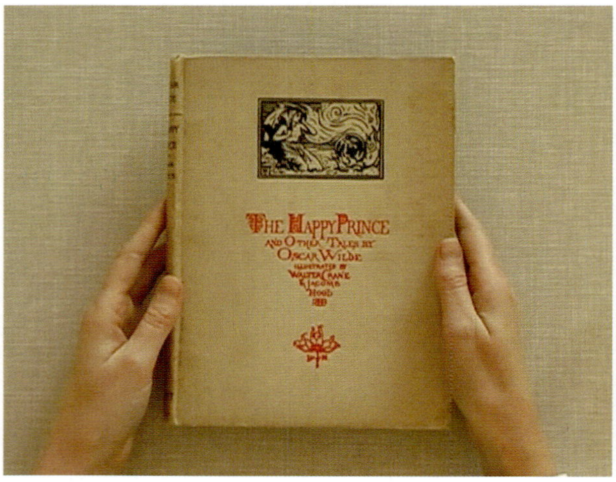
The Happy Prince
and Other Tales by
Oscar Wilde

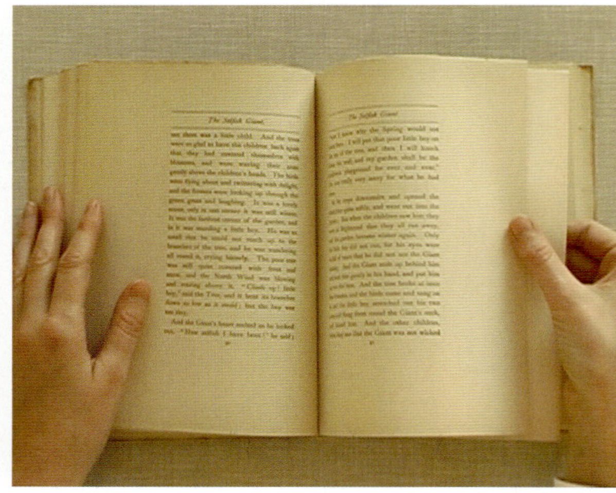

PHONETIC SKIN. A LIBRARY OF VOICES (2009) / ANNETTE STAHMER
video, 34 min 46 sec.

A kind of experimental set-up: a table and on it two hands which, one after the other, hold various books into the camera, open them and then – during an imaginary process of reading – rub two pages together. This gives rise to sounds with a phonetic quality; the paper speaks.

And just as the human voice always carries within it traces of the body that produces it and these also "speak", as it were, so too the different book-bodies here develop voices which are influenced by their respective materiality, paper, binding, etc.

The film *Phonetic Skin. A Library of Voices* deals with the process of reading and in doing so playfully and poetically interlinks spoken and written language and the materiality and corporeality of voice and writing.

Franz Kafka, *Das Schloß* (Frankfurt / Main: S. Fischer Verlag, 1968).
Clemens Brentano, *Briefe* (Leipzig: Insel Verlag, 1941).
Johann Wolfgang Goethe, *Sämtliche Gedichte* (München: Deutscher Taschenbuch Verlag, 1961).
Christian Morgenstern, *Palmström* (Leipzig: Insel Verlag, 1942).
Walter Benjamin, *Berliner Kindheit um neunzehnhundert* (Frankfurt / Main: Suhrkamp Verlag, 2006).
Erich Kästner, *Herz auf Taille* (Zürich: Atrium Verlag, 1985).
André Gide, *Corydon* (Frankfurt / Main: Suhrkamp Verlag, 1965).
E. E. Cummings, *Selected Poems* (New York: Liveright, 1994).
Eduard Mörike, *Sämtliche Werke* (München: Carl Hanser Verlag, 1964).
Hugo von Hofmannsthal, *Gedichte* (Wiesbaden: Insel Verlag, 1955).
Ovid, *Erotische Dichtungen* (Stuttgart: Kröner Verlag, 2001).
Paul Claudel, *Gedichte* (Klosterberg / Basel: Verlag Benno Schwabe & Co, 1942).
H. C. Andersen, *Gesammelte Märchen* (Zürich: Manesse Verlag, 2000).
James Joyce, *Ulysses* (Frankfurt / Main: Suhrkamp Verlag, 1977).
Jean-Jacques Rousseau, *Bekenntnisse* (Frankfurt / Main: Insel Verlag, 1985).
Heinrich Böll, *Erzählungen, Hörspiele, Aufsätze* (Köln / Berlin: Kiepenheuer & Witsch, 1962).
Thomas Mann, *Der Zauberberg* (Frankfurt / Main: S. Fischer Verlag, 1981).
Samuel Beckett, *Erzählungen und Texte um Nichts* (Frankfurt / Main: Suhrkamp Verlag, 1997).
Stendhal, *Das Leben des Henry Brulard* (München: Winkler Verlag, 1956).
John Cage, *Für die Vögel* (Berlin: Merve Verlag, 1984).
Oskar Pastior, *Lesungen mit Tinnitus* (München: Carl Hanser Verlag, Edition Akzente, 1985).
Raymond Queneau, *Zazie in der Métro* (Frankfurt / Main: Suhrkamp Verlag, 1975).
La Fontaine, *Hundert Fabeln* (Zürich: Manesse Verlag, 1997).
Gertrud von le Fort, *Die Letzte am Schafott* (München: Ehrenwirth Verlag, 1959).
Die Bibel (Stuttgart: Deutsche Bibelstiftung, 1978).
Joseph Freiherr von Eichendorff, *Werke* (Wien / München / Basel: Verlag Kurt Deich, 1955).
Marguerite Duras, *Der Liebhaber* (Berlin: Volk und Welt Verlag, 1986).
Hélène Cixous, *Weiblichkeit in der Schrift* (Berlin: Merve Verlag, 1980).
Gertrude Stein, *Autobiographie von Alice B. Toklas* (Leipzig / Weimar: Gustav Kiepenhauer Verlag, 1981).
Roland Barthes, *Die Körnung der Stimme* (Frankfurt / Main: Suhrkamp Verlag, 2002).
Marcel Proust, *Eine Liebe Swanns* (Frankfurt / Main: Suhrkamp Verlag, 1995).
Leo Tolstoi, *Meistererzählungen* (Zürich: Manesse Verlag, 1950).
George Sand, *Geschichte meines Lebens* (Frankfurt / Main: Insel Verlag, 1981).
Theodor Fontane, *Effi Briest* (München / Zürich: Droemersche Verlagsanstalt, 1958).
Oscar Wilde, *The Happy Prince and Other Tales* (London: David Nutt, 1908).
Bertolt Brecht, *Versuche 1–12*, (Berlin: Aufbau Verlag, 1963).

JANET BEIZER / THE TEXTUAL WOMAN AND THE HYSTERICAL NOVEL

In dreams, a writing tablet signifies a woman, since it receives the imprint of all kinds of letters.
ARTEMIDORUS, ONEIROCRITICA

In 1881, the journalist Jules Claretie published *Les Amours d'un interne,* a love story set in the hysteria wards of the Salpêtrière Hospital. Claretie had documented his novel in the best naturalist fashion, having long been among the faithful at Charcot's *leçons du mardi,* the *soirées du mardi,* and the *leçons du vendredi* as well. Accordingly, in his prefatorial claim to have pioneered the novelistic exploration of hysteria, the author gave priority to his medical confreres and subordinated his novel to a medical model:

On trouvera, étudiée dans ce volume, – et pour la première fois par un romancier, – une des formes les plus étranges de la grande maladie du siècle ... Il appartenait ... au romancier d'étudier, *après les savants,* ces manifestations inquiétantes, attirantes aussi, et ces cas bizarres.[1]

[One will discover in this volume the study – and for the first time by a novelist – of one of the strangest forms of the great *maladie du siècle* ... It was the novelist's turn to study, *after the scientists,* these foreboding but also seductive displays, and these bizarre cases.]

But an unexpected element intrudes upon this neat schema, a supplement that eludes both science and its pretended literary double: that "quelque chose *d'au delà*" ["otherworldliness"] to which Claretie alludes briefly in his preface (ii) – an apparition that contradicts the naturalist observation of material reality yet emerges from it – and to which we will have occasion to return.

In 1880, while Claretie would have been writing his novel, Dr. Charles Richet, one of Charcot's associates (and, incidentally, a closet novelist), published a medical expert's account of hysteria designed to redress popular misconceptions about the disease – misconceptions propagated in part, the author charged, by novelists.[2] The article, which appeared in the literary *Revue des deux mondes,* explicitly derives its authority from medical advances at the Salpêtrière. Rather unexpectedly, however, the doctor ends up deferring to the novelists, enhancing his clinician's perspective with examples culled from novels of the preceding quarter century. For there, Richet explains, one encounters "des descriptions exactes qui compléteront ce que nous venons de dire de l'état psychique des femmes nerveuses" (346) ["precise descriptions that complete what we have just said of the psychic condition of nervous women"]. As the novelist's and the doctor's approaches to hysteria intersect – that is, as they meet but also cross each other – they provide a glimpse of the complex interplay between literary and medical representations of the disease.

The novelist and the doctor

Together Claretie and Richet confirm the fact, too often overlooked, that the late nineteenth-century heyday of hysteria in France was not confined to the domain of pathology but was a literary phenomenon as well. Together the two presentations of hysteria bear witness to the popularization of a medical category: by 1880, the term had become not only familiar to a lay public, but fascinating, captivating. The ambiguous allure of Claretie's adjectives ("strange," "bizarre," "foreboding," "seductive") and Richet's stated effort to correct popular (novelistic) misrepresentations of the disease suggest that the diagnostic category had in fact become a vehicle for the imagination.

But here the coincidence ends. Claretie and Richet contradict each other in ways that preclude a clear-cut relationship between literary and medical discourses of hysteria. While the novelist draws his authority from the clinic, specifically from the much-publicized troupe of hysterics and their attendant doctors at the Salpêtrière, the clinician turns to the novel in order to corroborate medical research. While the writer in 1881 sees himself as a literary experimenter injecting an exotic pathological strain into the novel, the physician, at roughly the same time, finds considerable traces of hysteria in the novel well before the disease was in clinical vogue.

The *chassé-croisé* of scientific and literary positions in these samples is indicative of hysteria's elusiveness in the stories told about it: when one is about to locate it, to assign it to a time, place, or discipline, it turns out to have already been, elsewhere; and so the examining focus must be deferred or displaced. The disease is framed as conceptually recalcitrant as well; in literary and medical texts alike, it is represented as resisting circumscription.[3] Claretie and Richet once again furnish exemplary testimony.

The literary inability to define hysteria in direct, nonmetaphorical terms is explicit. Claretie's young physician-protagonist explains:

Une définition, c'est toujours difficile. Je vous dirai plutôt ce que l'hystérie n'est point. ... Ça peut être érotique – pour donner raison au vulgaire, – ça peut être sombre, ça peut être mystique, ça peut être religieux, ça peut être tout. C'est, si vous voulez, l'exagération de tout. L'hystérique ... est en dehors de la règle commune, et le monde et le demi-monde, le théâtre, les salons, tout Paris est plein d'hystériques ... C'est même la grande maladie moderne, l'hystérie! La société souffre d'une névrose ou d'une névrite gigantesque. (124)

[A definition is always difficult. I can more easily tell you what hysteria is not ... It can be erotic – to echo common opinion – it can be dark, it can be mystical, it can be religious, it can be everything. It is, if you wish, the exaggeration of everything. The hysteric is outside common norms, and both the world and the demi-monde, the theater, salons, all of Paris is full of hysterics ... In fact, it is the great modern ailment! Society suffers from a gigantic neurosis or neuritis.]

While this definition is less than precise, it does at least indicate two features of hysteria. The one, exaggeration, is clearly labeled. The other, contagion, is never named as such, but is evidenced by the spread of the disease from the clinic to high society, to the margins of society, to the theater and to salons, to all Paris and indeed to all of modern society. Even Claretie's style seems to have caught the disease, for it is noticeably afflicted with the only named symptom, exaggeration. Although his definition rapidly moves from the literal to the figurative, it is not evident, in this particular passage, to what metaphoric end the disease is being appropriated. Elsewhere in the novel, however, the metaphor is elucidated.

Les Amours d'un interne might more accurately be called (pastiching Balzac's *Comment aiment les filles*), *Comment aiment les internes,* for it is all about the illfated love choices of the young Salpêtrière doctors and their associates. To the question suggested by my substituted title – how do interns love? – the answer must be "badly," although Claretie implies that they could not do much better. It is not that they *all* love or lust after their patients (although some do), but rather that the boundaries between the Salpêtrière wards and the salons of Paris are extremely tenuous. While Combette's sexual exploitation of a young woman sets off her nascent hysteria, sending her straight to the Salpêtrière, where Mongobert then loves her as a patient, Combette eventually marries a high-strung heiress described as "cette petite hystérique du monde" (430) ["this little society hysteric"], and Pédro's infatuation for a beautiful if nervous young Russian ends in the debilitating discovery of this woman's particular brand of hysteria: Olga is a *skoptzy,* a religious fanatic who has had herself sexually mutilated. The protagonist, Pierre, speaks indirectly for Pédro (and for all the other interns as well) when, dually prompted by an inmate's attack on a colleague and his own unrequited love, he exclaims: "Tu vois, les femmes, ça vous déchire toujours quelque chose, la peau du front ou les muscles du coeur!" (291) ["You see, women always tear some part of you, the skin of your brow or your heart muscles!"]

In the course of the novel, "les femmes" and "les hystériques" become virtually interchangeable categories – so much so that the religious hysteric Olga is apostrophized as "cette idéale créature, plus femme que toutes les autres femmes" (379) ["that ideal creature, more of a woman than all other women"]. Despite its veneer of journalistic objectivity, *Les Amours d'un interne* clearly appropriates hysteria as a figure of woman.

It would be naive, however, to turn to the clinician's text as a likely source for an antidote to Claretie's metaphoricity. It is true that the opening of Richet's "Les Démoniaques d'aujourd'hui" promises to demystify hysteria, to make known "les faits positifs élucidés par les savans contemporains" (341) ["positive facts elucidated by contemporary scientists"], suggesting that the scientist will deliver the letter behind the figure. But the few concrete details he delivers about the affliction work essentially to reinforce age-old stereotypes about femininity. The hysteric, according to Richet, has a mobile and impressionable nature, lacks willpower, and is able to contain neither secrets nor secretions. Dominated by her passions, she is overly emotional, subject to frequent and unmotivated fits of crying, capricious, egotistical, fickle, and prone to exaggeration. She is excessively imaginative, histrionic, and dishonest. In fact, Richet insists, she is not only, like a child, insincere and deceitful; she is a forger of fictions and a lover of lies. Leaving nothing to chance, Richet goes on to interpret his data for us: "On peut même dire que les hystériques sont femmes plus que les autres femmes" (346) ["One can even say that hysterics are women more than other women"].

This is a startling definition for many reasons; most immediately because it almost exactly replicates Claretie's characterization of the hysteric Olga: "more of a woman than all other women." From novelist to clinician, we have come full circle. In vain do we move from literature to medicine in search of a scientific basis, a concrete or proper sense, a degree zero of hysteria. For when we begin to unravel the medical texts (and although he is writing for a largely literary audience, Richet is perfectly representative of the spirit if not the technical detail of such texts), when we comb through medical representations of hysteria, we find that the disease is in every case already a metaphor. Medical and narrative discourses each individually use hysteria as a metaphor that transcends them both, revealing glimpses of the imaginary of the period in which both are enmeshed.

I do not mean to contest the rapid and widespread diffusion of hysteria as medical term during the Charcot years at the Salpêtrière: neither the epidemie spread nor the wide-scale popularization nor the rapid narrative circulation of hysteria at this time can be denied.[4] But I do want to avoid attributing to the clinic the invention of a cultural concept that does not originate there, that is only belatedly taken over and disseminated by the clinic under the name of hysteria. Because Richet presumes that the lay public has a prior empirical if not technical knowledge of the subject, he can make accessible the arcana of medicine by mere allusion to colloquial conceptions: "Tout ce qu'on a coutume d'attribuer au tempérament nerveux de la femme rentre dans le domaine de l'hystérie" (343) ["All that is customarily attributed to woman's nervous temperament falls in the domain of hysteria"].

Contagions, rhetorical as well as literal, do not begin at plague levels. The medical term must be understood in relation to a more global sociocultural and aesthetic category. Figure of femininity correlatively associated (by way of traditional misogyny) with disorder, duplicity, and alterity, hysteria easily lends itself, in this fin de siècle society subject to convulsive upheavals, to a multiplicity of metaphoric uses: diagnosis of the assorted wounds of contemporary civilization, emblem of marginality, sign of expressivity and even of poetic furor. It is this last phenomenon – which we might more generally qualify as a poetics of hysteria or as the hystericization of aesthetics – that I want to approach in the second part of this text, in the form of a reflection on an excerpt from Claretie's novel.

Les Amours d'un interne stages that fascinating and perturbing practice known as dermographism, which appears here and there on the hysterical body in the pages of *L'Iconographie photographique de la Salpêtrière* as well as in other medical publications of the period. It consists of imprinting graffiti-like markings on the anesthetic but otherwise impressionable skin of the hysteric, following the vagaries of the doctor's will: doctor's signature, patient's name, diagnosis, invocation of the devil, ornamental design, and so on.[5] Neither a physiological explanation (malfunction of the vasomotor system) nor a potential therapeutic justification (which in any case was not offered) nor photographic documents (which do exist) succeed in exhausting the meaning of this experimental writing.

Inscribing the body

The following tableau is excerpted from a chapter of *Les Amours d'un interne*. We are in the hysteria ward along with a group of attendant interns gathered around Mathilde Mignon, a young and beautiful hysteric. She is in a comatose sleep after a night of delirium. Dr. Fargeas, the novel's eminent specialist in nervous disorders, uses Mathilde's supine body for a demonstration of dermographism.

> Mathilde était totalement anesthésique et il suffisait de tracer, sur sa peau blanche, d'une douceur pareille à une peau d'enfant, les caractères qu'on voulait pour qu'aussitôt, à la place touchée par l'ongle ou le crayon du docteur, une saillie rouge apparût, d'une proéminence teile qu'en tâtant ces caractères, on pût reconnaître la lettre que venait d'écrire là [le docteur].
> "Trouble trophique et qui durera plusieurs heures," disait le chef. "Le cas est assez fréquent." ...
> Et, pendant quelques heures, en effet, les caractères tracés sur cette peau blanche demeuraient visibles, comme une inscription parfaitement déchiffrable.
> "Un aveugle pourrait la lire!" disait Pédro.
> "C'est la *femme lithographique,* cette Mathilde," ajoutait le petit Finet. ...
> "Toi qui as inventé l'hystérie, Pauline," lui disait Pédro, "tu n'as pas ça, toi, la possibilité de servir de papier à lettres vivant!" (312)

> [Mathilde was completely anesthetic; and when the desired characters were traced on her white skin, soft as a child's skin, immediately at the spot touched by the doctor's nail or pencil, a red welt appeared so prominently that by touching the characters, one could recognize the letter that [the doctor] had just written there.
> "A trophic disorder that will last several hours," said the head doctor. "It is a rather frequent phenomenon." ...
> And for several hours, the characters traced on this white skin remained visible, like a perfectly decipherable inscription.
> "A blind man could read it!" said Pédro.
> "This Mathilde is a lithographic woman," added Finet. ...
> "Even you who invented hysteria, Pauline," said Pédro, "you don't have that – the ability to serve as living writing paper!"]

As Mathilde's hysterical body becomes a text to be deciphered by the attendant spectators, Claretie's text becomes an inscription on a woman's body, an allegory of the narrative appropriation of hysteria. Here as more generally, the expressive faculties of the hysterical body are overdetermined. Mathilde is not only a textual woman but "a lithographic woman." And her status as text and visual art object is further compounded by the narrative context, which turns the medical demonstration into a staged spectacle and Mathilde's displayed body into living theater.

In the hysteric's hyperfemale, hyperexpressive body, sex and text are joined. Mathilde's "peau blanche, d'une douceur pareille à une peau d'enfant" ["white skin, soft as a child's skin"] is at once a sexual and a textual marker: a sign of femininity, her white skin should also be read as a writing surface, a blank parchment or tabula rasa. Each time the sensual aspect recurs (in the repetition of "peau blanche," in the implied scratch of the doctor's nail, and in the verbs "toucher" and "tâter"), it is in the service of writing; for what is being touched, handled, or scratched into being is the flesh made word.

As the doctor writes upon the "living writing paper" presented by Mathilde's literally impressionable flesh, her woman's hysterical body *underwrites* Claretie's text; it gives form and authority to the writing, reading, and interpretive processes involved in textual production.[6] The inscription on Mathilde's skin, a text in the text of the novel, emblematizes the semiotic valorization of the nineteenth-century hysterical body, which writers perceived as a system of signs, an alphabet of gestures to be pressed into narrative service.

And yet, even while implying the crucial role played by the hysterical body in the nineteenth-century novel, Claretie's text does its utmost to complicate it – that is, to suggest that this body is never simply semiotic. It emits messages, but it also receives them. Let me elaborate by considering this body-text as production rather than product. When the doctor puts his mark onto Mathilde's flesh, the raised red letter that appears evokes a brand, a sign burned into the flesh. The allusion to branding within this allegory of the hysterical flesh made naturalist word points to an important connection between language and power, discourse and possession.[7] It reminds us once again – *pace* Aragon and Breton, who eulogized hysteria as a "supreme means of expression" – that when we are given the hysterical body to "read" in place of language, we are always in fact reading someone else's superimposed text.[8]

The interplay of hysteric discursivity and mechanisms of control is everywhere implied in this passage. Hysteria becomes discursive when the doctor imprints his message on the blank pad of Mathilde's body. This scenario, which opposes writing and blankness, pencil and paper, speech and speechlessness, male mastery and childlike submission (the child explicitly connoted by the woman's "peau d'enfant") is congruent with the traditional heterosexual oppositions of Western metaphysics: male/female, active/passive, subject/object, techne/physis, mind/body, and so on.[9] Although Mathilde crosses over into discursivity, any claim for a deconstruction of traditional dichotomies resulting from the fact that her body becomes intelligible strikes me as specious, for the potential scandal of the speaking body is neutralized by virtue of its production by an external agent. In fact the body does not speak; it is spoken, ventriloquized by the master text that makes it signify. The woman becomes a text, but she is a text within a text, a text *framed* as signifying source by another, mediating text.

The dermographic tableau framed by Claretie's text contains within it, however, a blind spot that opens a possibility for the semiotic process to elude authorial control, subverting classic paradigms and metaphoric structures. For although the text speaks insistently of the visibility, legibility, and transparency of the letters on Mathilde's skin, it simultaneously occults them. The message is never seen, read, or deciphered for us. Mathilde's signifying body, inhabiting the unexamined gap between Claretie's novel and the doctor's "perfectly decipherable inscription" then constitutes an element of excess, an inarticulate, unreadable space – a textual symptom. We might speak of *Les Amours d'un interne* as a hysterical novel because the hysteria thematized there eventually attacks the narrative, propagating its silences, its excesses, its incoherences.

The phantom letters carried by Mathilde's body do not need to be read to make known the threat they bear, a threat dimmed by the emphatic paleness of her skin but that can be articulated in the form of a question: what would happen if the hysterical body no longer allowed itself to be signed, labeled, diagnosed, but if, insubordinate, itself become a creator, a producer of meaning, this body assumed its own power and went on to deliver an unexpected, even fatal message? What would this message be – this message that uncannily recalls the "quelque chose d'*au delà*" that separated from "literal reality" to insinuate itself into the preface of the novel – and why does it inspire such fear?

It is critical to remember that the hysterical dermographic inscription is a text that must be replaced in the vaster context of the body-text, a concept or perhaps more accurately an intuition whose sources are lost in the mists of time and that manifests itself in such varied domains as popular wisdom and science, by such diverse notions as palm reading and the genetic code. But the best illustration of the body-text (the one that is both most graphic and most revealing) would be the apparatus that figures in Kafka's "In the Penal Colony": writing implement and torture implement simultaneously, whose macabre function is to inscribe in the flesh the sentence that the prisoner can read only when dying of the wounds inflicted by the inscription.[10] This sentence, both phrase and condemnation, is a violent figuration of the sentence every body bears. In other words, the body (which is to say, the material condition of life) *is* this sentence: its scars, its graying hairs, its wrinkles are the lexicon; its shiverings, its tremors, its death throes are the punctuation.

In the case of hysterical dermographism, the inscription is double; one is confronted with an inscription that covers another one – a palimpsest of sorts – a superimposed text that attempts to suppress the sentence, that originary (and doubtless final) text. For the message of a body semiotic in and by itself – whatever the sex – is death. Whence dermographism or invitation to a duel, struggle to the death with death played out on the field of the hysterical body. If the hysterical body is the chosen ground for this battle, it is because this paradigmatic woman's body is, as everyone knows, changeable, malleable, and impressionable. In the anticipatory words of Andreas Cappellanus, who spoke them some seven centuries earlier: "A woman is just like melting wax, which is always ready to take a new form and to receive the impress of anyone's seal."[11]

But the soft white skin is only apparently a tabula rasa, an unmarked pad. It bears a sentence, always already etched and always already repressed, which unpredictably returns from beyond the pale. That is why it is so necessary to efface the letters, reinscribe the body, prove that it could be the bearer of another message, that it could be the work not of God, but of men. By means of an eminently Promethean gesture, clinicians and writers alike struggle to steal God's word, labor to inscribe on the hysterical body a new gospel, which would say: "And the flesh will be made word; it will become the word of Men."

NOTES

[1] Jules Claretie, *Les Amours d'un interne* (Paris: Dentu, 1881), i-ii; my emphasis. All references to the novel will be to this edition, and will be provided in the text. Claretie was a novelist, playwright, and essayist as well as a journalist; he also became administrative director of the Comédie-Française in 1885.

[2] Charles Richet, "Les Démoniaques d'aujourd'hui," *Revue des deux mondes 37* (15 January 1880): 341. Further references will be provided in the text. Under the pen name Charles Epheyre, Richet was a prolific novelist, publishing, among other works, *Possession* (Paris: Ollendorff, 1887) and *Soeur Marthe* (*Revue des deux mondes 93* [15 May 1889]: 384-431), both of which leaned heavily on hysteria, hypnotism, and hallucination.

[3] I want to emphasize that it is not hysteria itself that is elusive, resistant, recalcitrant, and so on; a disease is after all not a person. If it appears to be vague or evasive, it is because it has been defined as such. And the fact that hysteria and women have overlapping attributes (the "characteristics" of hysteria are often borrowed from commonplaces about female nature so that the disease "behaves" like a woman) is one more indication of the metaphoric nature of the diagnosis.

[4] For an excellent survey of the diffusion of hysteria from the clinic to literature, newspapers, salons, and the streets, see Jacqueline Carroy-Thirard's "Hystérie, théâtre, littérature au XIXe siècle," *Psychanalyse à l'université 7* (March 1982): 299-317.

[5] See Georges Didi-Huberman, "Une Notion de 'corps-cliché' au XIXe siècle," *Parachute* 35 (1984): 8-14. Dermographism, as medical science understands it today, is a form of physical urticaria (an irritated, patchy condition of the skin) whose outbreaks are provoked by a release of histamines when the skin is stroked, rubbed, or scratched. There is a wheal-and-flare reaction sometimes accompanied by itching and burning at the site of such physical stimulation. The reaction may last forty-eight hours, but usually fades more quickly. While nineteenth-century doctors believed that hysterics were more prone to dermographism than others, because they were more "impressionable," late twentieth-century medicine finds the condition in approximately 5 percent of the general population. It is not sex-linked and is not correlated with any psychological disorder. When I spoke to doctors about dermographism today I discovered one element of continuity amid the changes that one hundred years have brought about: a fascination (which I share) with the ability of the human body to bear meaning. Doctors today continue to use the dermographic patient as writing pad, inscribing names, signs, and messages upon the skin. Two of the three doctors I talked with spoke of their collections of dermographic photographs.

[6] Although I am speaking of an authority that derives from the clinical domain, it is to be taken in sharp counterdistinction to the scientific or medical authority which Jean Starobinski, among others, refers to in his preface to Victor Segalen, *Les Cliniciens ès lettres* (Paris: Fata Morgana, 1980), 17. The authority of the hysterical body is a *counterauthority*, a source of truth whose power derives from its hidden value, its implicit contestation of received truths.

[7] See Elaine Scarry's fascinating analysis of the dynamics of power contained in the relationship between the body and language, in *The Body in Pain: The Making and Unmaking of the World* (Oxford: Oxford University Press, 1985).

[8] Louis Aragon and André Breton, "Le Cinquantenaire de l'hystérie," *La Révolution surréaliste 4* (15 March 1928): 20.

[9] For an elaboration on this dichotomy, see Hélène Cixous and Cathérine Clément, *La Jeune Née* (Paris: 10/18, 1975), 115-20.

[10] Franz Kafka, "In the Penal Colony," in *The Complete Stories,* trans. Willa and Edwin Muir, ed. Nahum N. Glazer (New York: Schocken, 1976), 140-67.

[11] Andreas Cappellanus, *The Art of Courtly Love,* ed. Frederick W. Locke, trans. John Jay Parry (New York: Frederick Ungar, 1957), 50. (Written ca. 1186).

JANET BEIZER / AFTERWORD
TEXTUAL WOMEN: TWENTY-FIRST-CENTURY REINSCRIPTIONS

When I teach my seminar on hysteria, students tend initially to approach the material with a nervous laugh and a distancing grimace, bemused by the nineteenth-century medical institution they read as the ancient history of another world. The greater part of my work in the course is slowly and gradually to foster the discovery that history evolves but does not end, that hysteria is framed and formed by inbred cultural discourses that die hard, and that if the diagnosis has faded from view, its ideological supports are firmly planted.

A short decade after I had finished writing about hysterical dermographism in *Ventriloquized Bodies*,[1] my attention was brought back to it by a brief news article about a contemporary legal suit. Although it does not address hysteria per se this case has everything to do with the phenomenon of nineteenth-century dermographism, which it graphically replays like a futuristic horror show. I offer it here, as I do in my seminar, in epilogue to my earlier reflections on medical presentations of women's dermographic bodies, and as prologue to a continuing conversation about writing, gendered bodies, power, creation, death, and the question of why words matter.

On January 29, 2003 the *Boston Globe* reported the following: "A surgeon in Louisville Kentucky being sued for branding a patient's uterus with the initials of his alma mater – the University of Kentucky – defended his actions yesterday as a routine part of a hysterectomy."[2] The grammatical structure of this opening sentence – its subordination of a clause announcing uterine branding to the dominant clause reporting the surgeon's justification of this action – all but banalizes the horror, almost sliding us past the astounding operation itself, nearly making us forget the implications that nevertheless beg to be read at once in the letter of their text and the spirit of their context.

For the record, then: first, the letter(s) of the text. After undergoing a hysterectomy in 2002, Stephanie Means was given a videotape of the operation by her surgeon, Dr. Michael Guiler. Only there did she learn, by witnessing the entire procedure, that during the operation Dr. Guiler had used a cauterizing instrument to brand her uterus with the letters "UK" – the initials of his alma mater – before going on to surgically remove the organ. To the charges of severe mental and emotional distress, embarrassment, and humiliation brought by Stephanie Means and her husband,[3] Dr. Guiler responded that the inscription was medically necessary to indicate the midline, left and right sides of the uterus as orientation for the surgery.[4] Other sources however (for example, Dr. Kim Alumbaugh, chair of the Kentucky chapter of the American College of Obstetricians and Gynecologists) specified that though some surgeons do indeed rely on markers to map tissue for removal, these more routinely take the form of stitches or other such neutral indicators, and went on to emphasize the need to respect a patient's dignity. In a statement to reporters, Dr. Guiler explained that his initialized branding served not only the interest of patient safety, but also that of institutional glory: "I felt that this was honorable since it made reference to the college of medicine where I received my medical degree."[5]

Much as members of a fraternity might spray letters on a wall or window or door, claiming – some might say desecrating – it in the alma mater's name, Michael Guiler imposed the initials "UK" on a surface of neither plaster nor concrete nor steel. Though I suspect that Dr. Guiler is not a great reader of Artemidorus, his act echoes the conviction that "a writing tablet signifies a woman" (and perhaps the converse) "since it receives the imprint of all kinds of letters."[6] It echoes as well the principle that women are more expressive than men, and hysterical women most expressive of all, as it appropriates the presumed site of hysteria itself and makes of it the space of projected expression: colonized territory, property, conquest, and the capture of meaning in the name of the medical school: the educator, the *alma mater*. How could we forget that *alma mater* translates as "nourishing mother" – and how could we ignore that here the alma mater is the *institutional* mother, or, in context and translating freely, the pater-mater, the patriarchal matter? The womb, by another common name "the mother" and by definition a nourishing mother, an "alma mater," is replaced here by another name, an "other" name that is ironically the same: a homonym burned over flesh that becomes word. "UK" inscribes the University of Kentucky or again the alma mater, a ghostly palimpsest whose rewriting can never completely overwrite the uncanny specter of the othered same.[7]

The letters, one to two inches high, searing white on rosy flesh, present with the more important "K" rising almost twice the height of the generic "U" – we have no need to do more than describe, for already, as a colleague remarked, "the imagination is so hurting."[8] Not surprisingly, this story generated a string of commentaries on the internet, ranging from Kathleen Parker's dismissal ("I can't get weepy over branding uteri that are bound for the incinerator") to Melissa Fried's indignation ("[Guiler] managed to debase a rather vital organ and transform it into a piece of collegiate paraphernalia") to – most usefully for my own reflection – Laura Pulfer's cheekiness:

> Perhaps the court could suggest that a really personal and important body part belonging to the doctor – say something roughly equivalent to a woman's uterus – could be similarly marked. Just to indicate his genuine remorse, just to prove he is the bigger person, maybe Dr. Guiler would submit to a brand with a few more letters: Hoosiers or UCLA or Bearcats or the University of Louisville.[9]

Pulfer's spirited suggestion is illogical – but in a very provocative way. For let us ask: what *would be* the male body part "roughly equivalent to a woman's uterus"? Though we might guess from the reference to a "really personal and important body part belonging to the doctor" that Pulfer has in mind his penis or his scrotum, neither in fact correspond – even roughly – to a uterus, for the simple reason that men cannot gestate babies, have no organ capable of this function. The point is that talion law is not applicable here, makes no sense, and its very senselessness reinscribes the fearful asymmetry that Dr. Guiler would destroy with his burning letters.

The doctor presents his markings on the uterine tissue of Stephanie Means as simple directional signals whose role, in the words of another physician, is merely "navigational."[10] The markings, Guiler insists, "were not intended to demean the patient in any way."[11] But demeaning is a slippery concept, not any more confineable to intent than is sense (*le sens*, direction, meaning) to a roadmap. If there is a single lesson that can be condensed from the case of Stephanie Means it is the one uncannily contained in her name: Stephanie *Means*; and demeaning Stephanie has meaning as well. What we write matters, whether "published" – on paper, in print, online, on skin – or clandestinely burned onto the internal tissue of private parts to be removed and discarded. Text indeed means tissue, but also, tissue means text, even when it is consigned to destruction. In the private auto-da-fe of a hysterectomy signing that is perversely captured on film, public and private, text and tissue, literary and medical, writing and erasure, meaning and demeaning – all cease to *mean* in predictable ways but never cease meaning.

Most startling perhaps is that nineteenth and twenty-first century distinctions collapse; over one hundred years of ostensible medical and cultural evolution take us right back to the same scene, dramatically replayed with medical amphitheater now replaced by home theater. The case of Stephanie Means (standing in emblematically for all of the women whose wombs were initialized by Dr. Guiler) re-enacts nineteenth-century hysterical dermographism to the nth degree. When I wrote earlier about Jules Claretie's descriptions of dermographic women, I suggested that "when the doctor puts his mark onto [the woman's] flesh, the raised red letter that appears evokes a brand, a sign burned into the flesh" and that "the allusion to branding ... points to an important connection between language and power, discourse and possession." Dr. Guiler's practice literalizes the figure of branding; his markings are not just *like* brandings, they *are* brandings. His practice of uterine graphics displaces the concept of hysteria, reveals the etiology of a diagnosis rather than of a disease.

A hysterectomy is that operation whereby the organ that routinely sheds its inner tissue (the placenta) after birth and then renews itself for and by birth, is itself, in an extreme version, shed entirely and irrevocably. To burn letters in the flesh of the presumed site of hysteria, the uterus, the mother, to claim it in the name of the other even as it is about to be excised: is this not anachronistically to betray the patriarchal roots of the diagnosis, the origin of the malady as *mal de pays*: a male malady of origins?

Hysteria, from the Greek word for uterus, *ustera*, is also related, by its neuter form *usteron*, to what comes after or behind, and by its neuter plural, *usteria* (literally, "things of the uterus") to the placenta and more specifically, the afterbirth.[12] Though I earlier spoke of the semiotic female body as bearer of a death sentence, I would now suggest that its first – its starkest – message may be life: a life lived after birth, or the afterbirth. The hysteria diagnosis might then be understood as a dermographic formulation applied over the original sentence: an abstract form of Dr. Guiler's womb-writing. But here demeaning Stephanie takes on more meaning than one can comfortably confront.

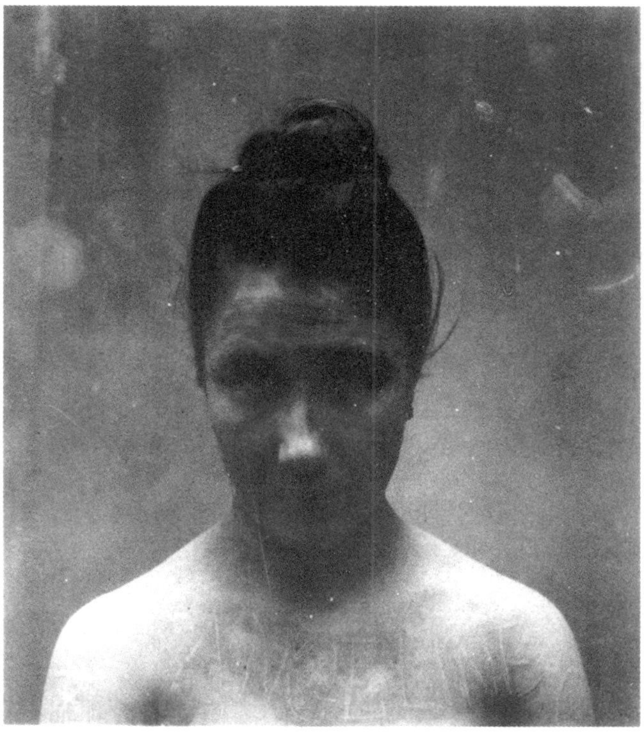

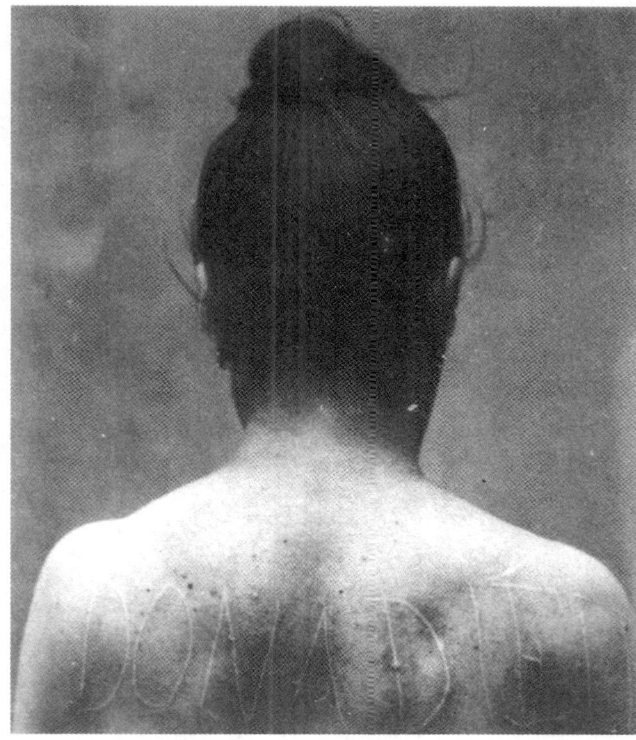

Figure 1: A dermographic woman who has been inscribed, recto/verso, with her first and last names: Angéline Donadieu.
(Published in: M. Lannois, *Nouvelle Iconographie de la Salpêtrière 14*, 1901; photo: Bibliothèque Interuniversitaire de Médecine, Université René Déscartes, Paris.)

NOTES

[1] Janet Beizer, *Ventriloquized Bodies: Nineteenth-Century Narratives of Hysteria* (Ithaca, N.Y.: Cornell University Press, 1994).

[2] *The Boston Globe*, Wednesday January 29, 2003, 19.

[3] Commonwealth of Kentucky, Fayette Circuit Court Division 8, Civil Action no. 03-CI-00285, January 22 2003. One month later nine women who had been similarly inscribed and had similarly discovered their branding upon viewing a videotape of their surgery provided by Dr. Guiler added their names to the lawsuit filed by Stephanie and David Means (Claim amended February 19, 2003).

[4] *Boston Globe.*

[5] Ibid.

[6] See my epigraph, above.

[7] The dictionary reminds us that "palimpsest" is derived from the Latin *palimpsestes*, "scraped again," from the Greek *palin* and *psen*, "to rub, scrape," and is defined as a "writing material (as a parchment or tablet) used one or more times after an earlier tablet has been erased"; but further, that it usually has "diverse layers or aspects apparent beneath the surface."

[8] E-mail from Annette Stahmer, May 13, 2010.

[9] Kathleen Parker, "Uterine Branding Bizarre, but not Criminal," Monday February 24, 2003, www.townhall.com; Melissa Fried, Wednesday February 12, 2003, www.thebatt.com; Laura Pulfer, Sunday February 2, 2003, www.enquirer.com.

[10] Dr. Bill Saye quoted by Kathleen Parker.

[11] Quoted by Garay.

[12] Martha Noel Evans, *Fits and Starts: A Genealogy of Hysteria in Modern France* (Ithaca, N.Y.: Cornell University Press, 1991).

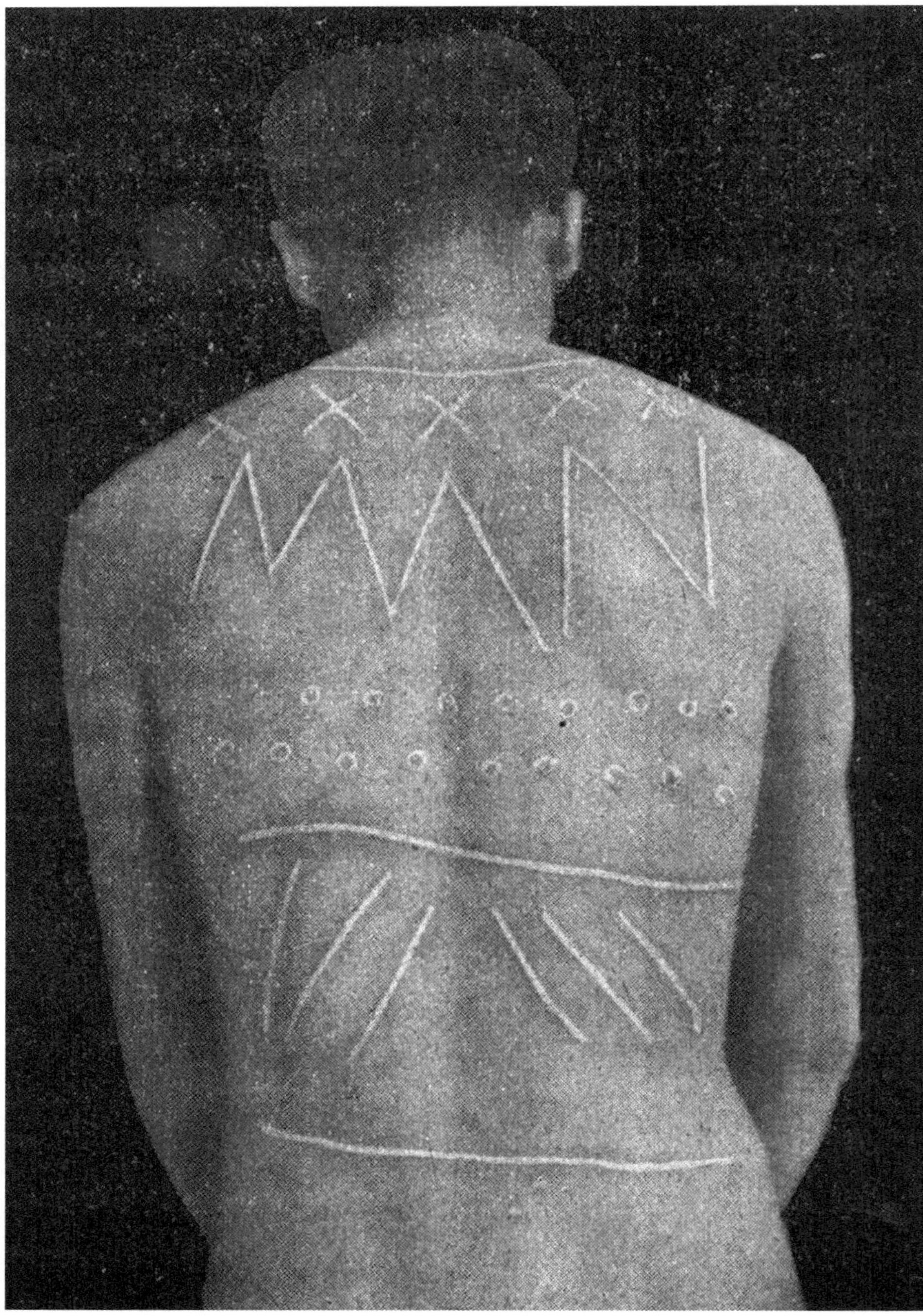

Figure 2: Although neither woman nor hysteric, this patient is described by his doctors as very nervous, excessively emotional, and deplorably impressionable – and so predisposed to dermographic manifestations.
(Published in: F. Allard and H. Meige, *Archives générales de médecine 2*, 1898; photo: B.I.M., Université René Déscartes, Paris.)

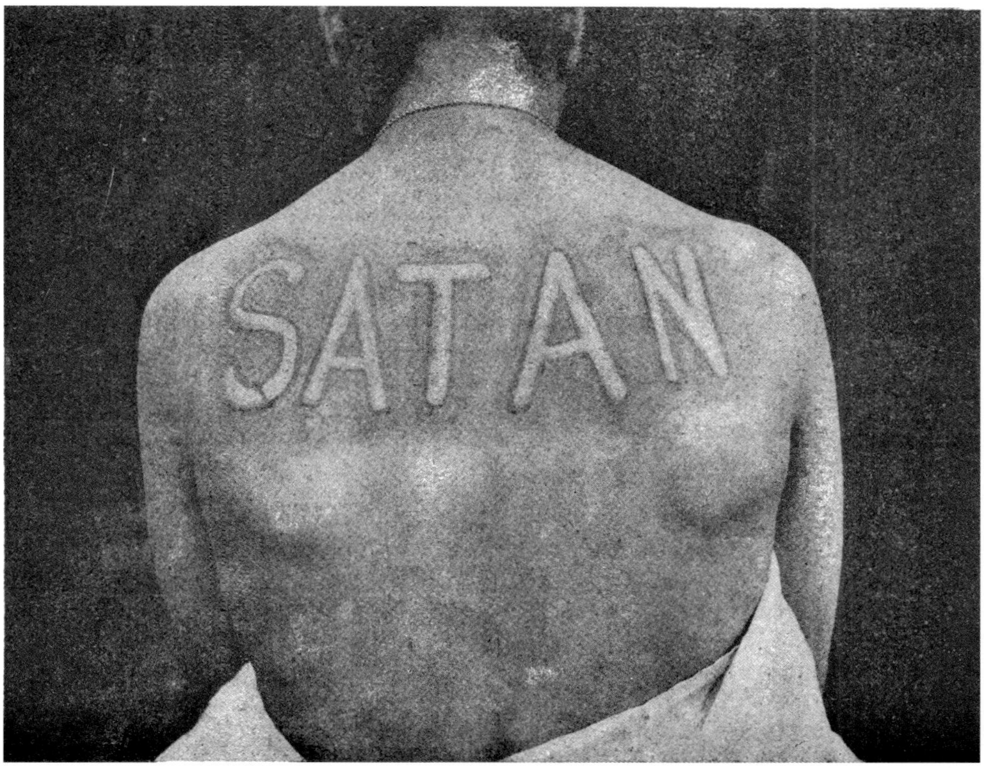

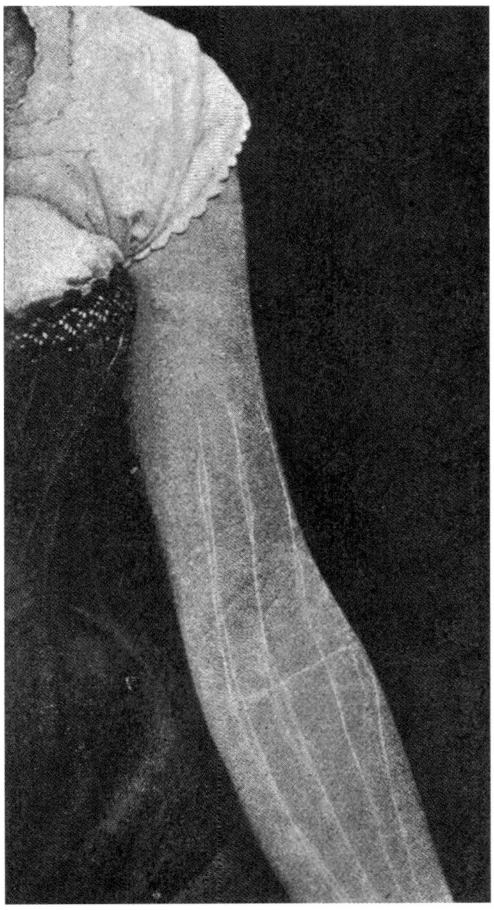

Figure 3: Doctors fascinated by dermographism often used the sign of the devil in their writing experiments. The clarity of this photograph suggests that it may have been retouched.
(Published in: T. Barthélémy, *Étude sur le dermographisme ou dermoneurose toxivasomotrice*, 1893; photo: B.I.M., Université René Déscartes, Paris.)

Figure 4: Etchings on young woman's arm. Women – especially hysterics – were said to be more *impressionable* than men; consequently they were thought to be more often subject to dermographism, the immune reaction that doctors appropriated as skin-writing or skin-drawing, and sometimes referred to as autography or lithography.
(Published in: T. Barthélémy, *Étude sur le dermographisme ou dermoneurose toxivasomotrice*, 1893; photo: B.I.M., Université René Déscartes, Paris.)

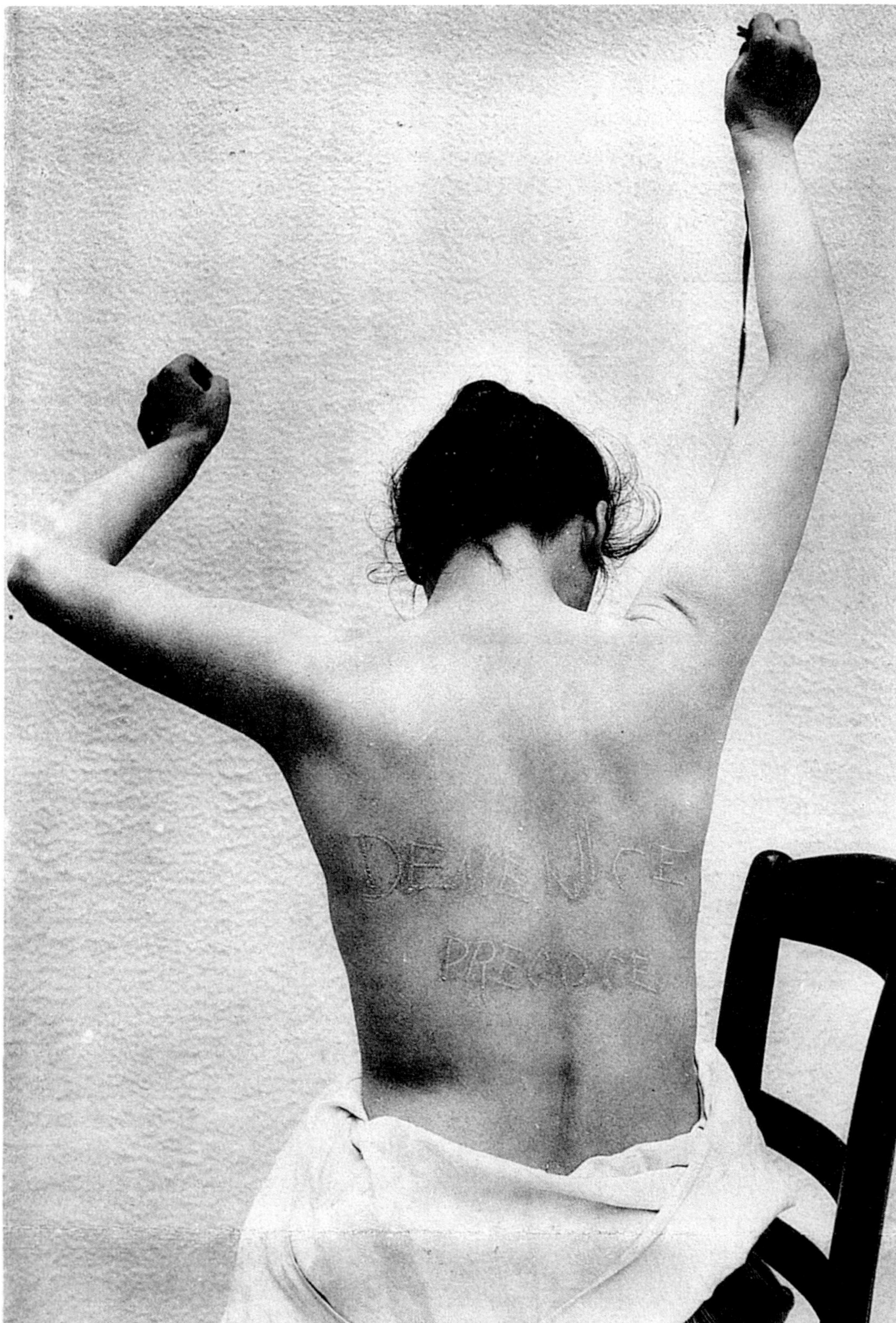

Figure 5: A dermographic woman made to bear the imprint of her own diagnosis: démence précoce. (Published in L. Trepsat, *Nouvelle Iconographie de la Salpêtrière* 17, 1904; photo: Pauline Page.)

LEIF ELGGREN / THE SUDARIUM OF ST. VERONICA

For many years I was doing engravings with a drypoint needle on 1 mm copperplates. It was mostly figurative images which came from my dreams. First I often made a drawing from a particular dream, and from that a small series of engravings developed, such as "The Gardeners", "The Knife Suite", "Street Dogs", "I and Me", "Africa", etc. From these images I started to make installations with furniture and objects. I even used the images as sketches or scores for performances – dressed up like the characters in the pictures. I started making books where I wrote down instructions for the performances. And soundtracks too. After a while I wanted to combine my work with the drypoint needle and all the other stuff that developed from it into a concentrated project. CM von Hausswolff took the first step and encouraged me to do it. It was very natural. I decided to do a piece where I recorded the sound from when I was engraving a small copperplate. I had for a long time been focusing on the images that I was scratching onto the reflecting metal. At the same time I was producing a lot of sound with the needle working in the soft reddish-coloured material, but without being aware of it. Now I wanted to totally focus on the sound that was generated through this working method. With the help of CM von Hausswolff and Erik Pauser we found an interesting place in Gothenburg for the recording. It was an old abandoned slaughterhouse on Haga Östergata. We had to climb over the rooftops to get there. All the doors and windows were blocked. We found a nice room where we installed the recording devices. We attached a contact microphone on the backside of the copperplate. The first recording was done in a light room. For seven minutes I tried to cover the plate as much as possible with the drypoint needle.

The second recording was done in a totally dark room. I used a burnisher and tried to erase as much as possible during seven minutes. This was done on the 23rd of November 1981. After this session I went back to Stockholm and printed the plate on a copperprint press. 252 copies were made. With lead types I put together the text for the different text sheets and printed it on my old letterpress, a Korrex from 1963. A seven inch vinyl record was made by a pressing plant in the North of Sweden. I had personal contact in Linköping, in the South of Sweden, with an old manufacturer of cardboard boxes. They made a very nice black box for me. On the top of the box I made a relief print with the chemical sign for copper: "Cu". In the box I placed the seven inch record, a print from the plate, a photo from the recording session, a text sheet with the instruction for the piece, a credit page with all the print information and a title page. It was released on Phauss. This was a simple but crucial point for my work. I could not only see the image, I could even hear it!

Several years after this I wanted to go further and bought two seven inch lacquers from a cutting studio in Solna, right outside Stockholm. I remember when I was there and picked them up. They were packed like a cake in a cardboard box. Very fragile. I took the box like a baker's delivery boy and walked carefully back home. I placed the lacquer on a record player and played it on the lowest speed. I took my drypoint needle and tried to act like a human cutting machine. I had a sentence that I screamed out loud over and over again. A true cutting machine draws an inexorable spiral from the periphery to the centre. The human version was not that easy. The needle was extremely difficult to control and the lines crossed each other constantly. But the thing was done and this was released in an edition of 618 copies as a handcut seven inch called "The New Immortality" on Anckarström / Firework Edition in 1992. Because of the crossed lines in the vinyl this was a very difficult record to playback. The pickup was jumping around on the surface and every playback produced a different sound. The record was more like a sound source, an instrument. No two playbacks sounded the same. So it was necessary to follow this up with a second release (553 copies) called "The New Immortality #2" on Firework Edition Records in 1998. This release was based on two playbacks of "The New Immortality".

As long as I can remember I have admired the print made by the French artist Claude Mellan (1598–1688), called "The Sudarium

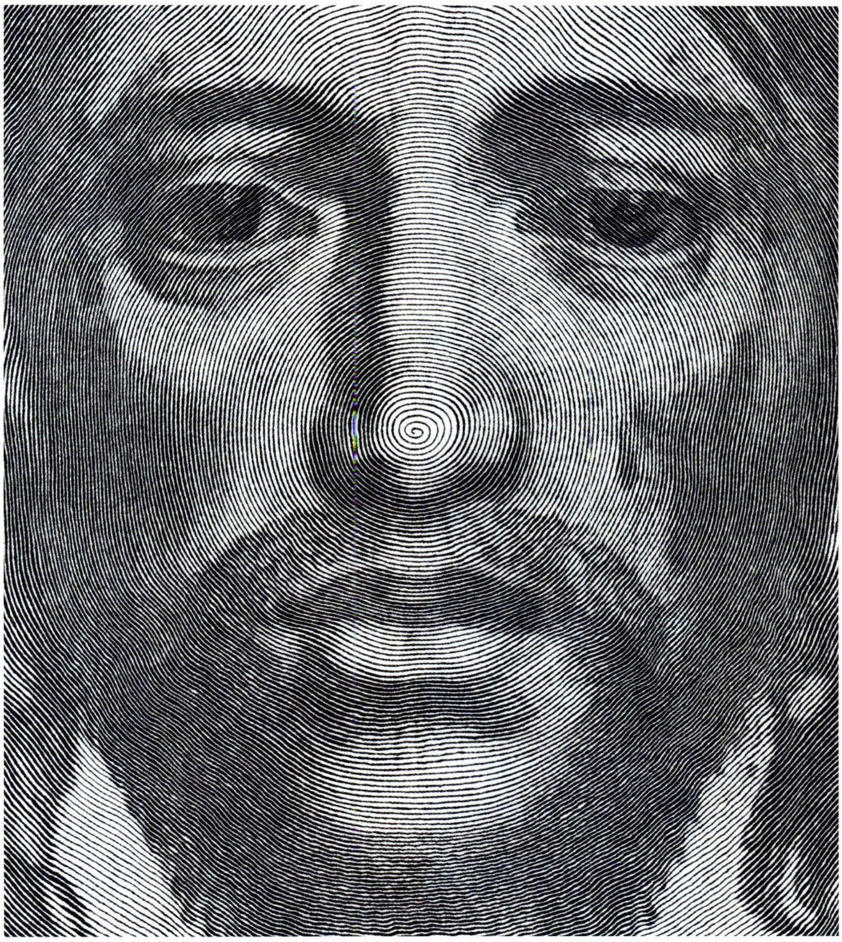

Fig. 1: Claude Mellan,
The Sudarium of St. Veronica (detail),
copper engraving, 1649.

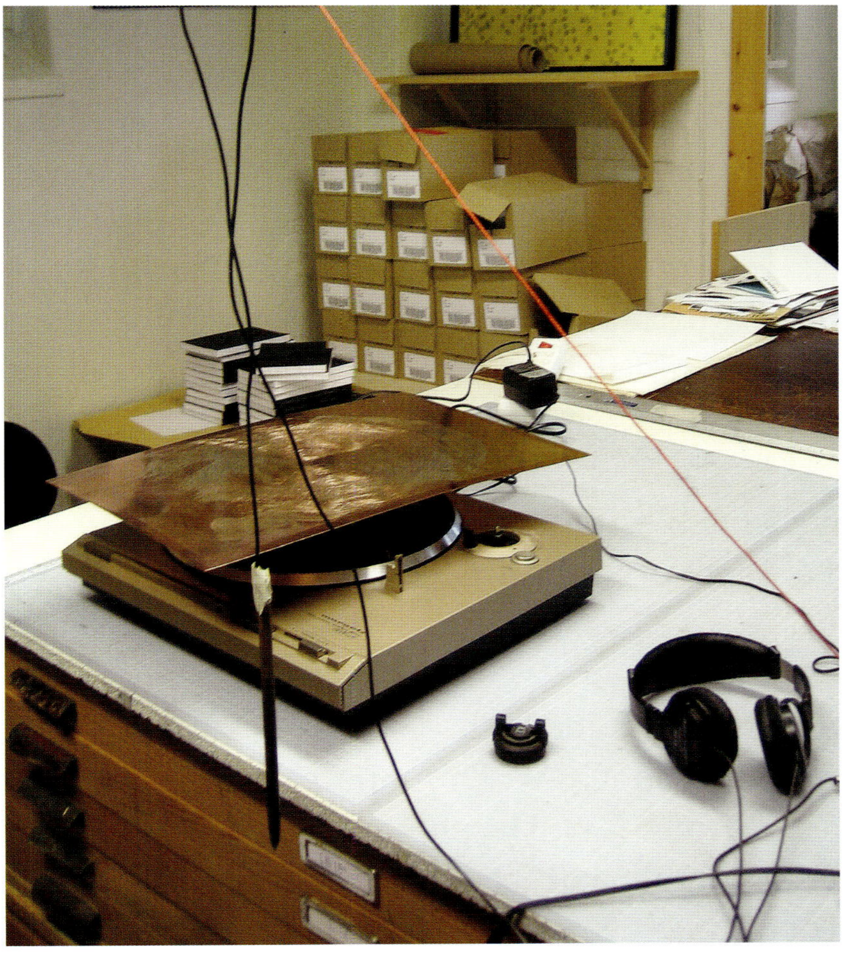

Fig. 2: Leif Elggren /
The Sudarium of St. Veronica, 2007.
Playback and recording of the replica
of the copper engraving
The Sudarium of St. Veronica,
cut by the French artist Claude Mellan
(1598–1688) in Paris 1649.

of St. Veronica", from 1649. A portrait of Christ engraved through a continuous spiral line that starts at the tip of his nose. I realized early that this must have been the first cut (maybe) ever done of a record (without being aware of it). So obvious and natural. And so beautifully done. Could it even be possible to playback the gravure in an old fashioned analogue way? But then I needed the plate. To play the plate! I was really excited by the thought of detecting what was hidden in that spiral line. To hear the image! But I needed a print that I could scan in order to make an etching and produce a new copperplate. I couldn't even contemplate using the original plate, even if it still existed. I tried to interest the people at the National Museum in Stockholm, because I knew that they at least had one print from the original plate in their collection. I talked to several of these guys including the manager. But they were not interested to help at all. Instead I tried to find another way through the library at the Academy of Fine Arts. I had heard about high quality heliogravures printed in old books. I did get very good assistance from the enthusiastic librarian Anneli Ekström. She finally found an old book with an acceptable print in it. I scanned the heliogravure in the highest resolution and worked with the image in Photoshop. For more than a year I was busy cleaning the image, trying to erase as much as possible of the blur around the spiral line, trying to get the line as clear as possible to make way for the pickup. When this was done I made a positive offset film and sent it to Svensk Industrigravyr in Hyltebruk in the South of Sweden and they made a perfect etching of the image. Not an exact copy of the original plate (that was an engraving) but a close replica, as close as I could get.

This plate was played back with a specially constructed record player and recorded at Firework Edition, Stockholm, July 17, 2007.

Three different recordings were made:
1: 21'34" (Turntable. By hand. CCW. Drypoint needle.)
2: 16'01" (Turntable. 33 rpm. CW. Drypoint needle.)
3: 14'48" (The plate on a table and the needle moving CW. Drypoint needle.) Total time: 52'23"

RESONANCE, AS IN SKIN (OR : PHONODERMATOGRAPHY)

BY ANDRÉ LEPECKI

It should be noted that when the material an artist directly assesses, works with, bends, folds, re-directs, assembles and invents is *time* then such an artist is inevitably working, assessing, re-directing, assembling and inventing also *a body* – that particularly vertiginous membrane of time, always on the edge of the moment, incorporating and expelling virtuals and actuals, and thus permanently re-aligning pasts and futures through its many actions, desires, inventions, expressions, gestures (whether intended or not). Cicatrix of one another, body and time suture the nervure of the present in the dissonance all friction produces. By creating a body-time, an artist assembles, defines and stitches together surfaces of sensation, provisional sensorial organs identifying as well as producing zones of aesthetic and political intensification. We can call these sutured and scarred surfaces a work's skin: the organ and matter where everything takes place, everything is inscribed as well as produced – times and subjectivities, gestures and vocalizations, violations and freedoms.

It should be noted that one of Maria José Arjona's main procedures is to harness time and thus to produce, in each and for each new work, a different body with its specific zones of sensation and of sense. She achieves this effect through a careful rhythmization of her gestures, pace, and cadence along with the rhythms and cadences she identifies in the apparently inert materials with which she creates her pieces: hybrids of sculpture, installation, painting, body-art, sound-art, performance art, drawing, and dance. It's as if Arjona's rhythms, deeply informed by her very specific mode of concentration when performing (concentration as a saturation of time around the performer's zone of presence) as well as by her careful choice of materials and specially of colors, invoke and secrete specific zones of temporality. By resonating the surrounding things' and materials' own temporal dimensions Arjona's works reveal the essential ethical nature of her mode of composing, where to compose equals to work along with the will of things. What sends Arjona's pieces into their pointed political dimension is that by producing before a public a cicatrix of time, a careful archeology of violence is revealed. In this archeology, a systematic confusion between visuality, corporeality and sonority becomes essential; for it is this confusion that produces the work's resounding skin.

Sight sound sight, sound sight sound: skin skin skin. There is something about skin and sound that is primordial, just as there is something about skin and the formation of the social that is primordial. "We must stretch the skin like a drum, in order that the 'great politics' begin," once wrote Deleuze. As if skin were that sonic surface where the heartbeat of politics is produced, rhythmized and broadcasted. On her back, between her shoulder blades, Arjona marked her skin with a tattoo that reads: *remember to remember*. Essential dermatography for every art(ist) of time. Essential dermatography for an ethics and for a politics of time – to remember to remember is what allows one to be always worthy of the event, and to never fall into the trap of compulsive resentment. The public can read this phrase on Arjona's back whenever it decides to be with her during one of the performances that composes her *White Series*: the work titled *Remember to Remember* (2008).

In this long-durational work (usually lasting several days), we will find Arjona, dressed in white, her back bare, scribbling with white chalk on a gallery's walls, for several hours a day, the very same sentence: remember to remember. Important detail: in this piece, the walls' whiteness is tainted by a vivid and uncanny band of splattered red paint, cutting a violent horizon across the entire gallery; it is over this red that Arjona writes. I will discuss in a moment how Arjona created this band of red splats during the performance of the piece in the *White Series* (*Untitled* 2008) that always precedes *Remember to Remember*. But, for now, let us stay a bit longer with Arjona scribbling the sentence that titles not only this particular work but also names her labor in it: remember to remember.

From the public's point of view remember to remember becomes a resonating refrain in several dimensions: grammatically, it is a sentence structured as a mirror doubling itself up to infinity; sonically, it produces a rumbling of the voice which echoes the material depths of memory; visually, one witnesses the reiterative reinscription of the sentence over itself, as Arjona scribbles remember to remember over and over again, sometimes even scribbling over the scribbles, so much so that remember to remember starts to slowly cover the violent red band of splattered paint on the walls – remember to remember, in white chalk, turns the red into a washed out pink, a quasi-white; still visually, the sentence tattooed on Arjona's back repeats and reflects its reiteration on the wall. A repetition that furthers the resonating power of the refrain – and that soon starts to gain the contours of an order-word.

Sight sound sight, sound sight sound, skin skin skin: remember to remember. The persistence of the sentence on Arjona's skin as she methodically works on writing it over and over again, over and over itself on the wall splattered in red, also functions as a suturing (or stitching) of memory-matters splayed over the entire performative/aesthetic situation. Remember to remember: a refrain functioning as a gesture functioning as a persistence doubling as a suturing of an order-word activating the time-body that is Arjona's entire performative act. Phonodermatography.

We may recall here that for Deleuze and Guattari the order-word activates two distinct, yet intimately linked, functions. On one hand, the order-word is a condemnation, like a judge's sentencing – Arjona performs this aspect of the order-word by taking for herself the task of having to perform her writing for hours in a row, for several days, silently, no matter how absurd this repetitive act may seem, following the sentencing present at the core of every order-word. On the other hand, the order-word is also and always a line of flight. Remember to remember thus becomes simultaneously a performative program, an imperative for an ethical stance before memory, but also a call for an urgent need to re-articulate our political bodies and our affective bodies into other modes of suturing a social skin and producing its temporal scar. Memory is the matter one needs to activate for the sake of the event of ethics. This is what one must remember to remember.

Because the skin of Arjona's back mirrors the gallery's walls as surface of inscription, the gallery wall becomes a skin – just as the artist's skin becomes a wall. And if the wall is the skin and the skin is the wall, then the red splatters over which Arjona writes (and by writing over, dilutes) acquire a corporeal dimension. The red indicates a kind of constitutive bleeding of those supposedly inert and supposedly neutral surfaces supporting and promoting

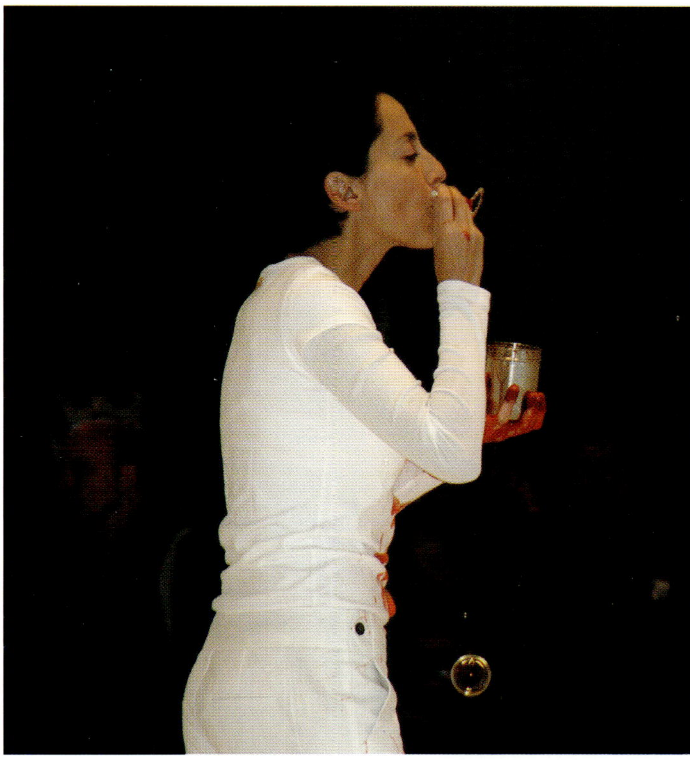

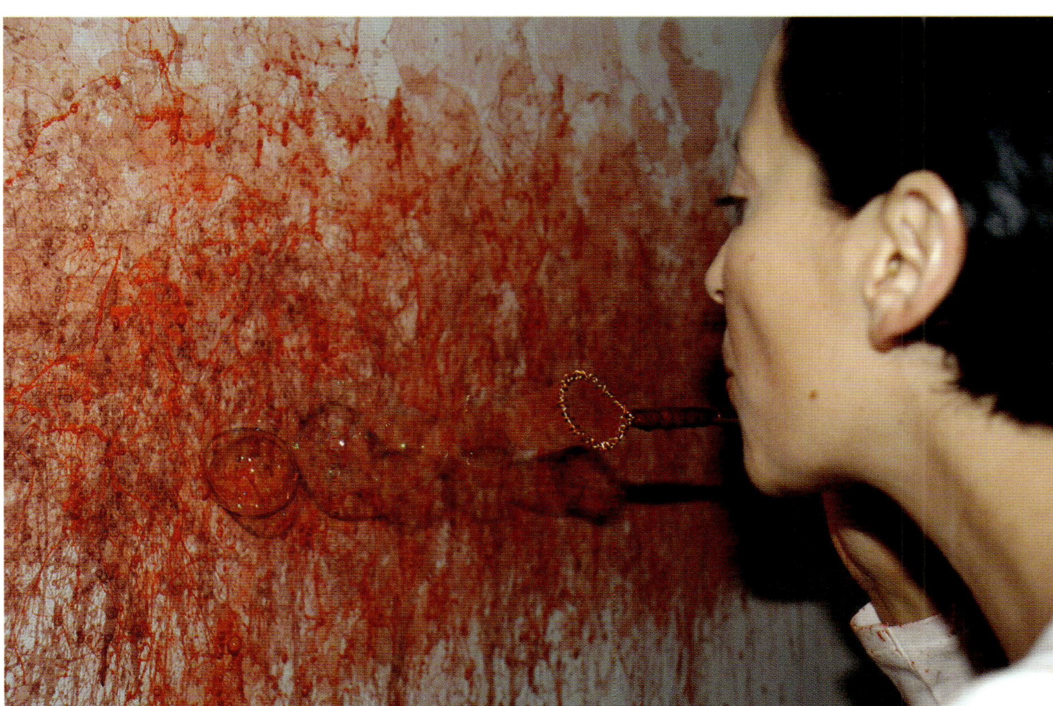

Fig. 1–3: Maria José Arjona, *Untitled*, IN TRANSIT, Haus der Kulturen der Welt, Berlin, 2009. Photos: David Bergé.

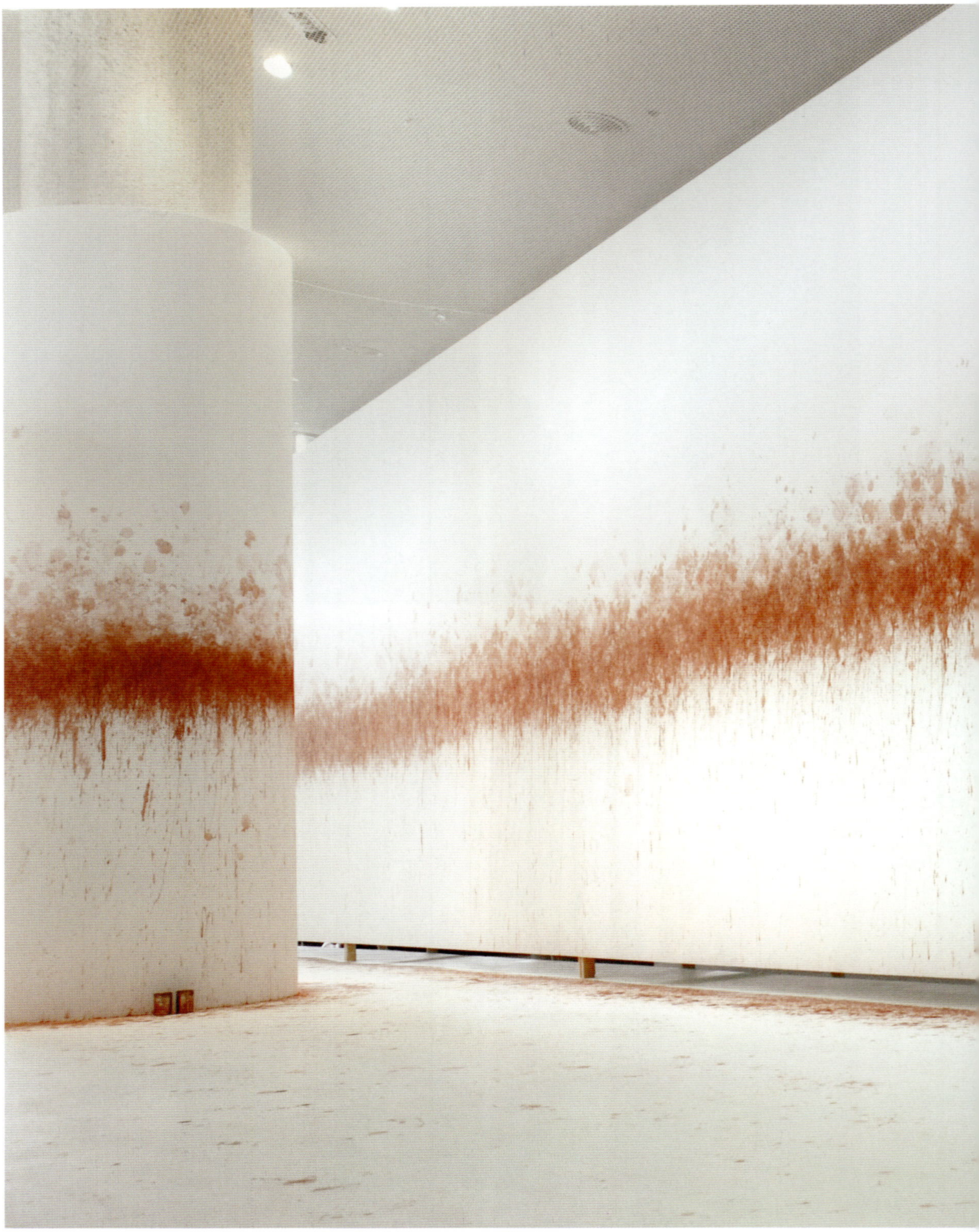

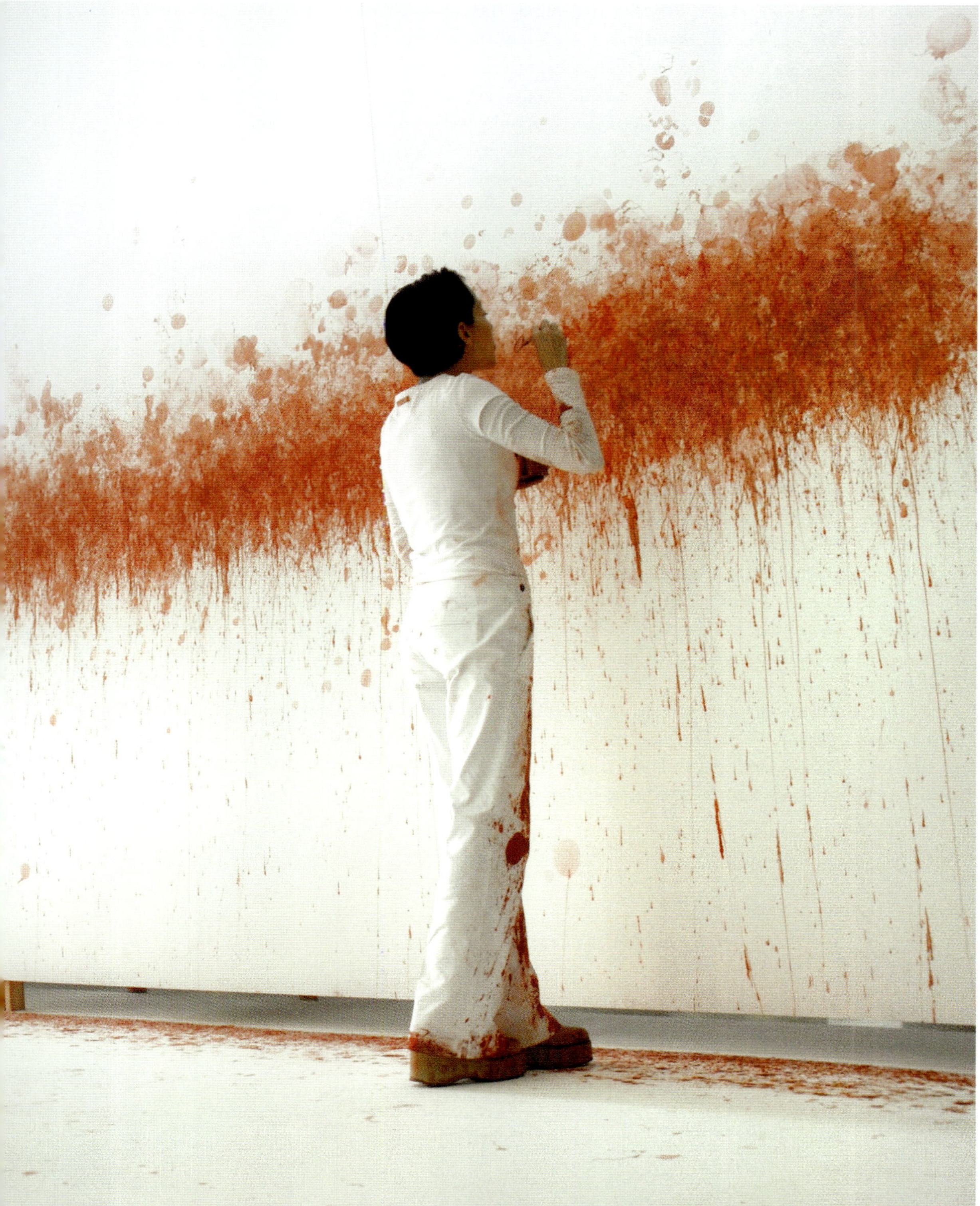

representation and inscription (Barthes had found the same corporeal dimension *and* violent dimension on the surface of photographic representation, when he described the *punctum* as simultaneously "prick" *and* "wound"). Thanks to the resonance wall/skin, we can now move in time and reveal the first "act" – or first action – that sets up the possibility of this particularly powerful work. For Arjona's work actually begins days before she starts to scribble over the band of red splatter with white chalk. Indeed, it starts with the performance *Untitled*.

In *Untitled*, Arjona, dressed in white, enters the white space of a gallery holding in her hand a cup containing a small wand with a little wire circle at one of its ends. Thus equipped, Arjona approaches one of the gallery walls, and slowly, methodically, carefully, gently, consistently, relentlessly and stubbornly starts to dip the wand in the cup, take it close to her lips, and through the circle, gently begins to blow soap bubbles against the wall. The bubbles are as transparent and fragile and beautiful as soap bubbles can be. However, as soon as they reach the white wall they burst in a splat of red. With each splat, a whole history of violence is made visibly audible.

Slowly walking along the walls, blowing and blowing and blowing and blowing, methodically, carefully, gently, consistently, relentlessly and stubbornly, Arjona starts to delineate three main zones of impact for the red bursts: an inexact band of about a meter wide on the white walls right in front of her; a narrower stripe of red on the floor, made by the dripping of paint from the cup, from the wand, from bubbles which explode in the air before reaching the walls, or from Arjona's hands; and finally red stains drenching Arjona's white shirt and pants, which gradually start looking more and more like a butcher's outfit, or a surgeon's in a war hospital at the frontline, or the clothes of the victim of a bloody crime. The delicacy of Arjona's movements while she paces along the walls blowing bubbles contrasts vividly with the visual end result of her action. (Depending on how she choreographs her pacing, the red splats may fall everywhere in the gallery, creating a truly charged environment.) It is in this discrepancy, in this friction between innocent act and violent result that a sonic reverberation inevitably comes across as walls visually scream as a slashed body. Even if Arjona's rhythm, her matter-of-factness and calm concentration, and the ethereal quality of the bubbles all help to temper this scream with a kind of suspension, one cannot help but to sense that within each silent floating bubble one more scream is at the edge of bursting.

skin
skin
skin: scream wall burst

bubble
bubble
bubble: burst white red

red
red
red: white scream wall

scream
scream

scream: remember to remember
remember to remember
remember to remember
remember to remember
remember to remember
remember to remember
remember to remember
remember to remember
remember to remember
remember to remember

Through the resonant refrain that activates the matter of memory, through phonodermatography acting as a bridge, we are now placed at the next piece composing the *White Series* – after several days of silent work by Arjona. This last piece is titled *Karaoke* (2008) and consists of the repetitive singing of one song, over and over, again and again, for hours, until Arjona's voice naturally falters in its joyful emission.

The very last performance of these three deeply inter-connected works that together compose the *White Series*, the farewell of *Untitled, Remember to Remember* and *Karaoke* from the world of actuals, took place during the festival IN TRANSIT, at Haus der Kulturen der Welt, between June 11 and June 21, 2009. As the curator of the festival in its 2008 and 2009 editions, I had invited Arjona to perform the *White Series* throughout those ten days of the festival – but I did not know then it would be the last iteration of the works. We installed a white space (designed by Christin Vahl) in the grand foyer of the Haus, a long corridor open at both ends. Arjona started blowing her bubbles on the Festival's opening day – and continued to do so for 7 hours a day, 4 days in a row. Then, on June 17th, Arjona started the second action: the writing of remember to remember in white chalk, for another 4 days, 7 hours a day. Finally, on the nineth day of work, one of the walls of the corridor was brought down. The space became a kind of stage, microphones were installed, and for more than four hours on that June 21st, as the sun set and the building became empty from the festival's public, Arjona sang without stopping – until her voice could no longer hold. She sang Edith Piaf's *Non, Je Ne Regrette Rien* as the festival's last day wound down and as she was joined by whoever wanted to sing along with her.

The work's skin was now stretching in yet another mode: a social skin was once again being sutured out of sound and sight and words through a song connecting mouth to mouth like a kiss or a language or a cicatrix. After the disclosure of violence contained even in the most innocent of gestures and in the most neutral of spaces (blood red in soap bubbles bursting supposedly neutral planes of representation, turning the artist into butcher and victim); after the ethical summoning of the matter of memory (remember to remember) Arjona's last call was not to regret: the affirmation of affirmation. The next day, the installation at HKW went down, planks and words and paint carried to a recycling center in Berlin. The beautiful red splattered painting that soap bubbles and air drafts and pigment and white walls and chalk and Arjona's breath, rhythm, concentration and actions had all assembled was now gone. In its absence, a zone of time still lingered, in the silent cave of HKW's modernist foyer. A silence filled with memory-matters, which is the same as to say a silence filled with the resonant phonodermatography called history.

PUBLIUS OVIDIUS NASO
Metamorphoses 6, 382–400, *Marsyas*

Sic ubi nescio quis Lycia de gente virorum
rettulit exitium, satyri reminiscitur alter,
quem Tritoniaca Latous harundine victum
adfecit poena. "quid me mihi detrahis?" inquit;
"a! piget, a! non est" clamabat "tibia tanti!"
clamanti cutis est summos direpta per artus,
nec quicquam nisi vulnus erat; cruor undique manat,
detectique patent nervi, trepidaeque sine ulla
pelle micant venae; salientia viscera possis
et perlucentes numerare in pectore fibras.
illum ruricolae, silvarum numina, Fauni
et satyri fratres et tunc quoque carus Olympus
et nymphae flerunt, et quisquis montibus illis
lanigerosque greges armentaque bucera pavit.
fertilis inmaduit madefactaque terra caducas
concepit lacrimas ac venis perbibit imis;
quas ubi fecit aquam, vacuas emisit in auras.
inde petens rapidus ripis declivibus aequor
Marsya nomen habet, Phrygiae liquidissimus amnis.[1]

When one of Lyce (I wot not who) had spoken in this sort,
Another of a satyr straight began to make report
Whom Phoebus, overcoming on a pipe (made late ago
By Pallas), put to punishment. 'Why flayest thou me so?
Alas!' he cried, 'It irketh me. Alas, a sorry pipe
Deserveth not so cruelly my skin from me to strip.'
For all his crying, o'er his ears quite pulled was his skin.
Nought else he was than one whole wound. The grisly blood did spin
From every part; the sinews lay discovered to the eye;
The quivering veins without a skin lay beating nakedly.
The panting bowels in his bulk ye might have numbered well,
And in his breast the sheer small strings a man might easily tell.
The country fauns, the gods of woods, the satyrs of his kin,
The Mount Olympus, whose renown did ere that time begin,
And all the nymphs and all that in those mountains kept their sheep
Or grazed cattle thereabouts, did for this satyr weep.
The fruitful earth waxed moist therewith and, moisted, did receive
Their tears and in her bowels deep did of the same conceive.
And when that she had turned them to water, by and by
She sent them forth again aloft to see the open sky.
The river that doth rise thereof, beginning there his race,
In very deep and shoring banks to seaward runs apace
Through Phrygie; and according as the satyr, so the stream
Is called Marsyas, of the brooks the clearest in that realm.[2]

Translation: Arthur Golding (1567)

Kläglich war, sehr kläglich, des Satyrs Marsyas Schicksal,
Der, von Apollo besiegt im Getön des tritonischen Rohres,
Jetzo die Strafe bestand. Was entziehst du mir selber mich? rief er.
Ah, mich gereut's! ah! schrie er, soviel nicht gilt mir das Schallrohr!
Doch wie er schrie, zog jener die Haut ihm über die Glieder;
Und nichts war, als Wunde, zu schaun. Blut rieselte ringsum;
Aufgedeckt lag Muskel und Sehn'; auch die zitternden Adern
Schlugen, der Hülle beraubt, aufzuckende Eingeweide
Konnte man zählen sogar, und der Brust durchscheinende Fibern.
Ihn wehklageten Faune, die ländlichen Mächte der Waldung,
Ihn die Satyrgebrüder, und du, ruhmvoller Olympus,
Ihn auch der Nymphen Geschlecht, und wer in der bergigen Gegend
Herden der wolligen Schaf, und gehörnete Rinder umhertrieb.
Aber das fruchtbare Land empfing die fallenden Tränen,
Durchgenetzt, und trank sie hinab in die innersten Adern:
Wo sie, zu Wasser geseigt, aufquellen an freiere Lüfte.
Jäh zu dem stürmischen Meer, im Hang abschüssiger Ufer,
Rollt der Marsyasstrom durch Phrygia lautere Wellen.[3]

Übersetzung: Johann Heinrich Voß (1798)

[1] Ovid, *Metamorphosen* (2–8 A.D.; Ditzingen: Reclam, 2010). [2] Ovid, *Metamorphoses* (London: Penguin Books, 2002). [3] Ovid, *Metamorphosen* (Frankfurt/M.: Insel Verlag, 1990).

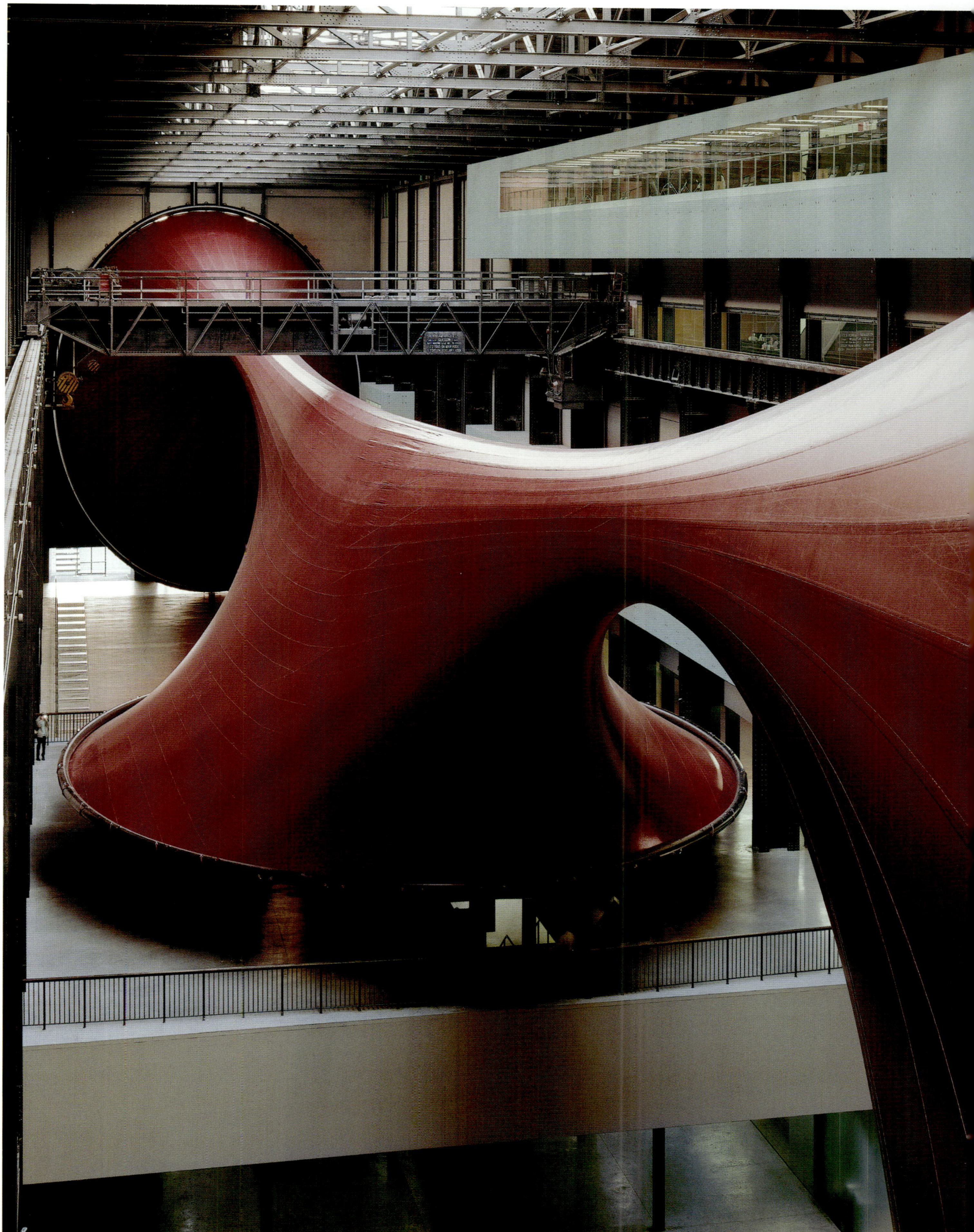

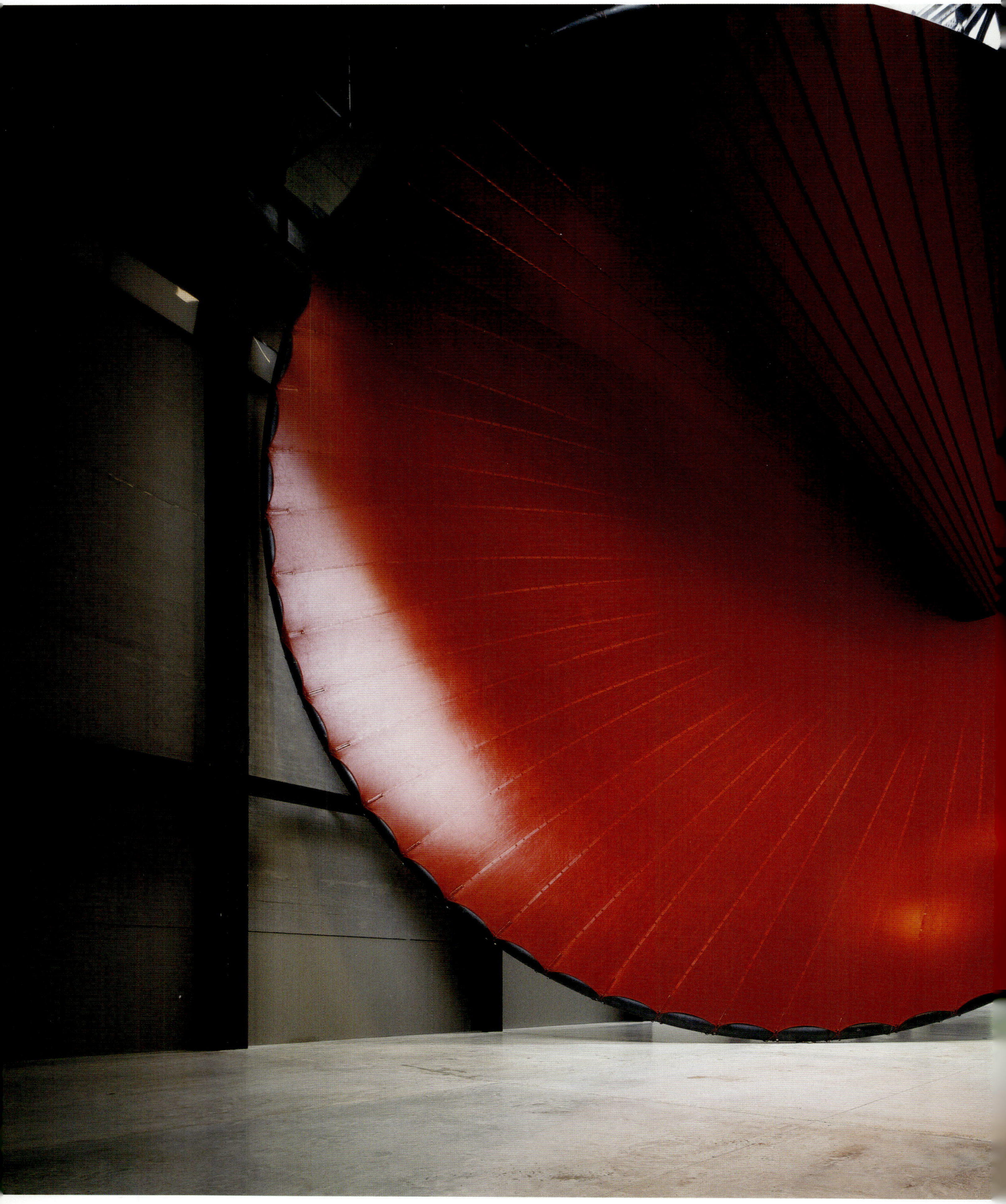

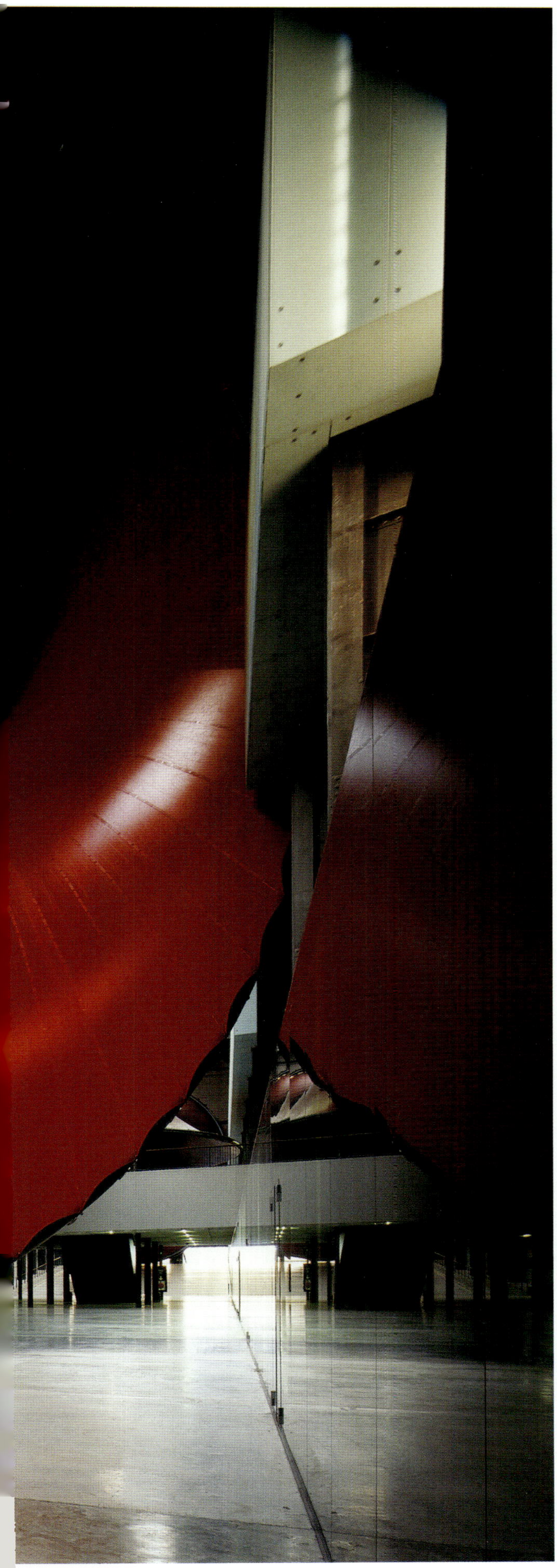

Anish Kapoor, *Marsyas*, 2002

PVC and steel.

Installation at the Tate Modern, London, 2002–2003.

Fig. 1–3: ANISH KAPOOR, *Marsyas*, 2002.
Tate Modern, London, 2002–2003. Courtesy: Tate Modern, London.
Photos: John Riddy.

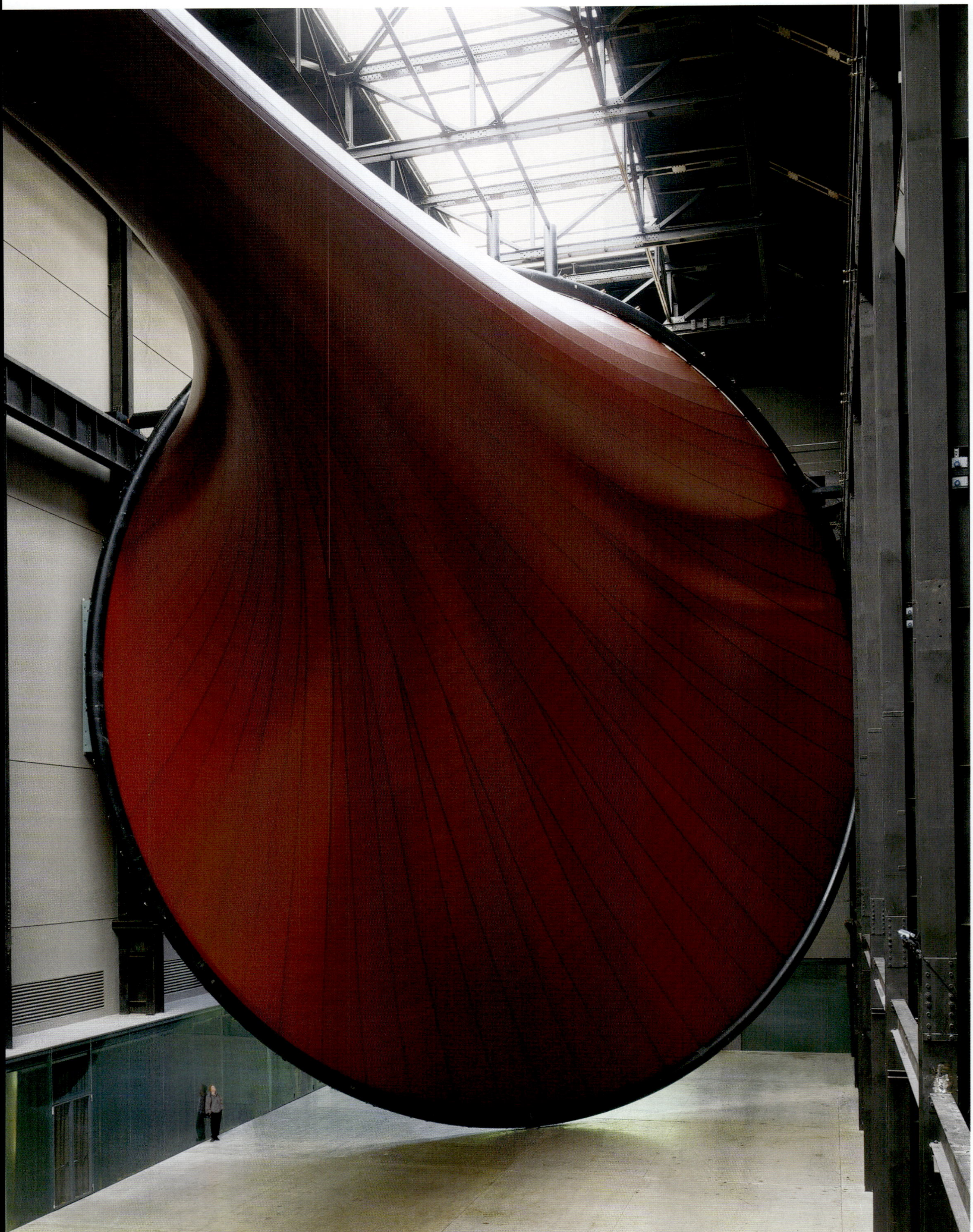

ALLEN S. WEISS / THE SONIC SKIN OF WATER

During the Showa period (1925–1989) there existed the custom of gathering during early summer at the Sinobazu-no-ike pond in Tokyo's Ueno Park to listen to the sound of lotus flowers blooming. This is described by musician and composer Imada Tadahiko:

> However, the frequency of that sound is approximately 9–16 Hz. As we normally hear sounds within a frequency range from 20 Hz to 20,000 Hz, people were unable to actually hear the sound of the bloom of a lotus flower. But they loved and wanted to listen to that phantom sound. The experience was a kind of communal auditory hallucination.[1]

Musicologist David Toop glosses:

> A prime listening site can be extraordinarily revealing. Minute actions click into focus. The clarity can slow pulse rate and perceived time. But loneliness may loom into view, also, and the deathly absence of significant activity.[2]

However, as the sound in question is far beneath the threshold of human auditory sensitivity, the event is actually about something other than flower music: the extreme concentration teaches one to hear the entire soundscape, such that background sounds are foregrounded, and the usually unheard sonic subtleties of the environment become the subject of attention. This is therefore a festival, striking in its extreme minimalism, that teaches one to hear anew, not unlike John Cage's famous Zen-inspired silent composition, *4'33"* (1952), where the musicians are instructed to make no sounds whatsoever, such that the ambient noise constitutes the music. We might wish to rethink the environment of the Zen garden according to the Zen-inspired ways of listening.

One of the great antinomies of the dry Zen garden (*karesansui*: dry mountain water) is that its symbolism is so profoundly aquatic. The very notion of a "sea" of sand or a "waterfall" rock, contradictions in terms, is particularly appropriate to the Zen koan spirit of paradox. Consider the actual and metaphoric use of water in the Japanese culture. I have always loved the way sake is often served: either overflowing a crystal glass into a wooden box (*masu*), or overflowing the wooden box into a saucer. The horizontal plane is materialized at the rim in an evanescent shimmering of liquid, while the vertical line of the receptacle is dynamized by the overflow, forming a small pool at the base – homologous to the everpresent form of irrigated rice-paddies, as well as to the overflowing of pools, wells, fountains, sculptures, baths, hollowed rocks, lavers (*chozubachi*), basins (*tsukubai*, the stone arrangements in which the lavers are placed), everywhere apparent in Japanese architecture and gardens.

Cognizance of such vast formal homologies across the arts is crucial in approaching the Zen garden. Metaphor, abstraction and stylization are always a matter of degree. Perhaps metaphor is too rhetorical a term, and the more complex *correspondence* (in the Baudelairean sense) would be more appropriate. Essential are both resemblances that create the correspondences at the core of Japanese aesthetics, and divergences that establish the conceptual gap within which the creative imagination may flourish. Consequently, incompatibilities and contradictions are as inspiring as resemblances. The old Zen adage attributed to the Chinese master Qingyuan Weixin is particularly apt:

> Before enlightenment, mountains are mountains and waters are waters. During the quest for enlightenment, mountains are not mountains and waters are not waters. After enlightenment, mountains are just mountains and waters are just waters.

Such is the very structure of metaphor. We might well apply this proverb to the stones (mountains) and raked gravel (sea) of Ryōan-ji and so many other Zen gardens, in order to reveal the profound polysemy of this garden, which can simultaneously represent utopia and the void, energy and ocean, landscape and painting, the site of intuition and the form of intuition. For in art, especially Zen art, the Aristotelian laws of non-contradiction do not hold. This might well explain a fundamental irony in Ryōan-ji, the fact that the bed of gravel on which the stones rest represents what the stones will one day themselves become: mere sand.

Daisen-in (a subtemple of Daitoku-ji), perhaps the most condensed and complex of all dry Zen gardens, represents in stones and pebbles a waterfall that cascades under a small bridge to divide into two branches of a river flowing in one direction out towards the open ocean, in the other to a closed pool. Here, where relative scale is a function of iconography and not perspective, such that the ocean to the right is no larger than the stream to the left, the varied use of stones and pebbles suggests the possibility of a catalogue to differentiate such effects: the large, irregular, vertical stones demarcating the waterfall; the small regular pebbles representing the cascading water; the slightly larger, slightly more irregular pebbles delineating the white water where the waterfall breaks under the flat stone of the bridge; the wave patterns of the small white pebbles that depict the flowing waters of the river. Perhaps most astonishing of all, at the left side of the garden, the small white pebbles of the flowing river end in a basin, represented by a circle of medium-size stones filled with large black pebbles representing deep, still water, with several ferns and a stone in the center. (Here the central stone is not a metaphor, but a stone.) This represented pond is juxtaposed to a large stone with a hollowed top (it is impossible to determine whether this hollow is natural or artificial, and such ambiguity is of the essence), in which rests a small pool of rainwater: a real, miniature "pond" alongside a figurative pond. The priest Zen, in one of the classics of Japanese landscape art, the 15th century *Illustrations for Designing Mountain, Water, and Hillside Field Landscapes,* goes so far as to suggest that sand alone may suffice to create a landscape scene:

> Another type of shoreline scenery is the ebb-tide beach, which has no striking features but simply creates the impression of the tide constantly ebbing and flowing. Here, if just by spreading fine and coarse grades of sand and without setting any rocks you can visually re-create a single scenic ambience.[3]

This central effect of dry gardens is well described by art historian Yoshinobu Yoshinaga:

> The garden is an attempt to represent the innermost essence of water, without actually using water, and to represent it at that even more profoundly than would be possible with real water.[4]

The potency of visual and auditory metaphors does not depend on the degree of verisimilitude, but on the differences between terms. Such is the space of dry water, still waves, proximate distance – the space of the impossible, the space of paradox, the space of Zen enlightenment.

One of the most stunning examples of this metaphor is to be seen in the 1964 film adaptation of Kōbō Abe's novel *Woman in the Dunes* (1962) by Hiroshi Teshigahara, where the protagonist is held prisoner in a sand pit in which the constantly flowing, spilling, falling, whorling sand acts just like water. And in case the spectator doesn't quite get the metaphor, at one point, to protect the meal from the sand leaking through the roof, the woman of the house opens an umbrella above the table. Teshigahara writes of this experience:

> In the course of struggling with the sand, I realized that sand flows like liquid, possesses will, and represents beauty and solitude. My creativity was stirred by the struggle with the sharply pointed, stinging sand.[5]

Whence the appropriateness in choosing Tōru Takemitsu to create the soundtrack, given that in 1960 he had composed *Water Music,* a work of musique concrète based on a variety of water sounds, creating effects not unlike those of a water zither. One particularly subtle and disquieting aspect of this manifestation of the sand-as-water metaphor in *Woman in the Dunes* is the fact that whereas on a sandy beach one hears the blending of both sand and water sounds, in the film – where water is the most precious commodity in the terribly arid landscape – the visual cues suggest sand-for-water, while the soundscape is one of pure sand and wind.

Writing of the age-old question of the origins of music, Leonard Bernstein claims:

> I believe that from the Earth emerges a musical poetry, which is by the nature of its sources tonal.[6]

This telluric music takes many forms, some of them paradoxically aquatic. One of the most beautiful, though relatively unknown, types of Japanese sonic installations is the *suikinkutsu* (water zither cave), said to have been created by the legendary tea master Kobori Enshu (1579 – 1647). The water from the laver (*tsukubai*) that is used to purify the hands and mouth before the tea ceremony overflows into a stone basin (*chozubachi*), and is then evacuated into the *suikinkutsu,* a small buried jar or chamber, where the water drips into the pool at the bottom, creating sounds akin to those of the koto, a type of zither. The *suikinkutsu* is usually made of pottery, with an irregular unglazed surface that causes numerous droplets of water to form and drip in irregular patterns, thus creating a complex sonic environment, where the earth resonates with the song of water. This aleatory music serves as purification of body and soul, anticipation of the pleasures of the Tea ceremony, and prefiguration of the rare sounds that punctuate the stillness of the tea pavilion, notably those of the boiling kettle, as described by Yasunari Kawabata in the following scene from *Snow Country*:

> The innkeeper had lent him an old Kyoto teakettle, skillfully inlaid in silver with flowers and birds, and from it came the sound of wind in the pines. He could make out two pine breezes,

as a matter of fact, a near one and a far one. Just beyond the far breeze he heard faintly the tinkling of a bell.[7]

This passage recalls (and might well be based on) another, from Kakuzo Okakura's classic, *The Book of Tea*:

The kettle sings well, for pieces of iron are so arranged in the bottom as to produce a peculiar melody in which one may hear the echoes of a cataract muffled by clouds, of a distant sea breaking among the rocks, a rainstorm sweeping through a bamboo forest, or of the soughing of pines on some faraway hill.[8]

These are all sonic tropes of Japanese poetry and music (especially the sound of wind in the pines as heard in *Matsukase,* one of the most famous compositions for shakuhachi flute), and they set the emotional and metaphoric stage for the performance of the tea ceremony, always a unique event, every aspect of which – flower arrangement, scroll imagery, pottery, kimono pattern, cuisine – is attuned to the season, weather, hour, and especially the tastes of the guests. Daisetz T. Suzuki, the great specialist of Zen Buddhism and John Cage's mentor, also evokes such sounds:

The breeze passing through the needles of the old pine tree harmoniously blends with the sizzling of the iron kettle over the fire.[9]

However, this depiction is rather banal and stereotyped, description rather than creation, as it operates on a strictly literal level, more attuned to the consciousness of a sound engineer rather than a poet. While the *sizzling* kettle might indeed harmonize with the sound of the wind, Suzuki hears no correspondences between sounds, seeks no poetic resonances, and imagines no musical variations. But after all, he is a philosopher rather than an artist, and his text fulfills a very different function.

All Japanese poetics depends upon such sonic correspondences: listening for the mimetic music of the world, where one of the central sonic figures of this infinite matrix of interconnections and resemblances is the sound of water, we conceive of the kettle as both musical instrument and proto-synthesizer. In this regard, the particular sounds of the *suikinkutsu* are even described, with a specific vocabulary, like the attack, sustain, and decay of musical tones: the attack of the first drops caused by the splash of the ladle upsetting the normal water flow, the crescendo of the cataract, and the final diminuendo as the water settles back into its normal trickle. But any description of the *suikinkutsu* must not remain totally abstracted from the broader environment in which it is found, and must be imagined within the soundscape of a Zen temple, with the ambient sounds of the wind, birds, crickets, and so forth, and perhaps even the sudden *clack* of a dear scarer (*shishi odoshi*), a pivoted bamboo tube that slowly fills with water and falls back upon a rock with a sharp sound once the center of gravity is surpassed. This latter device, with its unique sound and constant meter, provides a sort of sonic frame to the more diverse and aleatory sounds of the garden, a single metered beat set against the infinite sonic complexity of the world. Once again, the work of John Cage is useful in grasping these issues in a Western musical context. In the late 1940s, concurrent with his studies under Suzuki, Cage realized that rhythm need not be bound to metrics (i.e., to a sense of temporal regularity):

Rhythm is not at all something periodic and repetitive. It is the fact that something happens, something unexpected, something *irrelevant.*[10]

Rhythm, in its broadest definition, is the temporal relation between any two sound events whatsoever (no matter how many other sounds, or how much silence, or how much time or space, intervenes between the two.) Rhythm has to do with framing rather than counting. Cage's *Williams Mix* (1952) – a micromontage of hundreds of bits of tape from a stock of 600 recordings, all chance-organized and spliced into one-second segments – creates a new sort of polyrhythm: the mathematically regular metrics of the tape montage, with its 1/1 beat of one-second segments, is set in stark contrast against the nearly infinite scope of the microrhythms *within* the one-second segments, determined by the sundry, aleatory events of the recordings. In this context, *Williams Mix* is not so much polyrhythmic as *heterorhythmic*: the metric scansion of the one-second segments is a montage device that establishes a surreal articulation of disparate sites and sounds, each with its own internal rhythm and referential scope, not unlike the 1/1 meter of the *shishi odoshi* as it frames the complex rhythms of the *suikinkutsu* and the rest of the soundscape.

The most famous *suikinkutsu* extant is to be found in the Enkō-ji Temple in Kyoto. However, the changes wrought by modernization – vastly increased ambient noise and intensive tourism – have resulted in a radical transformation of the social and symbolic functions of this instrument as well as of its form. No longer does it offer an occult surprise for the happy few chosen to attend a Tea ceremony, as the guests kneel down in a gesture of ablution to be met with a mysterious aquatic music emanating from the earth; for the vast majority of tourists, it has been turned into the mere curiosity of an unusual musical instrument. The secret, symbolic, esoteric sounds previously linked to the Tea ceremony have been transmogrified into a public sonic event, a new form of music. This change is allegorized by the revised form of the instrument. Previously, the entirety of the *suikinkutsu* was underground, an invisibility that led to astonishment; but now wooden bamboo tubes have been inserted into the echo chamber to amplify and transmit the sound, and this tube system now ironically also serves as a barrier, so that the laver cannot be approached and utilized, reinforced by the fact that the ladle that normally would be laid across the bamboo support spanning the *chozubachi* has been removed. At Enkō-ji the *suikinkutsu* thus loses its surprise effect just as the *chozubachi* is deprived of its purifying function. It is no longer the splashing of the ladle into the water that creates the music, but rather the water's constant flow. We experience modern music, not poetic correspondence.

These sounds can be heard on a beautiful CD released by Steven Feld, *Suikinkutsu* (VoxLox 106, 2006), which begins with the "raw" recording of the sound that lasts 2'41", and continues as a constructed sound environment. Feld describes the sounds:

> i made the recording in august when there was maximum interaction acoustically between the water frequencies and the 2–zemi cicada species that paint all that zzzzzzzzzzz acoustic humidity [...] zzzzzzz is my acoustic memory of aburazemi and kumazemi i think that recording is a bit more dominated by kumazemi zzzzzzzzzz.[11]

The mixing procedure consisted of a Cage-inspired cutup of 17 different lengths sampled from the original raw recording and interwoven onto 8 tracks through a randomizing program, "successfully catching the intensity of the cicadas interacting with the drips, and the relationship between rhythmic random and the suggestion of a dance time."[12]

Since Japanese art and aesthetics are imbued with equivocation and paradox, so too should be our description, rhetoric and criticism, which is why I would like to conclude with the following haiku from one of the classics of Japanese literature, Matsuo Basho's, *The Narrow Road to the Deep North*:[13]

> In the utter silence
> Of a temple,
> A cicada's voice alone
> Penetrates the rocks.

The cicada here replaces humans as music maker, its sound penetrates the earth rather emerging from it, and the massive rock formation before the locked door of the Ryushaku-ji Temple near Obanazawa functions in a manner akin to the *suikinkutsu*. To restore the antinomy, equivocation and paradox between water and stone, one might say that the Ryushaku-ji cicada and the Enkō-ji water sing upon the sonic skins of water and stone, which in Japan may very well be the same thing.

NOTES

[The research for this text was partially funded by a generous grant from The Japan Foundation.]

[1] Cited in David Toop, *Haunted Weather: Music, Silence and Memory* (London: Serpent's Tail, 2004), 46. It was John Cage who first incorporated small sounds, those needing amplification in order to be heard, into music; many contemporary musicians, Japanese and others, are fascinated by sonic extremes, both loud and soft, as discussed in David Toop, *Aether Talk, Ambient Sound and Imaginary Worlds* (London: Serpent's Tail, 1995).

[2] *Ibid*, 46.

[3] Zen, *Illustrations for Designing Mountain, Water, and Hillside Field Landscapes* (15th century), cited in David A. Slawson, *Secret Teachings in the Art of Japanese Gardens: Design Principles, Aesthetic Values* (Tokyo: Kodansha, 1987), 74.

[4] Yoshinobu Yoshinaga, cited in *Secret Teachings*, 74.

[5] Hiroshi Teshigahara, cited in Dore Ashton, *The Delicate Thread* (Tokyo / New York: Kodansha, 1997), 95.

[6] Leonard Bernstein, *The Unanswered Question* (Cambridge, MA: Harvard University Press, 1976), 424. The magnum opus on the chthonic basis of music remains Friedrich Nietzsche, *The Birth of Tragedy* (1872). For a broad assessment of the symbolism of music, see Victor Zuckerkandle, *Sound and Symbol: Music and the External World*, trans. Willard R. Trask (Princeton: Princeton University Press, 1956), and Allen S. Weiss, *Varieties of Audio Mimesis: Musical Evocations of Landscape* (Berlin: Errant Bodies Press, 2008).

[7] Yasunari Kawabata, *Snow Country* (1956), trans. Edward G. Seidensticker (New York: Berkeley Medallion Books, 1960), 127.

[8] Kakuzo Okakura, *The Book of Tea* (1906; New York: Dover, 1964), 35.

[9] Daisetz T. Suzuki, *Zen and Japanese Culture* (New York: MJF Books, 1959), 274.

[10] John Cage interviewed by Daniel Charles, *For the Birds* (Boston: Marion Boyers, 1981), 222.

[11] From two emails to the author.

[12] From a letter to the author dated 30 September 2008.

[13] Matsuo Bashō, *The Narrow Road to the Deep North*, trans. Nobuyuki Yuasa (1694; London: Penguin, 1966), 123.

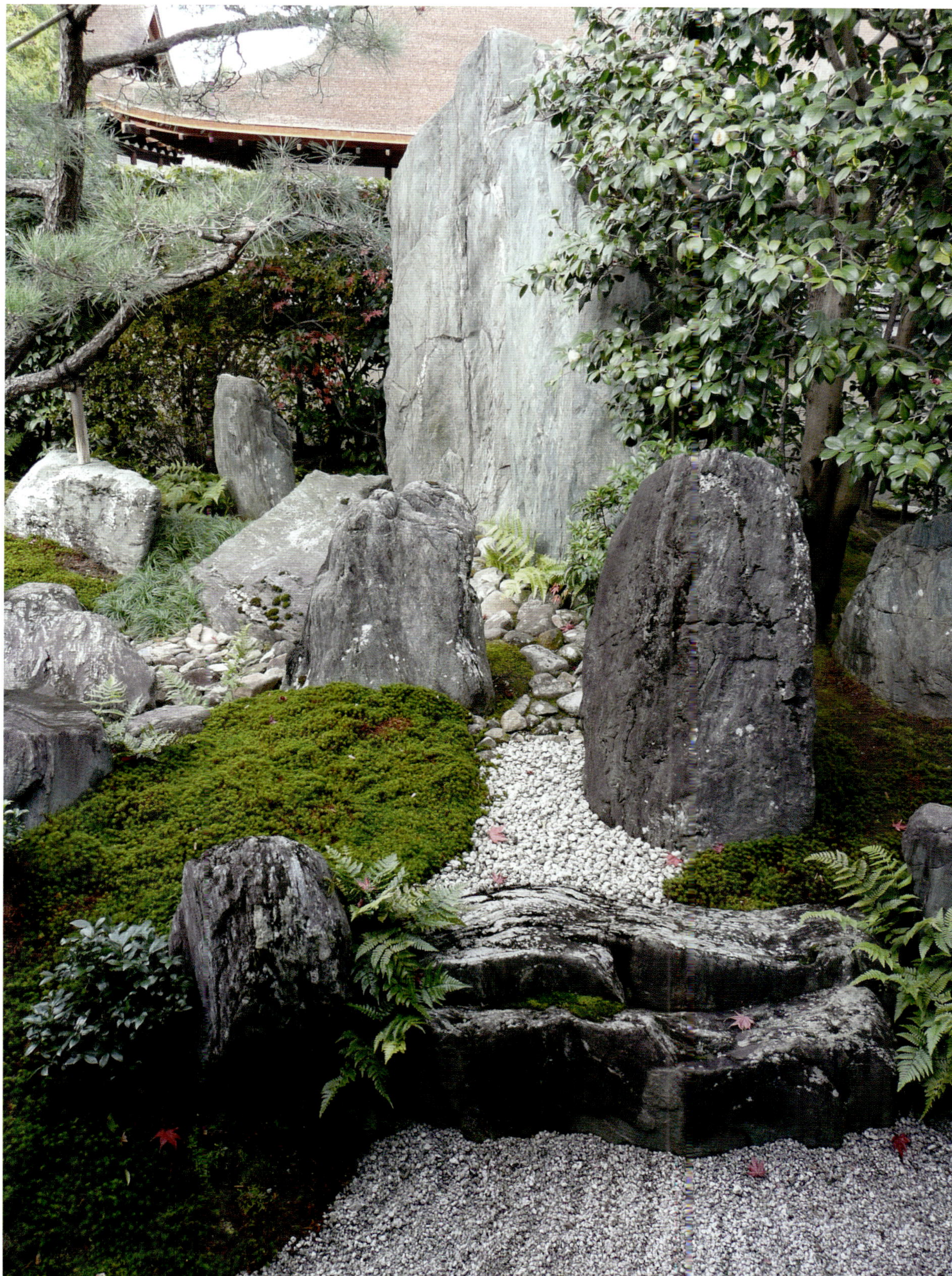

Figure 1: *Obai-in*, Kyoto, 2009.

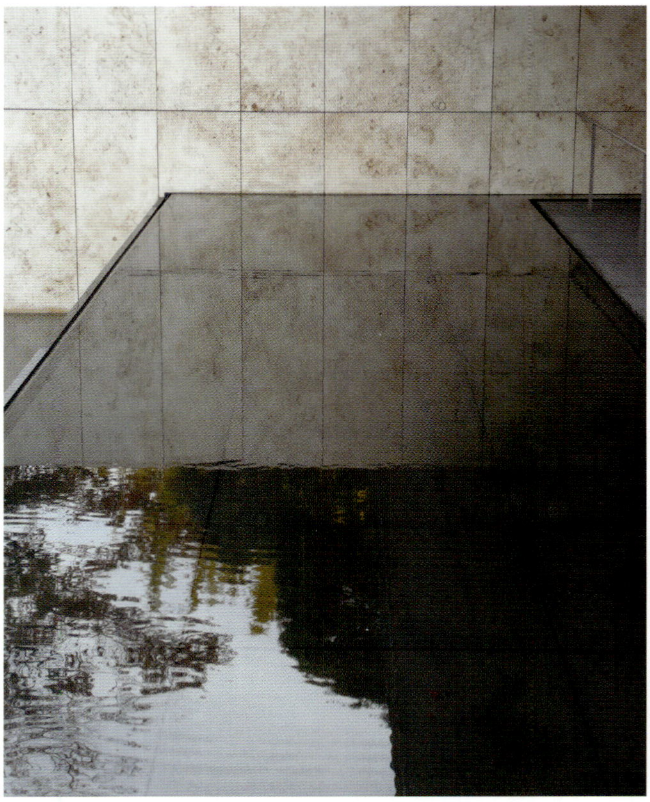

Figure 2: *Fountain of the Kyoto National Museum*, 2009.

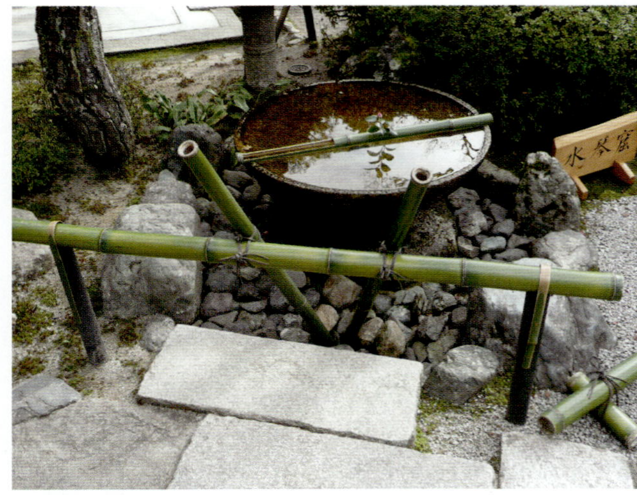

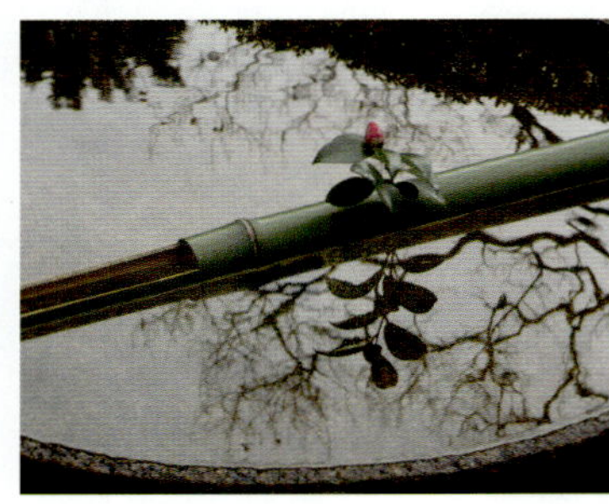

Figure 3/4: *Music-making laver in the garden of the Enkō-ji Temple*, Kyoto, 2009.

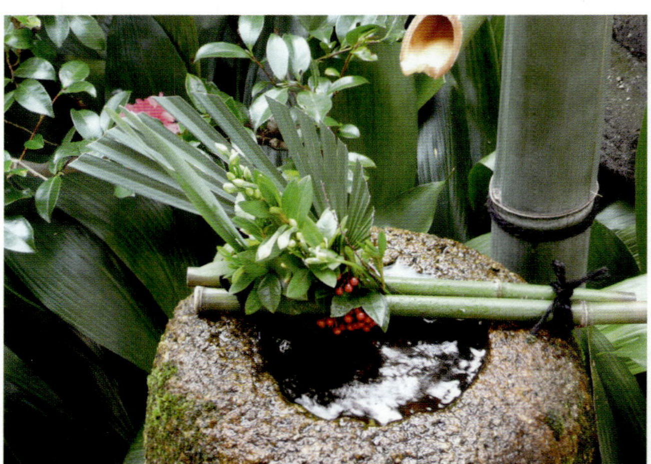

Figure 5: *Laver in the garden of the Sesshu-in Temple*, Kyoto, 2009.

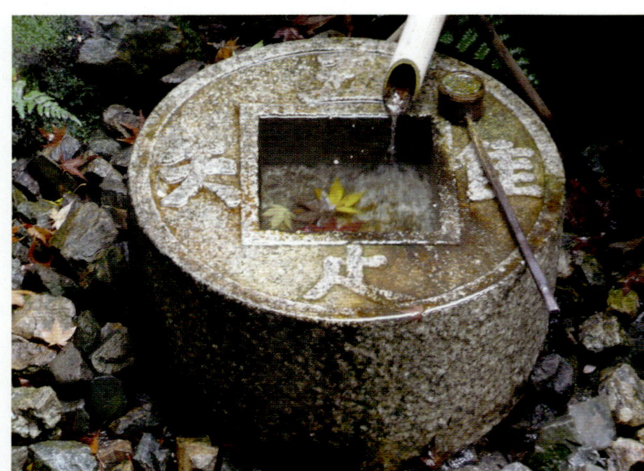

Figure 6: *Laver in the garden of the Ryoan-ji Temple*, Kyoto, 2009.

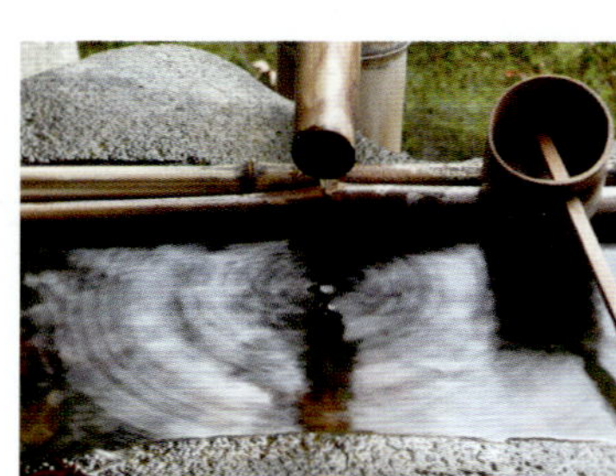

Figure 7: *Laver in the garden of the Kennin-ji Temple*, Kyoto, 2009.
Photos: Allen Weiss.

The foot taps, the hand hits, the knees bend, all of which signal a beginning, a transformation: the body filled with sound, on the verge of movement. I have always been fascinated by dancing – from junior high dances to late night parties, from dance clubs to weddings, these dance events that in their very ordinariness uncover an extraordinary energy: to reassemble the coordinates of the body and its place within particular settings. Yet because of this, dancing also brings forward embarrassment, awkwardness, uncertainty, as if to put on display the very undoing of the bodily form is to overstep, literally, certain limits. Yet the dance emerges, opening a space for inertia, collectivity, laughter and intensity: it transforms not only the gesturing composition of the body, but also, the entire spatial field – from the living room to the auditorium to the abandoned building, the thrust and twist, the gyrations and pivots, come to realign the perception and functionality of a particular place. Dancing may do so according to an energetic triangulation of sound, body and space: it brings these into energetic composition, makes them sweat, as a radical assembly that veers toward excess, collapse, transmutation.

For myself, dancing also dramatically says something about sound and music; it points the way toward a listening that is all-encompassing: the body in the midst of dance is totally propelled by a sonic infiltration; the music, the sound, the sonicity, drives the body into expression, it forces us outward, into a fullness always already on the threshold of oblivion, rapture, pain, love. Our body searches for the beat, it follows the rhythm, this sonic texturing of the air – it refigures itself as pure expenditure, delight, and in doing so, I might suggest, the body becomes sonic: it reaches for the other. Or, the sonic force finds its ultimate residence: to come inside, to resonate within, to break the seams of one's body-form to become uncontrollable, or porous, as a loose network that is extraordinarily intimate.

Such intimacy, such dis-figuring, forms the basis of this work. My idea was to nurture, among friends and strangers, this sonic-body-event: to research the dancing body as an auditory field full of suggestion. Might the dancing body be witnessed as the making of a body-environment, a loosening of the skin so as to become a horizon, a dispersed and ambiguous sensuality? A tender-body on the verge of a mysterious sociality. This in turn led to an interest in capturing the sonic body in sound only – to follow and trace that moment of movement-phenomena, the expenditure and dis-figuring at the heart of dance, the bursting of the body-seams, and to search for a way to render it back into sound: to hear the sonic body as a particular event generated from listening and that seeks its own diffusion, breakdown, climax, noise; where it carries all its built-in personhood, the multiplicities and the differences, the memories and the fantasies, and gives them amplified form, becoming a sort of crowd. Dancing is a search for what one could be.

A series of recording experiments were made throughout 2009 and 2010, inviting a range of participants, each of whom were given the task of dancing while listening to musical tracks of their choosing through headphones. The idea was to capture, through audio recording, the physical movements of each participant, within different settings, and to finally eliminate the musical material altogether from the work so as to concentrate on the moving body as a sound event. These movements may be highlighted as giving supplemental expression to the music heard, as sonic traces refiguring the musical work, embodying it through a radical incorporation: a sort of body-action that searches for points of contact in the music, following the beat while also beating back. May the body in the throes of such hyper-articulations, of burst-seams, expose the energies contained within music, and the dynamics of listening, as sonic forces that are immediately inside and that also find their way back out, through gestures, forms of collective contact, experimental moves? Music as a generative power that ropes the body in while giving it means for reinventing its own formation, for breaking loose with others.

Following these initial recordings of individuals, I was curious to work with different groups of people, some dancers and others not, creating various group situations. To do so, I also changed the conditions: instead of listening to music through headphones, the groups were invited to hear only themselves. Placing microphones throughout a space, the groups were given wireless headphones, thereby enabling them to hear their own actions, the physicality of the space, and to explore their movements as sound events. Aspects of group improvisation, performativity and spatial distribution all became further elements to consider, and to negotiate. The group dynamic also brought forward challenges to the individual ear: for it became increasingly difficult to fully locate one's own sounds or body within this collective and active space of movement and energy. Singularity quickly disappears within the rush and tumble of multiple bodies all resounding in space and against the ear.

As a final elaboration, I worked with additional groups, but this time taking away the headphones and live microphones altogether. The participants were asked to imagine their movements as sound-generating actions: that the movement of the arm, or the leg, were not visual actions to be looked at, but energetic expenditures whose movements extend beyond the body and into the air, as pressures or as a motion of imagined noise. This may open up to the understanding that music, as the instigator of dance, may already exist as an embedded bodily matter: that we are already composed as rhythmic assemblages, full of harmony, dissonance, vibration and melody. Listening may not only be an act directed outward, toward the world, but equally an internal process, of tuning self and surrounding; listening may search for an audible partnering found in the world, to mirror, complement or contrast that which is already within, as interior patterns, imaginings, biologies.

I imagine the sonic body as a sort of total reconfiguration resulting not in any recognizable image or arrested notion of self-hood, but constituting the subject as a noise in motion. The sounds presented here then might be heard as sonic skins thrown off from the full body, shaped and reshaped to form temporary or imaginary identities.

What is this shape, this matter, this expressive agitation? Limbs and appendages, slippery stuff and elegant grace, the wiggly digits and hairy elements? The body is an assemblage of force brought into formal arrangement: and given a name – I am myself.

To start again: I want to say something about how Georges Bataille upholds the big toe as a sign of animality – can I say, "I am my big toe"?

And yet, it disappears ... Or, distraction sets in, as another force, inside; to drift, to become, to change, to alternate, between this and that, you and I: the body is a gathering in whose wake multiple identities quiver, shake, rattle.

Where am I now? Who am I here? To what part of my body may I point to indicate the part of me that is myself? The knee, the breast, the neck? The tongue, the eye, the whisper?

To sketch the shape of a sonic body: where does it begin and where does it end? Its breath surprises me; it sends shivers down my spine; it causes me to dream, and at night, to remember the foghorns in the distance blowing through the darkness.

The sonic body is a splayed body: a big toe on the run? Shape-shifting. Masked. Secret.

To multiply, to fragment: all this gathering of force, that ripples from the inside of the skin, to the outside of the body, wants to burst with noise: a harnessed frequency, a musical assemblage, a measuring of dissonance to which the clouds vibrate on certain days.

To dance.

This is a beginning: a culmination, an arena for the gathering of the splintering of all those forces within, taut, tucked in, and then let loose, to unfurl in mighty thrusts and pivots. Robust. Erotic.

It comes forward – to break the floor, to rend the system, to follow the beat. The Beat: which gathers all the gathered force into another shape, aligning inside and out, you and I. My big toe follows the beat. It leads the way: this is its place.

Quiver. Shake. Rattle.

We are in a field: there is no grass here, though, no trees, or horizon. It is a field nonetheless: a field made in the moment of its agitation, its breaking, its occupation. The body washes over this space, it lays itself out, sprawling, piercing. It makes a field of this space, draw-ing lines across it, animating its emptiness with sweat, fidgeting against its seams.

The body becomes an environment, unfurled. Unmasked. It unfolds as a sonic body: the beginning of its charged potential. Elegant. Fantasy-Machine.

It pounds out a message: to make a culture.

From the curve of this line to the push of that movement, all the rhythms distribute themselves as points of contact: to diffuse, to reach out, to bring all surfaces into animation.

The lines grow fuzzy, the floor starts to quake, the tongue wags about – we enter a darkness full of light, a beginning that is also an end, a horizon looped back on itself; to become a new city.

Urban center. Solar anus. Pirate ships.

Oceanic, rubbing raw the edges of architecture, supplanting your perspective for his, their language for ours: multiplicity in the mouth, in the pores, circling around the ear.

Might the sonic body resound as a new kind of laughter? An emancipation of total dissonance?

Laughter from the mouth of the body.

Where am I now? Who is this gathering of matter? Particle and breath, spittle and sadness, longing, brushing, scratching and searching. A discourse of the scratch: what is that under the skin? All that uneasiness. Restless.

A feverish topography. Glowing.

To fall into the floor. To meld with the wall. To break with the breaking beat. Music might be thought of as the making of a new nervous system. A body-machine. A thought-patterning. Emotional geography. Inside and outside: hot breath.

My finger falls off. Your knee buckles. Quiver. Shake. Rattle.

To begin again, not with the big toe, but with the big ear: as membrane stretched and poked, a fluid flesh wrapped around, this collection of matter, and which resonates and flexes under the pushing and pulling of so much input and force. Like a sky.

Shivering with energy.

Your vibration changes the entire scene: I feel it over here.

The big ear falls all over the place – we stumble over it; we pick it up, toss it over the shoulder, pass it around. It becomes a new symbol, a body-narrative filling the imagination with new fantasy.

And back again, ducking underground, down the stairs, through this passage, and then inside, a forgotten space to be filled with a community with no name: like a new skin, wrapped everywhere.

To carry it along, to take it off, to make a tongue or a shoulder from its material.

I resonate, you vibrate, he echoes, she interferes, the other transmits, while they there start to receive, and the space is put on loop, and static is in the ceiling and the floor already in my shoe, as a voluptuous splinter.

I know this song, I have heard it before: that particular thwack, and melody, there, there it is – it finds its way into my heart, as a resonating caress, a driving thrust, making all the quivering matter of the emotional life quiver all the more: the skin unfolds in a river of soft energy, up and down, along the back of the neck, those words ringing across my chest as a shuddering lyric: to draw out all the fevers of longing, memory, or simply, the happiness found at the base of possible pleasure.

And you start to sing: lips pursed against the mysterious tangibility of all that is heard, following the words from another, as all that vocal force locked into the cascade of that song – I follow your lips as they follow those words, like an echo that never stops, to create new rivers and valleys, new fevers and dreams.

Primitive force. The disruption and ultimate bond of the surge of this and that.
The drum in the leg, the song in the tongue.
A globe of rapture.

The "k" or the "th" of the body-electric.

Eating the ear of the other.
The matter at hand is the matter already in the hand, in the foot, and along the walls: as matter no longer held but let go, to move between all these hands and feet, to collect and generate, like an immaterial vehicle taking shape suddenly, to foster new vocabularies of new identities that have also already been here before: to finally form what has always been formlessly circulating within.

The house starts to shake.

Willful anger, soft rapture, to break, to unfold, to destroy or to gather: the throng is a public emerging from so many private particles and breaths, here in the tide and flux of another beat, to drive the beat from within toward a without, to find the other, there too, as a beating longing, or a heart on the skin. Hold my breath in your shoe.

In your sweat.

FIGURES 1 – 12 (PROJECT RECORDINGS)

Figure 1:
movement in a concrete room
listening to "Diddle Li Di" by Suzi Hyldgaard
recorded on a spring afternoon with a single microphone held close to the participant

Figure 2:
same participant in the same space
listening to the same music
with the addition of a found piece of carpeting placed on the floor

Figure 3:
movement in a small room
listening to "Transmission" by Joy Division
recorded late evening

Figure 4:
movement in a quiet home
listening to "I Get Around" by the Beach Boys
recorded on a winter's evening

Figure 5:
movement in an extremely small empty space
listening to "Circular" by Hildur Gudnadottir
recorded afternoon

Figure 6:
movement in a concrete space with large windows overlooking a harbor
listening to "El Gran Varón" by Willie Colón
recorded on an ordinary day

Figure 7:
movement of a participant wearing multiple articles of clothing
listening to "Mani" by Paco Fernandez
recorded at night in a dark apartment hallway

Figure 8:
movement in an open light-filled studio
listening to "Young Man" by Epaksa
recorded privately by the participant

Figure 9:
movement in a cramped room
listening to "Ray of Light" by Madonna
recorded on a rainy morning

Figure 10:
movement of a group of five participants in a sound studio with carpeting
listening to "Can't Get Enough of Your Love" by Barry White
recorded early evening

Figure 11:
group action recorded in a large theater space with multiple participants
listening through wireless headphones to microphones located in the space
recorded in total darkness

Figure 12:
group action recorded in a small dance space with multiple participants
listening to the acoustic energies of their own movements
recorded in absolute brightness
note: the group was given the verbal instructions to stay together while trying to separate

Recordings included on the accompanying CD:
Figures 1/2/6/7/12

TRIKOTON. THE VOICE KNITTING COLLECTION / FROM VOICE PATTERN TO KNITTING PATTERN

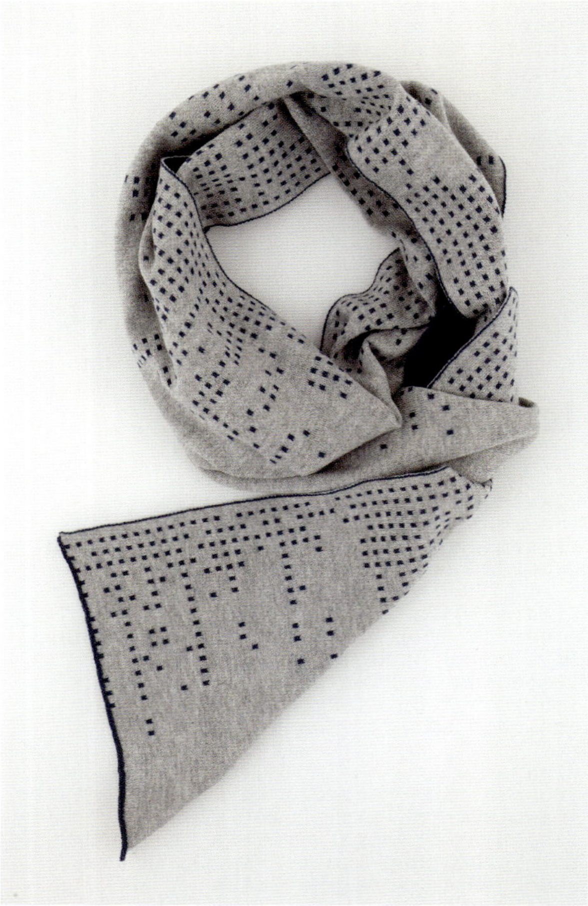

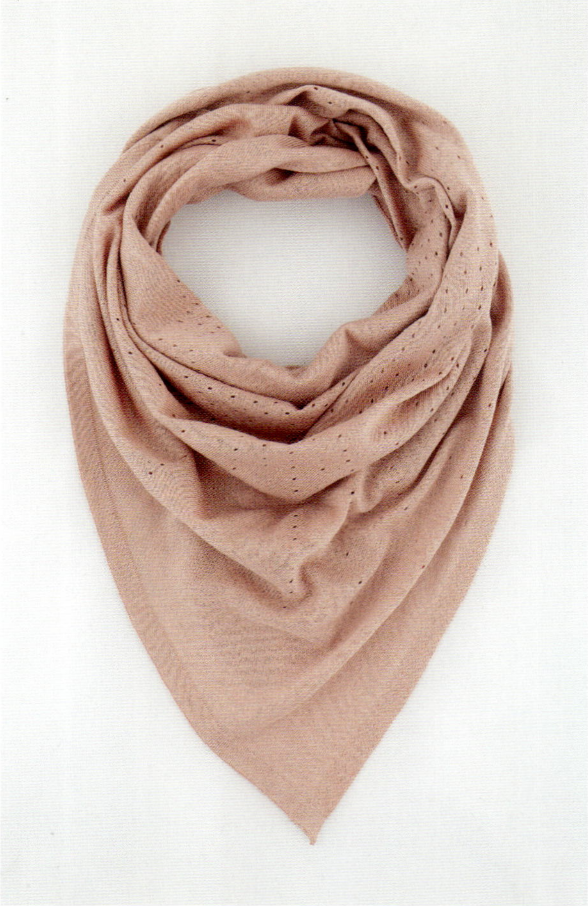

How does it feel when your pullover becomes a device for recording your own voice?

The focus of the project label TRIKOTON is on dealing with the human voice and its various methods of recording and producing sounds, as well as the connections between the voice, the act of speaking and the body. This entails integrating voices into the medium of clothing, leading to the creation of a new "recording aesthetic".

Modern media technologies have led to the human voice becoming increasingly distanced from the speaker's body, and often completely detached from the speaker's expressions and gestures when being transmitted or recorded. And yet we still automatically imagine the image of the person speaking when we hear a voice. If we know who is speaking, we picture the missing face and body in our head. And if we don't, then our own memories assist our imagination in providing the voice with a skin and "dressing" it. Sometimes we are subsequently amazed at what the speaker actually looks like when we finally see them, and realize that the friendly face doesn't at all fit to the scratchy, hard voice we've heard. Everyone has their own individual intonation, with accents, breaks and rough edges which distinguish their voice from others, making it unique. Our vocal fingerprint is at the same time linked to characteristics such as softness, hysteria, weariness, warmth or monotony, which we can, up to a point, influence and shape according to what is being said. These emotions and associations evoked by the voice are what help us navigate through the day's confusion of sounds, and which also allow us to recognize voices through these acoustic signals.

The project label TRIKOTON records this personal vocal code and converts it into knitting patterns, and, in a further step, to items of clothing. Knitting as an activity has always been closely linked to storytelling and communication through knitting circles, and punch-card driven knitting machines and weaving chairs were precursors of the earliest computers. In the installation GELSOMINA, created for the 2007 Ars Electronica, TRIKOTON combined computer and textile technologies in a surprising manner. The interactive knitting machine GELSOMINA combines speaking and knitting in real-time: the punch-card slot of an old mechanical knitting machine was replaced by 24 small motors, which receive the binary knitting code directly from a computer. Spoken audio messages materialize in the textile's pattern.

The link to clothing is a new approach to the connection between the speaker and the body – the identity of the voice is captured in a new medium, one which the body requires to express itself. In this way the voice is reconnected with the speaker's body.

At the same time, our clothing is also a language through which we daily express, design, isolate or integrate ourselves in a social context. TRIKOTON takes its theme of communication via clothing to a further level, the acoustic – here the material from which the clothing is made becomes itself a recording medium for the voice. The characteristics of each individual's intonation are reflected in the diverse forms the pattern takes, and form a second skin over the speaker's body, enabling a new visual and haptic experience of the creative quality of the voice.

THE URBAN BOOK OF PROPHET GENTILEZA – SCRIPTURE OF THE SELF AND THE CITY

Leonardo Guelman

In the second half of the last century, Brazil produced one of the country's greatest popular figures: the Prophet Gentileza. José Datrino – the name on his birth certificate – was born on 11th April 1977 in Cafelândia, a country town in the State of São Paulo, where he lived until his teenage years. From childhood, José was seen by his family as an odd child who foresaw that one day he was to fulfil his mission in the world. He was raised in a rural environment, helping his parents and 10 siblings cultivate the land, but at 19 years of age he decided to leave the countryside – against his family's wishes – and move to the big city.

He first arrived in São Paulo, later moving on to Rio de Janeiro, where he had a family and founded a small cargo transport firm. It was during this stage that signs of his life's mission began to manifest themselves. Living in the suburbs, married with 5 children, his lifestyle reached a point of crisis. According to his daughter Maria Alice's testimony, one day, after the visit of an individual who wanted to become his business partner, her father ran into the backyard, released the birds from their cages and covered himself in soil. Whilst this action was sculpting a different man, his family saw it as an act of madness. But José Datrino's real calling was his response to a horrendous tragedy in the city of Niterói, in the State of Rio de Janeiro, where approximately 500 people died due to a fire at a popular circus.

Prophet Gentileza's myth-poetics was born from this episode. Six days after the fire, which took place on 17th December 1961, José was called upon by voices emanating from the stars pleading for him to leave the material world behind and live in the spiritual world. The departure point for his mission was the site of the burned circus. José Datrino, who after this revelation became Prophet Gentileza, started his mission by comforting those who had lost their loved ones and approached the tragedy site in desperation. At the time, Gentileza wrote a verse that said: "It was once said that the world would come to an end and so it has. The defeat of the charred circus in Niterói is the representation of a world, because the world is round and the circus is round."

The world-circus in Niterói formed Gentileza's prophetic foundation. It was also on that desolate site that his designation as the Prophet of Kindness emerged from the ashes of a "world's end". After remaining for four years at the site of the fire, in an effort to purify both himself and the place, which he transformed into a garden, the Prophet started to wander the streets of Rio de Janeiro spreading his word as a reforming Prophet. He embarked on the defence of moral ethics and codes during the heyday of the hippies and of miniskirts.

However, the prophetic nature of Gentileza started to show its signs beyond his quaintness. As prophets do, he accused the world and proposed an alternative. In his case, his enthusiasm led him to condemn a crisis in human relations marked by "Devil-ism". He explained: "The word Capeta – the devil in Portuguese – comes from capital, cold hard cash makes the devil a devilish fiend and this is why humanity has gone wrong ..."

The alternative proposed by the Prophet was reflected in his words and writings, announcing his maxim: Kindness Breeds Kindness. According to Leonardo Boff, Gentileza was criticising – in the realm of popular culture – the paradigm of the domination of capital, intuitively pointing towards a new paradigm as the expression of a social ecology animating new ways of living. This is still our contemporary challenge.

Self-aestheticisation

Throughout the 35 years of his life's mission, the Prophet aestheticised everything he addressed spiritually. It was impossible to remain indifferent to his arrival or approach. As an allegory of himself, or even a mobile circus, carrying a plethora of hanging knickknacks, Gentileza stood out from the landscape in all his joy.

Several elements came together in the visual arrangement that composed his figure. Like a walking knight, he carried a profusion of accessories: a standard full of attachments – flowers, flags and weathercocks; a cape

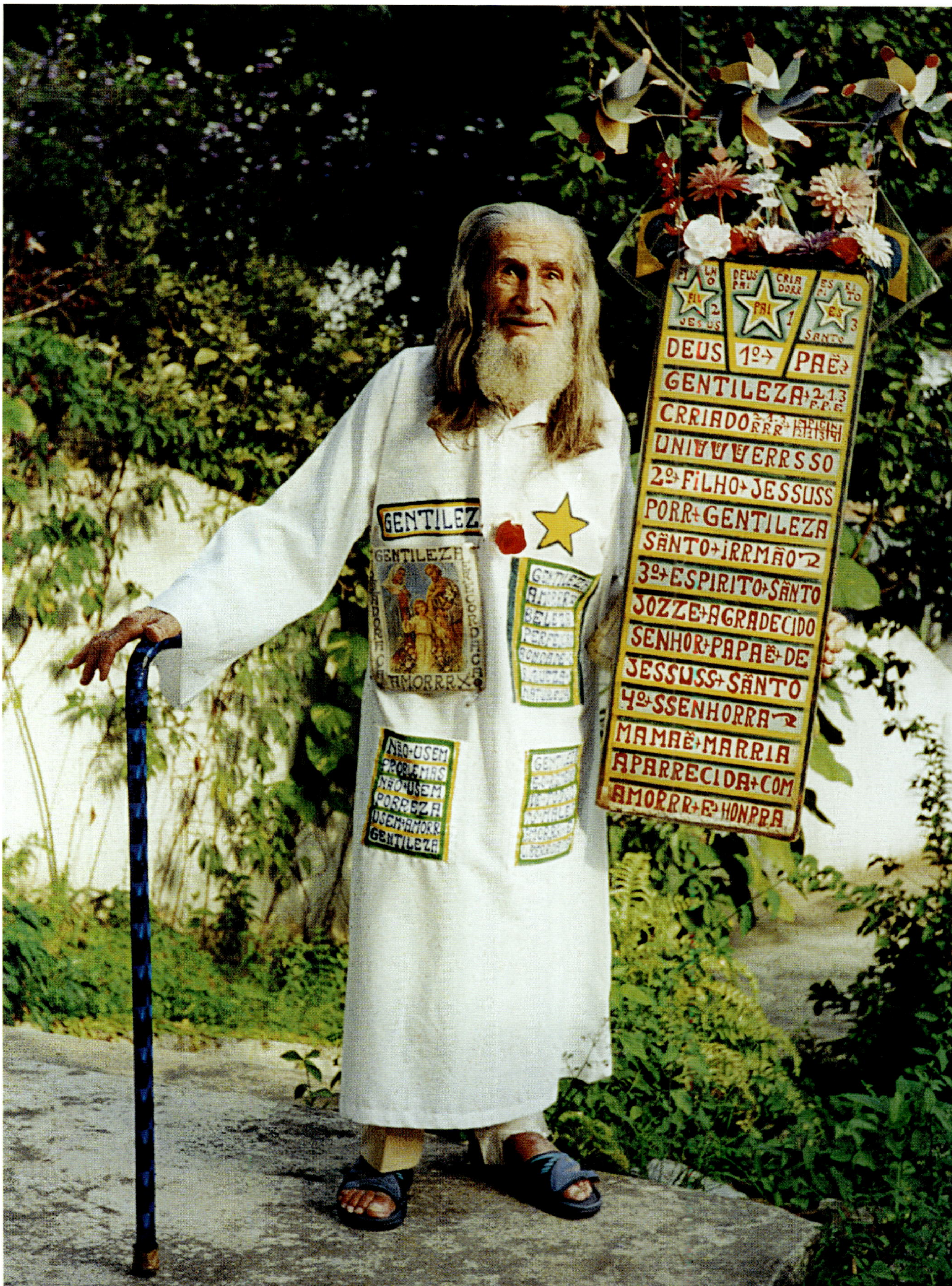

Fig. 1: *Prophet Gentileza*. Photo: Leonardo Guelman.

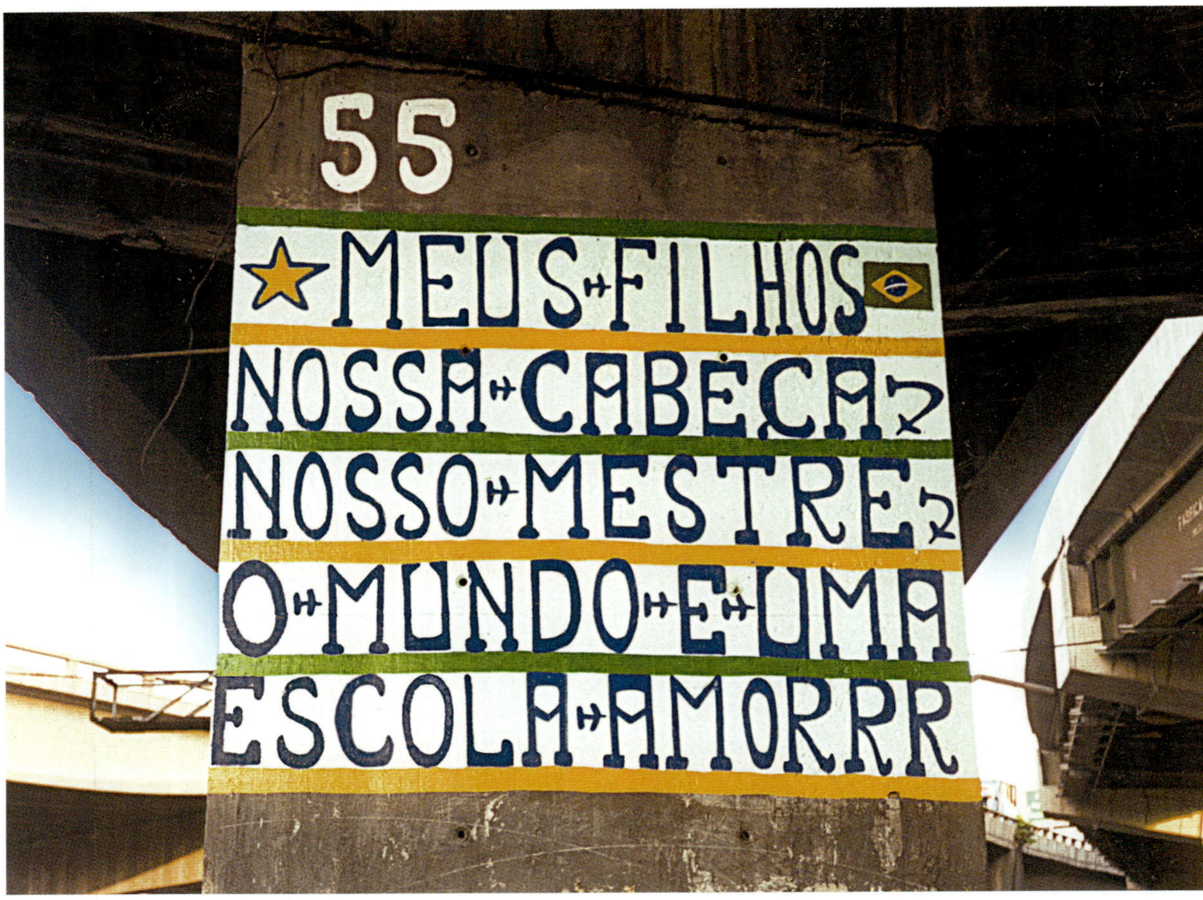

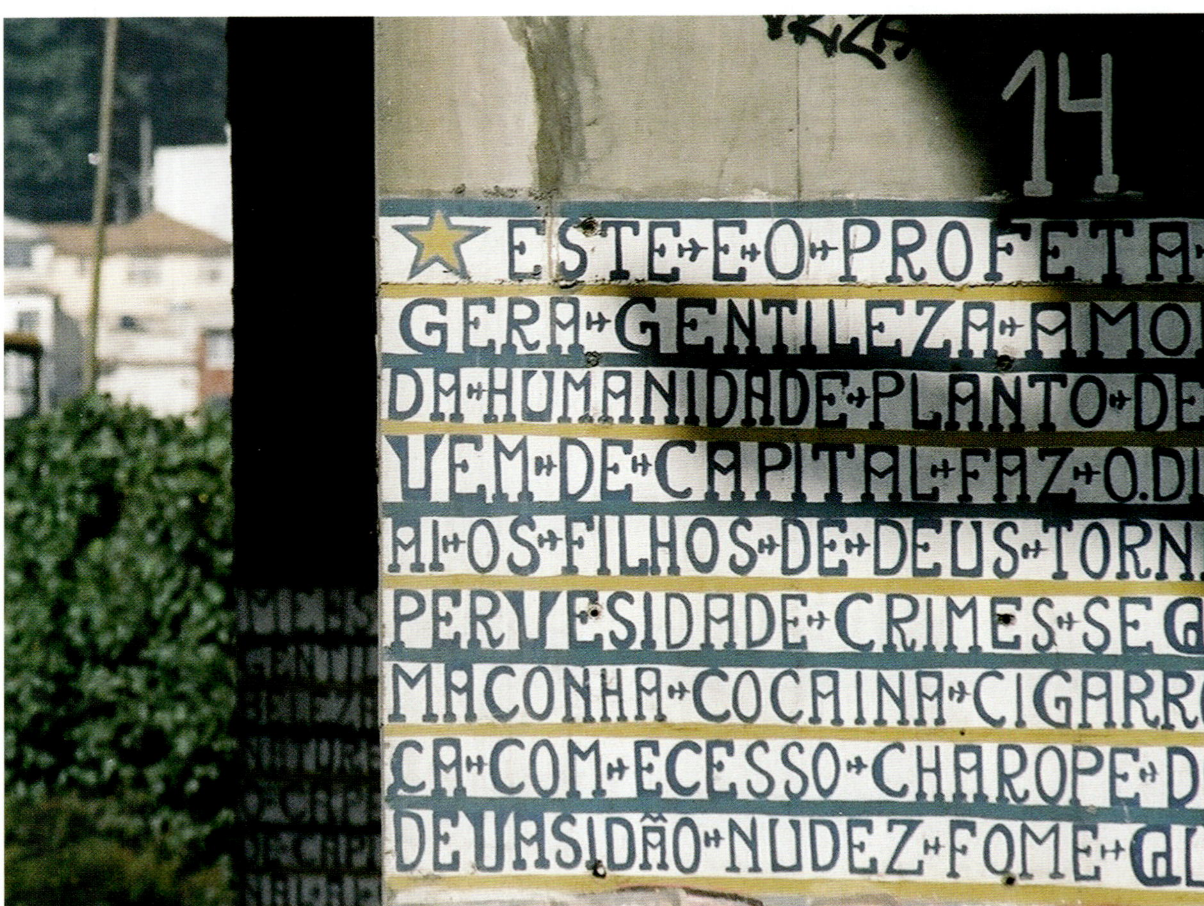

Fig. 2 – 3: *Pilastra 55* & *Pilastra 14* by Prophet Gentileza, Rio de Janeiro. Photos: Leonardo Guelman.

with pockets covered in inscriptions; shoes and a palm leaf. Through his appearance, Gentileza not only spoke about himself but also about universal religious values. Foucault's "aesthetics of existence" as the affirmation of ethics gained clear colours and shapes with Gentileza. His set of visual arrangements – his bricolage – expressed a synthesis of the principles adopted and conducted by him. His garments became the body of his symbolisation. Gentileza was both conductor and protector of his ethics, which also takes us back to the original meaning of ethos as *abode*.

The Graphic Invention of Gentileza

By becoming the bearer of kindness, the Prophet began to talk and write by means of a language of revelation. His writings therefore became a sacred expression, formally distinct from the usual profane language. The re-insertion of José Datrino (Gentileza) into this world is realised through the revelation and intuition of his ethical religious UNIVVVERRSS, which is the expression of an incipient language in which the Prophet draws on religious symbols that capture our attention because of the signs it uses and the addition of extra letters in words. This unique way of presenting itself marks the appropriation of a Trinitarian and Quaternarian symbolism developed by Gentileza in his language: the UNIVVVERRSS is the joint creation of S/F/S (Son, Father and Spirit) in the VVV and the double participation in RR and SS. The same would happen with LOVVVE to which he also referred: "material love is written with one V and universal love is written with three Vs".

Gentileza created an absolutely unique orthography. Like a typographer, he drew the words letter by letter, which were placed in a sequence of lines marking their boundaries. The text's internal movement was maintained by arrows or birds/planes that rejoined the words and generated a textual itinerary. The use of birds as a symbol (which also alludes to the representation of the holy spirit as a dove) spiritually reconnected his whole message. As Antônio Vieira suggested, when talking about holy writing more than four centuries ago: "feathers were taken from the wings of the holy dove".

The Prophet and Rio de Janeiro

The Prophet believed that Rio de Janeiro, with its tropical image, represented the national image. It was in Rio that a man from the countryside realised the antagonisms of the world. The city, beautiful by NATURE, gave back to the Prophet the belief in nature's WEALTH "that gives us everything for free". However, the big city, rapidly growing right in front of his eyes, crowded with intersected overpasses, also revealed the forces of the "Capital Devil". This was the space of contradiction where the need for kindness was revealed. By establishing a close identity with the city, the Prophet would say: "All the goodness in the world will come from Rio de Janeiro, Brazil, because the Prophet Gentileza is Brazilian."

The Prophet therefore identified the possibility of the "Marvellous City" of Rio de Janeiro being illuminated by his own destiny: a prognosis increasingly more untimely in a time when kindness was in exile. However, beyond the ferociousness of the metropolis, the unstoppable competition in which the Capital Devil shows his teeth, the Prophet was faced with the stupidity and indifference of those who lived there. All of his gestures in the big city were a response to this symptom. He was compelled to speak to the city, show and reveal himself to people; he had to touch them with his message. His street man feature was accentuated and the public space became the stage for his actions, as he moved constantly throughout the city.

His relationship with public space was always a performance. He appeared in different places and built an independent history followed by the press. He knew how to draw on the unusual and the new, which is what the press feeds on daily. However, the real difference lay beyond that, because to a certain extent he was the creator of his own media.

He began to experiment with intervention, using his writings in the city environment. Right at the start, his greatest accomplishment was his posters. He would post signs or stick large banners in the city as a different kind of advertisement. At this point, his main space of intervention was Avenida Brasil, a major road in Rio de Janeiro. As a former truck driver he had learned how to deal with road signs. His first signs and inscriptions were very aware of the drivers' angle of vision. His writing was slowly extended and started to establish a greater dialogue with the landscape itself. His language and aesthetics gained strength and expression. It was only when Gentileza tamed his desire to travel around Brazil that he was able to devote himself to the major writings of his body of work.

Gentileza's Urban Book

The early 1990s marked the period of his greatest intervention in Rio's urban landscape. The Prophet's place of choice between Novo Rio Bus Terminal and the Caju Cemetery – which covered approximately one mile – represented the city's entrance gate, the "ground zero" of Avenida Brasil. And given the universal content of his work, the Prophet was writing from Rio de Janeiro to the world.

At this point, Gentileza started working on his 56 murals by writing on the columns underneath the Caju Overpass. His spelling and symbols, which were already present on the standard he carried and on the signs he produced earlier, were now inscribed on the city itself, turning the overpass column into his teaching boards. The Prophet painted directly onto the concrete surface in his attempt to make his message permanent. However, even at that moment, his writings were regularly removed, forcing him to rewrite them over and over again. But in the end his everyday persistence and dedication prevailed.

By painting the columns the Prophet established a new emotional link with the city of Rio de Janeiro. A great number of people followed him in his daily endeavours. Once again, his intervention surprised people, spotlighting his aesthetics and his message. The extent and the body of his work are equally striking. His work was previously planned in a sketchbook in the form of manuscripts. Nothing was random. The reading followed the flow of cars and was curiously presented with an inverted numbering. The book "starts" on column 55, stating the Prophet's understanding that "THE WORLD IS A SCHOOL AND OUR HEAD IS THE MASTER", and opens itself up to the ceiling by opposing KINDNESS and FAVOUR, which he denounces as being an exchange of interests linked to the "Capital Devil".

His themes unfold and culminate on column 1, next to Novo Rio Bus Terminal, with the passage "GRRREEN IS LIFE" and "WELCOME TO RIO". Each one of his murals does not present an end in itself as an isolated picture; they only make sense in the proposed sequence of reading. In addition, pictures are not framed, allowing you to read from one column to the other, therefore transposing the message and contents from one to the other.

This work is a reference book containing Gentileza's basic principles. It is an Urban Book where each column is a page that can be read through the windows of vehicles that continuously drive by. At the start of the 1990s, once his work was completed, Gentileza used to stay next to column number 1 seated on a chair, waving at everyone as if he were on his own balcony.

There's a final aspect of his work that is worth mentioning. Gentileza's efforts were aimed at the humanisation of life in the contemporary city. For the Prophet, cities marked by violence and by the indifference of their inhabitants were a world to be restored. This is exactly what he did with the place where the circus once stood in Niterói and the overpasses in Caju, Rio de Janeiro. Through the ashes and the smoke of the megalopolis' flyovers, in its most inhospitable and desolate places, the man from Cafelândia made his exalted "announcement" in blue letters and green and yellow banners. The perspective of a simple man – based on his experience of reality and Brazilian culture – was established as a fundamental counterpoint to a lifestyle that involves us all. KINDNESS BREEDS KINDNESS, shouts the Prophet through his writings in Rio de Janeiro.

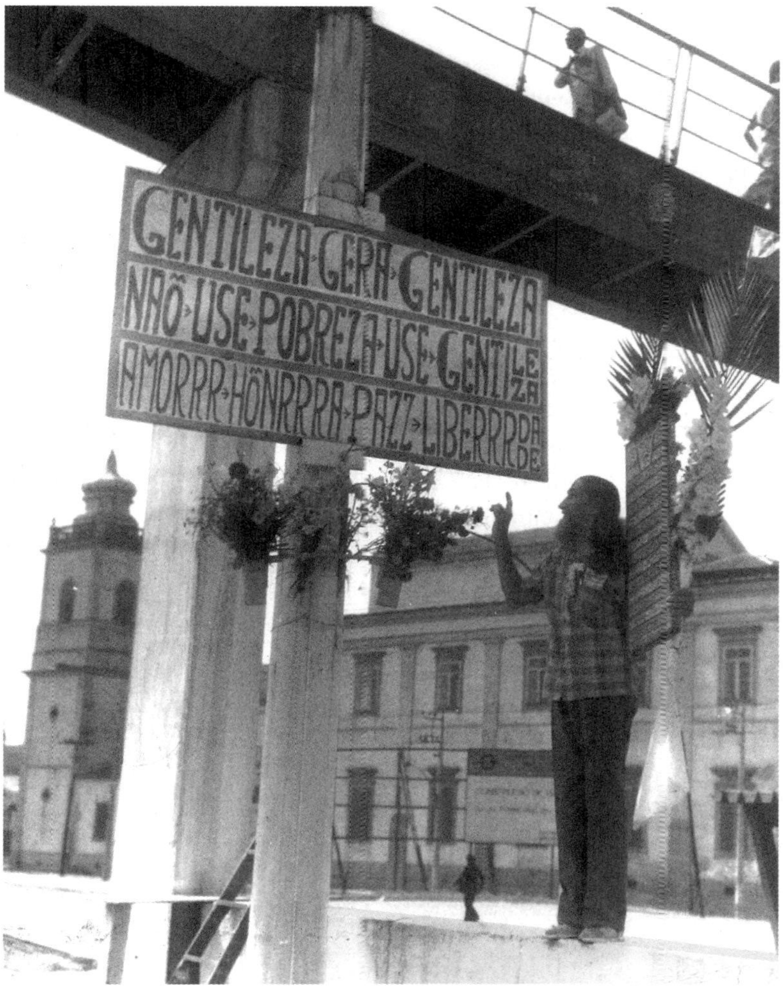

Fig. 4:
Prophet Gentileza, Avenida Brasil, Rio de Janeiro.

Fig. 5:
Sequences of Pilastras by Prophet Gentileza,
Rio de Janeiro.

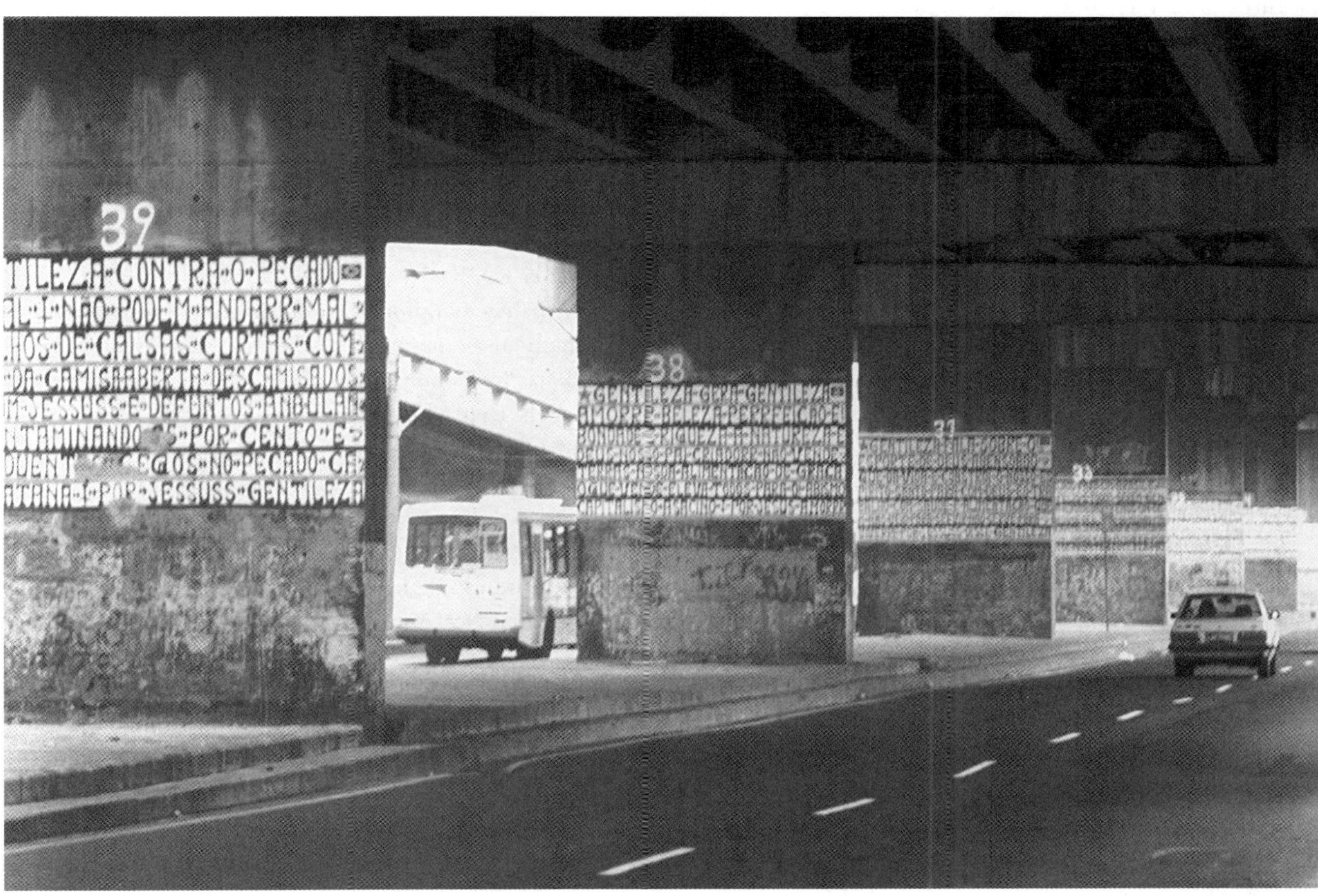

MARIA JOSÉ ARJONA
is a performance artist focused on affirming the body through long durational exercises addressing process, time, memory and power. Her performances have been exhibited in museums and galleries in South America, Europe, China and the United States. She participated as a re-performer at Marina Abramovic's retrospective at The Museum Of Modern Art in New York and started touring with her own work at The Madre Museum in Naples (Italy) as part of the program *Corpus, Arte In Azione.*

JANET BEIZER
is Professor of Romance Languages and Literatures at Harvard University, where she teaches nineteenth and twentieth-century French literature and cultural studies. She is currently working on the fugue epidemic in France at the turn of the nineteenth-century, and on the travel writer Alexandra David-Neel. Her publications include *Thinking through the Mothers: Reimagining Women's Biographies* (Cornell University Press, 2009), *Ventriloquized Bodies: Narratives of Hysteria in Nineteenth-Century France* (Cornell University Press, 1994), and *Family Plots: Balzac's Narrative Generations* (Yale University Press, 1986).

DE GEUZEN
is a foundation for multi-visual research and the collaborative identity of Riek Sijbring, Femke Snelting and Renée Turner. Since 1996 they have employed a variety of tactics to explore female identity, narratives of the archive and media image ecologies. Exhibitions, workshops and online projects operate as thematic framing devices where the group investigates and tests ideas collectively with different publics. Characterizing what they do as research, their work is open-ended and values processes of exchange and critical interrogation.

PAUL DICKINSON
is an American sound artist and Zen Shiatsu practitioner. He is particularly interested in the physical and psychic spaces where these two diverse practices overlap: how the body listens and responds to environments both immediate and reconstructed, and how that act of listening can affect the healing process. His previous works have included "Sleep Talk", a collection of his sleep talk utterances collected over 20 years, and "Music for Worms and Compost", a sound installation based on amplified sounds from worm composting bins. His work has been presented at the Museum of Contemporary Art in Chicago and many galleries and institutions in the US and Europe.

MLADEN DOLAR
is a Slovenian philosopher, cultural theorist, film critic and expert in psychoanalysis. He was the co-founder, together with Slavoj Žižek and Rastko Močnik, of the Ljubljana school of psychoanalysis. He has taught at the University of Ljubljana since 1982. In 2010 Dolar began his tenure as an Advising Researcher in theory at the Jan Van Eyck Academie, Maastricht, The Netherlands. His main fields of expertise are the philosophy of G. W. F. Hegel and French structuralism. His publications in English include *Opera's Second Death* (with Slavoj Žižek), Routledge 2001, and *A Voice and Nothing More*, MIT 2006.

LEIF ELGGREN
is a Swedish artist. His work has been shown in Venice (Nordic Pavilion, Biennale di Venezia 2001 and 2003), Stockholm (Fargfabriken), Berlin (Podewil, NK), Johannesburg (2nd Biennial), Siena (Palazzo delle Papesse), etc. His music has been released through labels such as Ash International (London), Firework Edition Records (Stockholm) or Insofar Vapour Bulk (Moscow). Over the years, he has collaborated with artists such as C. M. von Hausswolff, Lotta Melin, Charlotte Engelkes and Tetsuo Furudate.

STEVEN FELD
is a musician, filmmaker, and anthropologist who teaches at the University of New Mexico and University of Oslo. His anthropology of sound research and recording has focused on Papua New Guinea, Southern Europe, Japan, and West Africa. His most recent book is *Jazz Cosmopolitanism in Accra* (Duke University Press). He is director of VoxLox documentary art, www.voxlox.net.

LEONARDO GUELMAN
is Professor of the Department of Arts of the Federal University of Niterói and Master in Philosophy from the University of Rio de Janeiro. His extensive research about Gentileza, that covers a period of two decades, was reprinted in the publication *UNIVVVERRSSO GENTILEZA*, by Editora Mundo das Idéias.

ANISH KAPOOR
is a British sculptor of Indian birth. He exhibits internationally at venues such as the Tate Gallery and Hayward Gallery in London, Kunsthalle Basel, Haus der Kunst Munich, Deutsche Guggenheim in Berlin, Reina Sofia in Madrid, MAK Vienna, and the ICA Boston. He represented Britain in the XLIV Venice Biennale in 1990, when he was awarded the Premio Duemila Prize. In 1991 he received the Turner Prize. Notable public sculptures include Cloud Gate, Millennium Park, Chicago, and Sky Mirror at the Rockefeller Center, New York.

BRANDON LABELLE
is an artist and writer working with sound, performance and sited constructions. His work has been featured worldwide, at IMT Gallery (London), Sonic Acts (Amsterdam), A/V Festival (Newcastle), Museums-Quartier/Tonspur, (Vienna), 7th Bienal do Mercosul (Porto Allegro), Netherlands Media Art Institute (Amsterdam), Center for Cultural Decontamination (Belgrade), Casa Vecina (Mexico City), etc. He is the author of *Background Noise: Perspectives*

on Sound Art (Continuum, 2006) and *Acoustic Territories: Sound Culture and Everyday Life* (Continuum, 2010), as well as editor of Errant Bodies Press, Berlin. He is currently Professor in New Media at the Bergen National Academy of the Arts, Norway.

ANDRÉ LEPECKI

is an author and curator and one of the leading theoreticians who view performance as a political act in the field of tensions of post-structuralism, anthropology and post-colonialism. His widely-read treatise *Exhausting Dance* (translated into 6 languages) deals with the subversive potential of works by choreographers such as Vera Mantero and Xavier Le Roy and calls for closer exchanges between artistic practice and theoretical reflection. He is Associate Professor at the Department of Performance Studies at New York University.

DAVID LOCKE

is an ethnomusicologist specializing in the traditional music and dance of Africa, especially Ghana. He is the author of the African chapter in the textbook *Worlds of Music*, and three books of theory, documentation and instruction published by White Cliffs Media (*Drum Gahu* 1988, *Drum Damba* 1990, *Kpegisu* 1992). His doctoral dissertation is about the Ewe masterwork *Atsiagbekor* (Wesleyan University 1979). Locke's 35 year study of Dagomba music with Alhaji Abubakari Lunna has culminated in a website of audio, text, and staff notation (http://dagomba.uit.tufts.edu). He is an Assistant Professor in the Music Department at Tufts University.

PETRA MARIA MEYER

is Professor of Cultural and Media Studies at the Muthesius Academy of Fine Arts and Design in Kiel. Among other things, she has been active as an editor, playwright and author for the "Studio Akustische Kunst" at WDR, Cologne and has held various professorships for theater, film and television studies. Media aesthetics of the voice is one of her main fields of research for nearly twenty years. Among her books are *Die Stimme und ihre Schrift* (1993), *Gedächtniskultur des Hörens* (1997) and *Intermedialität des Theaters* (2001). In 2006 she published the book *Performance im medialen Wandel*, and in 2007 *Acoustic Turn*.

JÜRGEN PARTENHEIMER

is an internationally acclaimed artist. His work emerged in Germany in the 1980s and is distinguished by a minimal abstraction. He participated in the Paris Biennial, the Venice Biennial and the São Paulo Biennial. Among others his work was included in exhibitions at The Museum of Modern Art, New York; National Gallery, Washington; San Francisco Museum of Modern Art; The Singapore Art Museum; Gulbenkian Foundation, Lisbon; Fondacion Miró, Barcelona; Museum of Contemporary Art, Madrid; Museum Ludwig, Cologne and the National Gallery of Art Berlin.

NAOMI SEGAL

is Professorial Fellow at Birkbeck, University of London. From 2004 to 2011 she was founding Director of the Institute of Germanic & Romance Studies; before that, at the University of Reading, she created and directed an MA on the Body & Representation. Since the 1990s, she has served on numerous national and international committees within ESF, HERA, the British Academy, AHRC and AUPHF. She has published 73 articles and 12 books, most recently *Consensuality: Didier Anzieu, gender and the sense of touch* (2009), *Indeterminate Bodies* (2003), *Le Désir à l'Œuvre* (2000) and *André Gide: Pederasty & Pedagogy* (1998).

ANNETTE STAHMER

is a designer and artist, working in the interdisciplinary field of language, with a focus on the relation between voice and script, the act of writing, synästhesia and the materiality of language. She is co-founder of the design office *fliegende Teilchen* in Berlin together with André Heers. Since 2009 she is Professor for Typography at the Muthesius Academy of Fine Arts and Design in Kiel.

IMOGEN STIDWORTHY

is a British artist based in Liverpool. She has exhibited at Documenta 12 (2007), and during 2010/11, in solo exhibitions at Matts Gallery, London; Arnolfini, Bristol (UK); Galerie Akinci, Amsterdam and Kunstpavillon Innsbruck. Recent group exhibitions (2010/11) include *Terminal Convention*, Cork Airport; *Eternal Tour*, East Jerusalem; *No Longer Empty*, Liverpool Biennial; *Life: a Users Manual*, Art Sheffield 2010 etc. She is currently working on an exhibition, *In the First Circle*, with Paul Domela, for Fundacio Antoni Tapies, Barcelona (Oct-Feb 2012). Her new book *(.)* will be published in the autumn. She is currently an Advising Researcher at the Jan van Eyck Akademie, Maastricht.

TRIKOTON

is an interdisciplinary project and Berlin-based fashion label, consisting of Magdalena Kohler (Fashion design), Hanna Wiesener (Product design), Hannes Nützmann (Interactive Media) and Achim Amman (Business Administration) who are exploring new ways of designing and production by transforming audio files into knitting codes.

ALLEN S. WEISS

is a writer, editor, translator, curator and playwright, and is the author and editor of 40 books in the fields of performance theory, landscape architecture, gastronomy, sound art and experimental theater, including *Phantasmic Radio* (Duke University Press); *Breathless: Sound Recording, Disembodiment, and the Transformation of Lyrical Nostalgia* (Wesleyan University Press); *Varieties of Audio Mimesis: Musical Evocations of Landscape* (Errant Bodies Press). He directed the *Theater of the Ears* and *Danse Macabre*. Allen S. Weiss teaches in the Departments of Performance Studies and Cinema Studies at New York University.

Parole #2: Phonetic Skin / Phonetische Haut is based on a design concept which works with the idea of a "phonetic skin". Most of the articles quote in their design from the layout of an extant linguistic book. The textual bodies of the books are dissected, form and content are separated from one another and the old layout is "filled" with the new text. In this manner, the design of *Parole #2: Phonetic Skin / Phonetische Haut* contains the following books:

Petra Maria Meyer / *Mit Haut und Hören [Listen to Your Skin]*

R. H. STETSON, *Motor Phonetics. A Study of Speech Movements in Action* (Amsterdam: North-Holland Publishing Company, 1951).
Design: unknown.

Paul Dickinson / *Sleep Talk*

KNUT FINTOFT, *Fonetikk. Oppgaver med Svar* (Trondheim: Tapir Akademisk Forlag, 1982).
Design: unknown.

Mladen Dolar / *The Phonetic Burrow*

R. H. STETSON, *Motor Phonetics. A Study of Speech Movements in Action* (Amsterdam: North-Holland Publishing Company, 1951).
Design: unknown.

Naomi Segal / *Playing the Strange Statue*

R. H. STETSON, *Motor Phonetics. A Study of Speech Movements in Action* (Amsterdam: North-Holland Publishing Company, 1951).
Design: unknown.

David Locke / *Skin as a Metaphor*

R. H. STETSON, *Motor Phonetics. A Study of Speech Movements in Action* (Amsterdam: North-Holland Publishing Company, 1951). (modified version)
Design: unknown.

Janet Beizer / *The Textual Woman*

R. H. STETSON, *Motor Phonetics. A Study of Speech Movements in Action* (Amsterdam: North-Holland Publishing Company, 1951).
Design: unknown.

Leif Elggren / *The Sudarium of St. Veronica*

MATS EEG-OLOFSSON, *Word-Class Tagging* (Göteborg: University of Göteborg 1991).
Design: unknown.

André Lepecki / *Resonance, as in Skin*

WILLIAM G. MOULTON, *The Sounds of English and German* (Chicago / London: The University of Chicago Press, 1962).
Design: The University of Chicago Press, Chicago.

Allen S. Weiss / *The Sonic Skin of Water*

R. H. STETSON, *Motor Phonetics. A Study of Speech Movements in Action* (Amsterdam: North-Holland Publishing Company, 1951).
Design: unknown.

Brandon LaBelle / *The Sonic Body*

KENNETH L. PIKE, *Phonemics. A Technic for Reducing Language to Writing* (Ann Arbor: The University of Michigan Press, 1947).
Design: unknown.

Trikoton / *The Voice Knitting Collection*

GEORGE N. CLEMENTS & SAMUEL JAY KEYSER, *CV Phonology. A Generative Theory of the Syllable* (Cambridge / London: The MIT Press, 1983).
Design: George N. Clements & Samuel Jay Keyser.

Leonardo Guelman / *The Urban Book of Prophet Gentileza*

DIANA MARIA DE SOUSA MARQUES PINTO DOS SANTOS, *Tense and Aspect in English and Portuguese: A constrastive semantical study* (Lisbon: Technical University of Lisbon, 1996).
Design: Diana Maria de Sousa Marques Pinto dos Santos.

Parole #2: Phonetic Skin / Phonetische Haut
Annette Stahmer (editor)
Salon Verlag, Cologne
in cooperation with Errant Bodies Press, Berlin / Los Angeles

Bibliographic information published by *Die Deutsche Bibliothek. Die Deutsche Bibliothek* lists this publication in the *Deutsche Nationalbibliografie*, detailed bibliograhic data are available in the internet at http://dnb.ddb.de.

ISBN: 978-3-89770-375-9

www.salon-verlag.de / mail@salon-verlag.de
www.errantbodies.org

Design: Annette Stahmer
Text back cover: Annette Stahmer
Pictures inside covers: Marcel Proust, *À la recherche du temps perdu / À l'ombre des jeunes filles en fleurs 2* (Paris: Gallimard, 1919).

Translations: Pauline Cumbers: "Introduction" / "With Skin and Hearing"
Patrick Charles: "Trikoton – The Voice Knitting Collection"
Adriana Francisco: "The Urban Book of Prophet Gentileza"

Print: Druckerei Conrad, Berlin

Thanks to: Brandon LaBelle, André Heers, my parents Eilith le Fort and Carsten Stahmer, Octávio Camargo, Bryndís Sigurjónsdóttir, Henning Reinke and to the authors!

Kindly supported by: Druckerei Conrad, Berlin